Use of the
Mass Media by
the Urban Poor

PRAEGER SPECIAL STUDIES IN
U.S. ECONOMIC AND SOCIAL DEVELOPMENT

Use of the Mass Media by the Urban Poor

FINDINGS OF THREE RESEARCH PROJECTS, WITH AN ANNOTATED BIBLIOGRAPHY

Bradley S. Greenberg
Brenda Dervin

With the assistance of
**Joseph R. Dominick
John Bowes**

PRAEGER PUBLISHERS
New York · Washington · London

The purpose of Praeger Special Studies is to make specialized research in U.S. and international economics and politics available to the academic, business, and government communities. For further information, write to the Special Projects Division, Praeger Publishers, Inc., 111 Fourth Avenue, New York, N.Y. 10003.

PRAEGER PUBLISHERS
111 Fourth Avenue, New York, N.Y. 10003, U.S.A.
5, Cromwell Place, London S.W.7, England

Published in the United States of America in 1970
by Praeger Publishers, Inc.

© 1970 by Praeger Publishers, Inc.

Library of Congress Catalog Card Number: 73-127804

Printed in the United States of America

PREFACE

The war on poverty of the 1960's has not ended
in victory. In the 1970's, millions of veterans
will remain in the battle zone of the disadvantaged.
Of vast welfare and educational programs begun in
the past decade, a much smaller subset continues the
fight against poverty. Current attention focuses
sharply on the lack of communication that presumably contributed to the death of some programs and
the curtailment of others. This lack of communication exists between people from different walks of
life, between the races, and between poverty practitioners and their intended clients.

An interesting paradox exists in the social
science and social action literature. There is an
extensive body of information available on the poor
largely provided by psychologists and sociologists.
Yet this literature tends to ignore the specific
communication behaviors of the poor. Similarly, the
extensive literature available in communication
fields has virtually ignored the segment of the
population that is poor and/or black. Looking for
an interface between these two areas--communication
and poverty--is like looking for the proverbial
needle.

Thus, few sources are available to the poverty
program practitioner who is looking for empirical
evidence on which to base his efforts to reach the
poor and gain acceptance for his programs. Indeed,
the Kerner Commission on Civil Disorders could point
to only one study as background for describing the
media behaviors of ghetto residents.[1] Our own careful search of a ten-year array of literature in both
communication and poverty yielded only a handful of
studies directly focused on poverty and mass communication.[2] There are also a number of media usage
studies that focus on the general relationship of
socio-economic class variables (e.g., education,

v

occupation, race, and income) to media behaviors.
These studies provide some baseline data.3 However,
the sum-total of work available on poverty and mass
communication is small.

Furthermore, the available literature has some
serious limitations:

1. Many studies include too few blacks and/or
low-income respondents for legitimate comparisons.
This is particularly true of studies concerned with
demographic correlations of media use based on random
sampling of the general population. For example, one
study contrasting black and white television and newspaper use reports only 10 percent blacks for comparison purposes.4
2. Most studies lack controlled comparison of
low-income blacks to whites and low-income respondents
to general population respondents. Some look only
at black respondents; others look at both black and
white respondents but do not control for the inher-
ently lower socio-economic position of blacks; still
others draw samples of low-income respondents but
give no general population comparison; and one presents a sample almost entirely composed of females.
3. The studies focus on a very limited set of
media behaviors: Jack Lyle looks only at Negro use
of weekly newspapers; Maxwell McCombs looks only at
frequency of newspaper and television use; and Leslie
Sargent and Guido Stempel III look only at television,
radio, and newspaper use.5 No one study focuses on
a large set of media behaviors--use, access, content
preferences, functions, and attitudes--across a more
complete range of media.
4. The studies do not give a developmental comparison of the media behaviors of the poor at different age levels.

Thus, empirical evidence available on poverty
and communication is of limited comprehensiveness
and has many methodological shortcomings. The purpose of this book is to begin to fill in this information gap. The book is divided into two parts. Part
I reports the results of three research projects on
the mass media behaviors of the poor. The studies
attempt to circumvent certain major problems in previous studies by: (1) focusing on a more complete
range of media behaviors--media use, availability,
content preferences, functions and attitudes; (2)
considering a more comprehensive set of media--radio
television, newspapers, magazines, phonographs, and

movies; (3) explicitly comparing low-income blacks to low-income whites and low-income respondents in composite to general population samples; and (4) focusing on respondents at three age levels--childhood, adolescence, and adulthood.

Our goal in presenting these studies is to provide as complete as possible a baseline picture of the mass communication behaviors of the poor. Chapter 1 focuses on urban poor adults; Chapter 2 on adolescents; and Chapter 3 on children. Chapter 4 draws together the findings of these three studies and discusses future research directions. For the reader who wants an overview of our three studies, Chapter 4 is suggested as a starting point.

Part II offers a representative picture of findings on the communication behaviors of the poor currently available in the social science literature. This overview summarizes the results of approximately 80 studies and reports. In Part II, the focus goes beyond the mass communication behaviors of the poor to communication behaviors in general. Chapter 5 is a summary of research on intra-family communication patterns, outside family relationships, and mass communication behaviors. Readers seeking an overview of the communication behaviors of the poor might start with Chapter 5. Chapter 6 presents extensive abstracts of the some 80 studies summarized in Chapter 5.

In sum, this book presents an overview of the communication behaviors of the poor with particular emphasis on mass communication behaviors. In this sense, the book is primarily descriptive. Its purpose is to give the poverty practitioner and the social scientist a realistic picture of the communication behaviors of the poor. It is done with the hope that future research and poverty programs may be built on concrete information about these behaviors.

NOTES

1. National Commission on Civil Disorders, Report of the National Commission on Civil Disorders, (New York: Bantam Books, 1968).

2. These pioneer studies dealing with the media behaviors of the poor break down into three general types: (1) studies focusing on poor respondents in general--Lewis Donohew and B. K. Singh, "Modernization of Life Styles. An Appraisal of the 'War on Poverty' in a Rural Setting of Southeastern Kentucky" (Lexington: University of Kentucky, August, 1968); Leslie W. Sargent and Guido H. Stempel III, "Poverty, Alienation, and Mass Media Use," Journalism Quarterly XLV, 2 (Summer, 1968), 324-326; (2) studies focusing on black respondents only--Jack Lyle, The News in Megalopolis (San Francisco: Chandler Publishing Company, 1967); T. H. Allen, "Mass Media Use Patterns and Functions in a Negro Ghetto" (Master's thesis, University of West Virginia, 1967); (3) studies comparing black and white respondents--James W. Carey, "Variations in Negro/White Television Preference," Journal of Broadcasting X, 3 (1966), 199-212; Maxwell E. McCombs, "Negro Use of Television and Newspapers for Political Information, 1952-64," Journal of Broadcasting XIII, 3 (Summer, 1968), 261-266; Arnold M. Barban and Werner F. Grunbaum, "A Factor Analytic Study of Negro and White Responses to Advertising Stimuli," Journal of Applied Psychology XLIX, 4 (1965), 274-279; Walter Gerson, "Mass Media Socialization Behavior: Negro-White Differences," Social Forces XLV, 1 (September, 1966), 40-50; Russell Middleton, "Alienation, Race, and Education," The American Sociological Review XXVIII, (December, 1963), 974-977.

3. Among these studies are: Lotte Bailyn, "Mass Media and Children: A Study of Exposure Habits and Cognitive Effects," Psychological Monographs LXXIII, 1 (1959); Walter M. Geiger and Robert Sokol, "Social Norms in Television-Watching," The American Journal of Sociology LXV, 2 (September, 1959), 174-181; Bradley S. Greenberg, "Media Use and Believability: Multiple Correlates," Journalism Quarterly XLIII (1966), 655-670; Merrill Samuelson, Richard F. Carter, and Lee Ruggels, "Education, Available Time, and the Use of the Mass Media," Journalism Quarterly XL (Fall, 1963), 491-496; Gary A. Steiner, The People Look at Television (New York: Alfred A. Knopf, 1963); Bruce H. Westley and Werner J. Severin, "Some Correlates of Media Credibility," Journalism Quarterly XLI (Summer, 1964), 325-335.

4. McCombs, op. cit.

5. Lyle, op. cit.; McCombs, op. cit.; Sargent and Stempel, op. cit.

ACKNOWLEDGMENTS

Project CUP (Communication Among the Urban Poor) has been active in the Department of Communication at Michigan State University for three years. This volume contains the best of the efforts from that project. The first data were gathered by uncoerced volunteer student interviewers in a dozen inches of snow in bitter weather during February, 1967. Their goals were to find out what poverty was like, who were the poor, and what were some of their communication modes and behaviors.

Initial funding for this work came in a direct allocation of funds from Fred Siebert, then Dean of the College of Communication Arts at Michigan State University. Without his personal assistance, this project would not have been started. Additional support throughout the past three years has come from the Department of Communication through its chairman, David K. Berlo. Whenever research assistants, computer resources, hourly labor, and other aids have been needed, they have somehow been made available.

More recently, various portions of this research have been financed through a substantial grant from the Educational Foundation of the American Association of Advertising Agencies and through small grants from the National Association of Broadcasters and the Michigan State University All-University Research Grant program.

Other assistance took the form of personal help in the conduct of research in the cities to which we went. In Philadelphia, John Hayman and Alan Solomon of the Philadelphia Board of Education facilitated our work and Karen Woodson gathered data for us. In East Cleveland, Mandell Sperling and Jack Jirus of the East Cleveland school district made arrangements for us and Mrs. Mandell Sperling, Sally Davidson, Paula Bacon, and William McEwen gathered data for us.

    The preparation of the bibliographic abstracts
was largely a graduate student effort. In particular,
we wish to acknowledge the time and energy given by
Richard Allen, Edward Bodaken, Betty Crawford, Lytton
Guimaraes, Gerhard Hanneman, William McEwen, Gustavo
Quesada, K. S. S. Raju, Gonzalo Rivero, and Edward
Wotring. Miss Crawford also did a precise editing
of the entire set of abstracts.

    The authors wish it to be known that there are
substantial numbers of university students, both
graduate and undergraduate, who will apply themselves
to work, scholarship, and research solely for the
sake of learning. We are in daily contact with many
of them and this has been one of the larger rewards
for us.

    Three young ladies--Mrs. Jessica Gard, Mrs.
Claudia Gean, and Mrs. Linda Omura--have been our
persistent trouble-shooters for many kinds of secre-
tarial, proofing, and administrative tasks.

    Three more young ladies--Delight, Beth, and
Shawn Greenberg--have been too often without a husband or father during evenings and weekends, but
remain understanding and supportive. A fourth,
Debra, does not yet know what she's missed.

CONTENTS

PART II: RELATED RESEARCH ON COMMUNICATION
           BEHAVIORS OF THE POOR

LIST OF TABLES AND FIGURES

PART |

RESEARCH PROJECTS ON MASS MEDIA BEHAVIOR

CHAPTER **1** THE ROLE OF THE
MASS MEDIA FOR
URBAN POOR ADULTS

Bradley S. Greenberg
and Brenda Dervin

Increasingly, national attention is being focused on the problems of ghettos, criminal violence
in the streets, and poverty in general. Much of this
attention has emphasized the sub-cultural nature of
the ghetto--the notion that the behaviors, attitudes,
and feelings of the poor are different from those of
the majority society.[1] Yet for one important class
of behaviors and attitudes--those dealing with the
mass media by which the majority society communicates
with the poverty sub-culture--our information level
is disturbingly low. The study described in this
chapter was the first of three that attempted to fill
the information gap about the role of the mass media
for the urban poor.

PURPOSE OF THE STUDY

This chapter focuses on urban poor adults and
has the following purposes: to fully describe the
media behaviors and attitudes of a sample of low-income urban adults; to compare these with a sample of
general population adults living in the same urban
area; and to compare the media behaviors of low-income blacks with those of low-income whites. Prior
research provided two general working hypotheses to
guide our approach:

1. Considerable difference was expected in the
mass media use and attitudes of low-income versus
general population adults. Support for this working
hypothesis came from a number of classic media use
studies that focus on general populations[2] as well

3

as the few studies that focus solely on the poor.[3]
Typical findings of these studies are: the poor use
more television and are more favorable to it; they
use less print media; and they tend to use more radio.
    2. Considerable similarity was expected in the
media behaviors of low-income black and white adults.
Given the attention to blacks in the current press,
this working hypothesis may seem surprising. However,
a considerable body of literature suggests that the
poor--the some one-fifth of the nation's families
living below anti-poverty program standards--live in
a sub-culture that makes them much alike regardless
of race or ethnic origin. Elizabeth Herzog prepared
a strong case for the theory that socio-economic status is a stronger variable in relation to family patterns and life styles than race.[4]

    The intersection of several studies suggests
that both variables--poverty and race--operate together.[5] Because of their poverty, low-income whites
and blacks are more similar to each other than either
is to the general population. However, being black
makes most of the characteristics that differentiate
the poor function more strongly. This is certainly
true of the demographic characteristics that differentiate the poor: low-income blacks are more likely
to be from larger families, from broken homes, less
educated, and on welfare than are low-income whites.
In short, to be poor is to be different from the
general population; to be black is to be even more
different.

METHODS AND PROCEDURES

Scope and Design of the Study

    No available prior study looked at a relatively
complete range of mass media behaviors and specifically compared low-income blacks to whites as well as
low-income to general population adults.[6] The study
reported in this chapter was designed explicitly to
test our two working hypotheses across a comprehensive set of mass media behaviors. In our basic design, poverty and race were considered predictor
variables and the mass media use and attitude measures
were considered criterion variables. In other words,
the intent was to predict media behaviors on the
basis of race and poverty.

Implementation of the Study

Questionnaire Development

A first version of the questionnaire was developed in consultation with personnel in the Lansing,
Michigan, Office of Economic Opportunity (OEO). The
questionnaire was revised twice after pretests with
low-income respondents. The final version was a
structured combination of free-response and closed-
ended items. Two general classes of questions were
created. One tapped media behaviors; the other tapped
race, income, and other demographic variables related
to poverty.

Media Questions. Mass media questions were about
ownership, use, content preferences, and attitudes.
Questions were developed to tap these four dimensions
of media behavior for the mass media of television,
radio, newspapers, magazines, phonographs, and movies.

Media ownership questions dealt with the number
of television sets, radio sets, phonographs, and
phonograph records owned and the frequency of newspaper delivery. Typical questions were: Do you have
a television set at home? How many TV sets do you
have? How many are actually working? Do you have
a color TV set?

Media use questions tapped the frequency of use
of television, radio, newspapers, magazines, phonographs, and movies. Typical questions were: Did you
listen to the radio yesterday? For how many hours?

For two of the media--television and newspapers--
media content preference questions were also asked.
Typical questions asked respondents which of a set of
top-rated television shows they watched regularly and
what parts of the newspaper they read regularly.

The final class of media questions dealt with attitudes. These questions pitted the various media
against each other by asking respondents which media
they preferred. A typical question was: If you heard
a news report on television that did not agree with a
news report in the newspaper, which would you believe
most?

Demographic Questions. The two basic predictor vari-
ables--race and poverty--were actually constructed by

the sampling design which is outlined in full below.
Briefly, the sampling design yielded a sample of low-
income respondents and a sample of general population
respondents. The low-income sample was divided into
two sub-samples--low-income whites and low-income
blacks. It was necessary to establish whether the
low-income sample was indeed a low-income sample;
whether the general population sample was a good representation of the general population; and whether
the low-income black sample was comparable to the low-
income white sample. Prior research on poverty suggested that such variables as family size, education,
occupation, income, and place of birth were good indicators of the differences between low-income and general population adults and between low-income blacks
and whites. For this reason, questionnaire items
tapped these demographic variables.

Sampling and Questionnaire Administration

Sampling and questionnaire administration was
divided into two major phases. The first phase con-
centrated on the low-income sample; the second on the
general population sample.

Low-Income Sample. The final low-income sample was
obtained by a three-stage process. First, three 20-
block areas within urban Lansing, Michigan, were identified by local OEO personnel. These areas marked the
geographical confines of three OEO action areas--i.e.,
they were the areas of the city having the highest
concentration of low-income residents. Next, ten
blocks were randomly sampled within each of the three
OEO action areas and a starting point for interviewing
was selected randomly for each block. The third and
final stage of sampling was carried out in the field.
Interviewers began knocking on doors at the random
starting point, moving counter clockwise until they
had completed ten interviews on the designated block.
Only English-speaking persons at least 18 years of
age were interviewed.

The half-hour questionnaire was personally administered by trained interviewers during a three-week
period from February 16 to March 14, 1967. Interviews
were conducted on Thursdays, Fridays, and Saturdays
only. Interviewers averaged one refusal for each two
interviews obtained. By these procedures, a low-
income sample of 312 respondents was obtained--131
blacks, 150 whites, and 31 Spanish-origin respondents.
The Spanish-origin respondents are omitted from this
analysis.

General Population Sample. The general population
questionnaire was a shortened version of that used
for low-income respondents and was administered by
phone. First, a systematic probability sample of
285 telephone numbers from Lansing and East Lansing
was drawn from the 1967 Lansing phonebook. Interviewers were told to interview the first adult who
answered the phone. On the third day of interviewing, interviewers asked specifically for the "man of
the house" to increase the number of males in the
sample.

     The phone survey was done on April 18-20, 1967,
by eight experienced female interviewers. At least
three callbacks were made for each number. Of the
285 numbers sampled, 206 (72 percent) were completed.
There were 15 percent refusals; 8 percent phones that
could not be reached because of busy signals or no
answers; and 5 percent numbers where the phone was
disconnected, not residential, or where no one could
speak English or was over 18 years old.

Data Coding and Statistical Analyses

     Responses from the two samples--low-income and
general population--were coded first by a team of
eight coders. Two other coders independently recoded
a 14 percent sub-sample from each main sample. The
measure of interjudge coding reliability used was the
Percentage Agreement Index.[7] For the general population sample, 40 variables were coded with reliabilities on all 40 above 92 percent.* For the low-income
sample, 71 variables were coded with reliabilities
for all 71 variables above 82 percent and 60 above
90 percent.

     The primary method of statistical analysis was
the use of cross-tabulations with the Chi-square test

----

     *For the intercoder reliability checks, n for
the general population sample was 29 and n for the
low-income sample was 45. The reliability check
sub-samples were drawn randomly. The criterion for
agreement was a "point agreement" or agreement on
the actual code for all but two of the communication
variables. For these two variables--amount of television viewing yesterday and amount of radio listening yesterday--agreement was measured within ½ hour
of viewing or listening time.

of significance. Since most variables were measured
continuously, collapsing of categories was necessary.
All collapsing was done empirically by dividing variables into categories with frequencies as near equal
as possible.*

Demographic Comparison of the Samples

Before analyzing the results, the various sub-
samples--low-income blacks and whites and general
population--were checked to determine if they were
representative of their population groups.

Comparison of Low-Income and
General Population Samples

No very adequate means was available for check-
ing the representativeness of the low-income sample.
Recent highway construction meant that low-income
families were even more mobile than usual, making a
check to the outdated 1960 census tract data unsound.
We therefore compared the demographic characteristics
of this low-income sample with the general population
sample obtained at the same time. With equivalent
sex distributions, the low-income sample differed significantly from the general population in that it had
a higher proportion of older respondents and larger
families, more children per family, more one-adult
households, more households with more than two adults,
more households with no one working, less education,
and lower occupational prestige. Much literature on
the poor validates these differences as characteristic
of the poverty class.[8]

The quality of the low-income sample is most
clearly suggested by education and occupation comparisons. In the low-income sample, 61 percent had 11
years or less education compared to 18 percent in the
general population sample. Only 10 percent of the
low-income sample reported jobs that fit white-collar
descriptions as compared with 67 percent in the general population sample.

----

*In most cases, category n's were kept large
enough to prevent cell expecteds from dropping below
10. When a cell expected dropped below 10, Yates'
correction was applied.

Comparison of Low-Income Black and White Samples

Low-income blacks differed from low-income whites
in that they were younger, had larger households and
more children, and were more likely to have more
adults living in the household. .Low-income blacks
also had more job-holders per household, lower occupational prestige, and were more likely to be unemployed or on welfare. They had lived in the city
fewer years and most were originally from the south.
All these differences should be found in a sample of
low-income blacks as compared with low-income whites.9
No difference in current weekly income was found for
these two sub-groups, making a comparison between
them valid in terms of poverty status.

Comparison of General Population Sample
to Census Data

The general population sample was comparable to
1960 census data in terms of age, sex, marital status,
and size of household.10   The sample had more young
people but respondents included in the sample were
those 18 years or older compared to those 20 years
or older for the census. The sample had 8 percent
fewer single people than the census but the census
age baseline was 14 years of age compared to 18 for
the sample. The education level in the sample was
higher, partly because the sample included those 18
years or older whereas the census included those 25
years or older in its education breakdown. In sum,
the demographic discrepancies between the sample and
the census were small and could be largely accounted
for by differing sampling baselines.*

RESULTS

Media Ownership

First, we determined what media are regularly
available. Table 1 reports the availability of TV
sets, radios, daily newspapers, phonographs, and
phonograph records for the low-income and general

---

*Complete statistical data on these demographic
comparisons of the samples are available from the
authors.

TABLE 1

Media Ownership Comparison:
Low-Income Versus General Population Adults;
Low-Income White Versus Low-Income Black Adults

Variable	Low-Income Versus General Population			White Versus Black Low-Income		
	LI[a] (percent)	GP (percent)	X^2p	W (percent)	B (percent)	X^2p
No. of working TV sets						
None	3	3	n.s.	3	2	n.s.
One	63	58		66	60	
Two or more	34	39		31	38	
Color TV ownership						
Don't own one	91	78	<.001	91	91	n.s.
Do own one	9	22		9	9	
No. of radio sets						
None	7	0	<.001	6	8	n.s.
One	31	17		30	32	
Two	29	26		30	27	
Three or more	33	57		34	32	
Newspaper delivered daily						
No	25	14	<.01	20	31	<.05
Yes	75	86		80	69	
Phonograph ownership						
None	23	14	<.02	29	16	<.01
One or more	77	86		71	84	
No. of phonograph records owned						
000	22	17	<.05	29	13	<.01
001-049	27	21		23	31	
050-099	18	38		17	20	
100 or more	32	24		31	35	

[a]Total LI n=281; n's for these crossbreaks range from 271 to 281. Total GP n=206; n's for these crossbreaks range from 180 to 206. Total W n=150; n's for these crossbreaks range from 144 to 150. Total B n=131; n's for these crossbreaks range from 127 to 131. Incomplete n's result from missing data. All tables in this report use these abbreviations: LI=low-income; GP=general population; W=low-income white; B=low-income black; X^2p=the probability level at which the obtained X^2s were significant; n.s.=not significant.

population samples as well as the black and white
low-income sub-samples.

Comparison of Low-Income and
General Population Samples

   In comparing the low-income sample with the general population, two findings stand out. First, the
low-income respondents were as likely as general population respondents to own at least one TV set--97
percent of both samples did. Second, the general
population adults were significantly more likely to
have available all types of media other than TV.
These two findings indicate the relative prominence
of television within the media-environment of the
poor.

   Although the general population was more likely
to have more media available, the low-income population was certainly not media-poor. Only 3 percent
of the low-income sample reported not owning a TV; 7
percent did not have at least one radio; 25 percent
did not have a newspaper delivered;* 23 percent did
not own a phonograph; and 22 percent had no phonograph records. Thus, although the general population
generally had more media available, a majority of the
low-income respondents were relatively affluent in
terms of availability of media.

Comparison of Low-Income
Black and White Samples

   Fewer and smaller media ownership differences
existed between low-income black and white respondents. Neither lacked media availability. A majority
of both sub-samples had TV, radio, newspapers, and
phonographs available. Their ownership of radios and
working TV sets was high and equivalent. However,
the low-income whites were more likely to have a

----

   *About 75 percent of the low-income respondents
reported having a newspaper delivered, a figure that
may seem high. Unfortunately, there are few studies
available with which to check this figure. T. H.
Allen reports that only 14 percent of his Pittsburgh
black ghetto sample got a daily newspaper but Sargent
and Stempel report that 67 percent of their sample of
welfare recipients in Athens, Ohio, read the newspaper
daily.11

newspaper delivered. Interestingly, low-income blacks
(84 percent) were significantly more likely than
whites (71 percent) to own one or more phonographs
and to own more phonograph records.

It is possible that low-income whites reflect
the general population on newspaper access because
the whites are more attuned to or interested in a
predominantly white majority society and/or the
papers are perceived as "white" papers. The blacks'
significantly greater ownership of phonographs may
have a parallel explanation. Through phonograph
records, blacks may obtain sub-cultural materials
such as black music not available in the majority
media.

TV Use and Content Preferences

Table 2 lists the amount of television use for
each group and the regularity with which each group
viewed 12 top-rated shows.

Comparison of Low-Income and
General Population Samples

For the low-income versus general population
comparison, the most striking finding is the considerable difference in viewing time. Forty-one
percent of the general population sample reported
that they did not watch TV yesterday compared with
24 percent of the low-income sample. Only 17 percent of the general population reported viewing 4
or more hours yesterday compared with 53 percent of
the low-income sample. The mean viewing time for
the general population was 2.0 hours compared with
a mean of 5.2 hours for the low-income sample.* If
16 hours are considered a waking-day, the low-income
adults spent an average of almost one-third of that
day viewing TV in comparison with one-eighth for the

_____

*General population TV viewing time computed
from this sample compares well with that obtained
for other general population samples. The considerably higher low-income viewing time is also well
supported. Comparable data come from the research
of Maxwell McCombs, Leslie Sargent and Guido Stempel
III, Gary Steiner, and Bruce H. Westley and Werner
J. Severin.12

TABLE 2

TV Use and Content Preference Comparison:
Low-Income Versus General Population Adults;
Low-Income White Versus Low-Income Black Adults

Variable	Low-Income Versus General Population			White Versus Black Low-Income		
	LI (n=281)	GP (n=206)	x^2p	W (n=150)	B (n=131)	x^2p
Hours TV viewing yesterday						
None	24%	41%	<.001	23%	25%	n.s.
1/4-3 3/4	23%	42%		25%	20%	
4-7 3/4	26%	12%		29%	24%	
8 or more	27%	5%		23%	31%	
No. of 12 top TV shows[a] watched regularly						
0-4	31%	58%	<.001	33%	28%	n.s.
5-6	18%	20%		21%	15%	(<.10)
7-8	27%	15%		29%	26%	
9-12	23%	7%		17%	30%	
Ranking of 12 top[b] TV shows						
Beverley Hillbillies	1.5	8	Rank order	2	1	Rank order
Andy Griffith	1.5	1.5	correlation	1	2	correlation
Green Acres	3	10	(RHO) = .03	4.5	5	(RHO) = .72
Bonanza	4	10		6	4	
Daktari	5	3	n.s.	3	8	<.01
Ed Sullivan	6	5		7.5	3	
Lucy Show	7	10		7.5	6	
Red Skelton	8	7		4.5	9	
Jackie Gleason	9	1.5		9	7	
Walt Disney	10	5		10	10	
Lawrence Welk	11	12		11	12	
Bewitched	12	5		12	11	

[a]The TV shows listed are among the top-rated shows in the nation for the period October, 1966-January, 1967. Since TV ratings vary greatly depending on any given week's TV fare, four different weeks of TV ratings were used in compiling this list--the Arbitron ratings for January 18, 1967 and October 23, 1966 and the Nielson ratings for December 18, 1966 and November 5, 1966. Specials and movies were deleted. Of the remaining shows, any show that was ranked in the top 12 on two or more of the rating lists was included.

[b]To compare the popularity of the 12 shows across samples while controlling for the widely disparate total viewing times, the proportion of viewers watching each show regularly was converted to ranks, with the TV show having the highest proportion of regular viewers receiving a rank of 1. Rank order correlations (RHO's) were computed with correction for ties.

general population. More than one-fourth of the low-
income respondents spent more than one-half their day
watching TV.

A possible bias in these results might have resulted from the particular days for which TV viewing
data were collected. Each respondent was given the
TV program log for the day preceding his interview
and he indicated each show watched. Viewing data
for the general population referred to shows watched
on Mondays, Tuesdays, and Wednesdays; viewing for
the low-income samples referred to Wednesdays, Thursdays, and Fridays. To check this possible bias
source, exposure times were recomputed by day (see
Table 3).

TABLE 3

TV Exposure Time for Low-Income and
General Population Samples by Day
for Which TV Viewing Was Measured

Low-Income Sample	Mon.	Tues.	Wed.	Thurs.	Fri.	Total
Mean hours	---	---	5.9	6.9	4.5	5.2
(n)	---	---	(46)	(64)	(170)	(281)
General Population						
Mean hours	2.0	2.1	1.4	---	---	2.0
(n)	(59)	(99)	(48)	---	---	(206)

The discrepancy between days surveyed actually
served to suppress the overall viewing time difference
between the two samples. For the one day on which
both samples were measured--Wednesday--the TV exposure time difference was greater than the average
computed across three days. Further, the largest
number of general population respondents were measured for the day on which their TV viewing was highest (Tuesday) and the largest number of low-income
respondents were interviewed on the day on which
their TV viewing was lowest (Friday). Any bias introduced by measuring TV viewing on different days
certainly did not inflate the average difference in
hours spent watching TV. Consequently, the noted
average difference--2.0 hours (general population)
versus 5.2 hours (low-income)--is even more striking.

The low-income sample also watched a significantly greater number of the 12 top TV shows (see Table 2). Only 22 percent of the general population regularly watched 7 or more of these top shows in comparison with 50 percent of the low-income sample. A comparison of the viewers for each of the 12 top shows generally confirms this finding: the low-income adults were significantly more likely to be regular viewers of 8 of the 12 shows. From 51 to 73 percent of the low-income sample reported regular viewing of these 8 shows, compared with 30 to 43 percent of the general population.* More important, however, is the relative popularity of the 12 shows in each sample. When the proportion of regular viewers for each show was converted to ranks, the resulting rank order correlation was .03. Thus, the favorite shows of the low-income adults were not the favorites of the general population.

One further observation is of interest in terms of television usage. More viewing was done throughout almost the entire day by the low-income sample (see Figure 1). The low-income adults started their viewing earlier, continued their viewing at a higher level throughout the day, and ended their viewing later. The largest differences in viewing occurred in the morning and afternoon when general population viewing remained stable at around 4-10 percent; viewing in the low-income sample ranged from 14-36 percent during these time periods. Indeed, the peak afternoon viewing for the low-income sample (36 percent) was not far different from its peak evening viewing (49 percent). These data suggest that in terms of using TV to reach low-income respondents, afternoon time may serve almost as well as evening time.

Comparison of Low-Income Black and White Samples

The television usage and content preference findings of the white and black low-income sub-samples show no consistent differences. Blacks were not significantly more likely than whites to watch more television although the mean difference (5.7 versus 4.8 hours a day) indicates such a trend. Nor were the

---

*These figures are not reported in Table 2. All differences on the 8 shows were significant at p <.001 by the Chi-square test of significance.

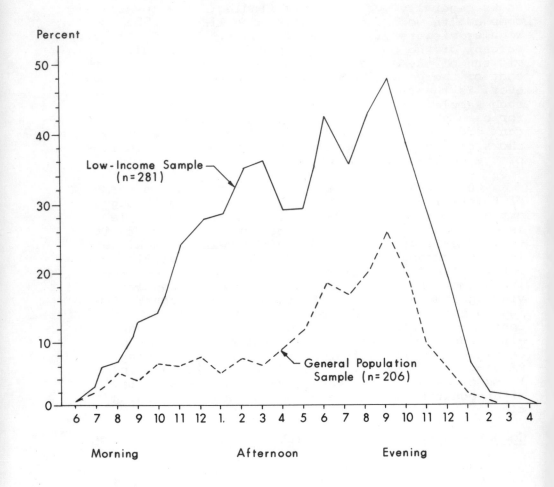

FIGURE 1

Percentage of Low-Income and General
Population Adults Viewing TV Each Hour During Day

two sub-samples different in terms of the number of
top TV shows they watched regularly. The proportion
of black respondents regularly viewing 6 of the 12
top TV shows equalled the proportion of whites. The
pattern of differences on the remaining shows was not
interpretable. However, when the proportion of viewers regularly watching a show was converted to ranks,
the rank order correlation was .72. This indicates
that the popularity order of these 12 shows was very
similar for low-income blacks and whites.* This result is even more striking when compared to the correlation of .03 obtained between the low-income sample
and the general population ranks.

These data suggest that low-income blacks and
whites are quite similar in their TV behaviors and
collectively quite different from the general population.

Newspaper Use and Content Preferences

Comparison of Low-Income and
General Population Samples

Table 4 presents the newspaper usage and content
preference results. Again, there was greater difference between the low-income and general population
respondents than between the low-income blacks and
whites. For two of the three newspaper-use items,
general population usage was significantly greater:
77 percent read a newspaper each day (compared with
65 percent of the low-income sample); 39 percent read
all of the newspaper regularly (compared with 17 percent of the low-income sample).

Although the two income samples were not significantly different in terms of the number of newspaper
sections they reported reading regularly, they differed in terms of the content and popularity of particular sections read. The general population was

---

*This finding contradicts that of James W. Carey
who concluded on the basis of his analysis of nation-
wide poll data that Negro and white viewing preferences were quite different. However, Carey's black
respondents were a sub-sample from general population
samples. Thus, his data have no control for the necessarily lower economic status of blacks.[13]

TABLE 4

Newspaper Use and Content Preference Comparison:
Low-Income Versus General Population Adults;
Low-Income White Versus Low-Income Black Adults

Variable	Low-Income Versus General Population			White Versus Black Low-Income		
	LI[a]	GP	X^2p	W	B	X^2p
No. of days a week newspaper is read						
Never	7%	5%	<.05	7%	7%	n.s.
1 day a week	13	8		12	14	
2-6 days a week	15	10		11	20	
Every day	65	77		69	59	
Portion of newspaper read regularly						
None	7%	5%	<.001	7%	7%	<.05
Some	76	56		70	83	
All	17	39		23	10	
No. of newspaper sections read regularly						
None	7%	5%	n.s.	7%	7%	n.s.
One	17	12		17	18	
Two	27	23		22	32	
Three	19	24		20	18	
Four or more	29	35		34	25	
Ranking of newspaper sections						
Front page	1	1	Rank order	1	1	Rank order
Headlines	2	7	correlation	3	2	correlation
Sports	3	2	(RHO) = .23	2	3	(RHO) = .74
Ann Landers	4	11.5		7	5	
General news	5	4	n.s.	9	4	<.01
Classified	6.5	13		6	7.5	
General ads	6.5	10		4	7.5	
Local news	8.5	11.5		5	9.5	
Comics	8.5	3		9	6	
Society news	10.5	5		9	12.5	
Editorials	10.5	7		11	11	
Obituaries	12	7		12	9.5	
Food pages	13	9		13	12.5	

[a]Total LI n=281; n's for these crossbreaks range from 279 to 281. Total GP n=206; n's for these crossbreaks range from 204 to 206. Total W n=150; n's for these crossbreaks ranged from 149 to 150. Total B n=131; n's for these crossbreaks range from 130 to 131. Incomplete n's result from non-responses.

significantly more likely to read regularly the front
page (60 percent, versus 41 percent low-income), comics
(25 percent, versus 12 percent low-income),* and sports
(30 percent versus 19 percent low-income). The low-
income sample was significantly more likely to report
reading regularly the headlines (22 percent versus 12
percent general population) and classified ads (12 percent, versus 4 percent general population).

The overall popularity of any one newspaper section tended to be on the low side (front page, headlines, comics, and sports were the only sections with
regular readership above 20 percent in at least one
of the samples).** When the proportions of regular
readers were converted to ranks, the resulting correlation between low- and higher-income samples was .23.
Again, we find that the media content preferences of
low-income adults are quite different from those of
general population adults.

Comparison of Low-Income Black and White Samples

As expected, there were fewer differences between
the two low-income groups. The only variable showing
a difference was the portion of the newspaper read regularly. The two low-income sub-samples did not differ
in terms of the number of days of the week they read
newspapers or the number of sections they read.

This lack of difference between the low-income
sub-samples was sustained in an analysis of the content of their newspaper reading. The proportion of
black versus white respondents regularly reading any
of 13 newspaper sections was not significantly different. In general, their completeness of newspaper
reading was quite low. (For blacks and whites combined, the three major reading categories were the
front page (41 percent), the headlines (22 percent),
and the sports news (19 percent).

When the proportions of regular readers for the
13 sections were converted to ranks, the correlation

----

*The low use of comics by the low-income sample
was verified by another item not reported in Table 4.
When asked if they had a favorite comic strip, only 49
percent in the low-income sample reported that they
did.
**Allen's study of black ghetto residents resulted
in very similar newspaper content preferences.[14]

between the two groups was .74. Thus, low-income blacks and whites had similar newspaper content preferences just as their preferences among various television programs were much the same.

Other Media Usage

Table 5 describes use of radio, magazines, movies, and phonographs for the low-income white, low-income black, and general population samples.

Comparison of Low-Income and General Population Samples

Although the general population tended to use radio only slightly more than did the low-income sample, there were consistent differences in the usage of the other three media.* The general population sample read magazines more frequently. Only 17 percent of the general population had not read a magazine within the past week compared with one-third of the low-income sample. Overall movie attendance was infrequent--70 percent or more of both samples had not attended a movie for at least a month. However, the general population indicated significantly more recent attendance. The low-income sample reported significantly more phonograph use yesterday (as with television). Fifty-nine percent of the low-income adults had spent at least some time on phonograph use compared to 23 percent of the general population. This finding is especially intriguing in light of the significantly greater ownership of both phonographs and phonograph records by the general population. The significant difference in phonograph usage was maintained when non-owners were excluded from the analysis.

Comparison of Low-Income Black and White Samples

Again, there were few media use differences when low-income whites were compared to low-income

----

*Results on radio are only partly supported by other available data. Samuelson, Carter, and Ruggels found a non-significant relationship between radio use and education--one index of poverty.15 Recent media use studies have shown generally non-significant relationships between socio-economic variables and radio use.16

TABLE 5

Other Media Usage Comparison:
Low-Income Versus General Population Adults;
Low-Income White Versus Low-Income Black Adults

Variable	Low-Income Versus General Population			White Versus Black Low-Income		
	LI[a] (percent)	GP (percent)	x^2p	W (percent)	B (percent)	x^2p
Hours radio listening yesterday						
None	39	30	n.s.	40	37	n.s.
1/4-3/4	11	17	(<.10)	14	8	
1-1 3/4	19	24		19	19	
2-3 3/4	16	12		13	19	
4 or more	15	17		13	18	
When last read magazine						
Never	16	10	<.01	19	13	n.s.
More than week ago	17	7		13	21	
Week ago	12	14		14	11	
Few days ago	16	16		15	17	
Today or yesterday	38	53		38	38	
When last attended movie						
0-3 weeks ago	14	30	<.001	12	16	n.s.
4 or more weeks	86	70		88	84	
Time spent on phonograph use yesterday						
None	41	76	<.001	54	29	<.001
Less than one	41	9		33	48	
One or more	18	14		13	23	

[a]Total LI n=281; n's for these crossbreaks range from 277 to 280. Total GP n=206; n's for these crossbreaks range from 199 to 205. Total W n=150; n's for these crossbreaks range from 148 to 150. Total B n=131; n's for these tables range from 129 to 131.

21

blacks. The two samples were different only for
time spent on phonograph use--71 percent of the
blacks reported spending some time listening to
records yesterday compared with 46 percent of the
whites.

Attitudes Toward the Media

Comparison of Low-Income and
General Population Samples

The low-income sample was consistently more
favorable than the general population toward television on all media attitude measures (see Table 6).
For example, two-thirds of the low-income adults
cited television as the medium preferred for world
news in comparison with one-third of the general public. For local news, the low-income adults cited TV
more frequently than did the general population.

Radio was the most frequently cited medium for
local news among the low-income adults (34 percent),
followed by television, newspapers, and people. In
contrast, the general population indicated newspapers
as the most preferred medium for local news (41 percent), followed by radio, television, and people.

This general pattern of attitudes was supported
by three items asking respondents to choose which
medium they would believe in the case of conflicting
reports. The low-income sample chose television over
radio and radio over newspapers* more often than did
the general population. When asked how they generally
felt about TV, 52 percent of the low-income respondents compared with 14 percent of the general population said they like it "a lot." Only 21 percent of
the general population said they liked TV "only a
little" or "not at all."

Comparison of Low-Income Black and White Samples

In general, low-income respondents overwhelmingly
preferred TV for world news and there was no difference by race. The lack of attitudinal difference between blacks and whites was maintained for the items

---

*These differences were all significant at p
< .001 by the Chi-square test of significance.

TABLE 6

Media Attitudes Comparison:
Low-Income Versus General Population Adults;
Low-Income White Versus Low-Income Black Adults

Variable	Low-Income Versus General Population			White Versus Black Low-Income		
	LIa (percent)	GP (percent)	x^2p	W (percent)	B (percent)	x^2p
Medium preferred for world news						
Television	69	38	<.001	68	68	n.s.
Radio	16	28		13	21	(<.10)
Newspapers	15	34		19	11	
Medium preferred for local news						
Television	30	21	<.001	33	27	<.01
Radio	34	31		34	32	
Newspapers	22	41		26	19	
People	14	7		7	22	

aTotal LI n=281; n's for these two crossbreaks are 269 and 277, respectively. Total GP n=206; n's here are 190 and 203. Total W n=150; n's here are 143 and 148. Total B n=131; n's here are 126 and 129. Incomplete n's for the world news item result from non-responses and a small proportion of respondents who specified "people" as their preferred world news source. Incomplete n's on the local news item result entirely from non-response.

that asked respondents to choose the most believable
of two media. The low-income respondents consistently
chose TV over newspapers (74 percent for TV), TV over
radio (65 percent for TV), and radio over newspapers
(62 percent for radio). In none of these comparisons
were the blacks and whites significantly different
from each other.

However, there was a clearly significant difference between low-income blacks and whites for one
media attitude item. The whites gave almost equal
preference to TV, radio, and newspapers and low preference to people (7 percent) as the preferred source
for local news. In contrast, 22 percent of the blacks
cited people as their preferred medium for local news
(see Table 6).* This is another indication that although black and white low-income media behaviors are
very similar there are certain situations in which the
black sub-culture turns to sources outside the majority society for its information.

SUMMARY

In general, the media behaviors of low-income
adults are markedly different from those of the general population. The two samples were not significantly different on only two variables--ownership
levels of black-and-white TV sets and amount of radio
use yesterday. For every other media ownership, use,
content preference, and attitude variable, the two
samples were different. A brief summary of these
differences follows.

1. In terms of media ownership, except for black-
and-white TV sets, the general population had significantly higher media ownership and availability levels.
However, the low-income population was certainly not
media-poor as its ownership and daily availability
levels were all above 70 percent.

_____

*Although no specific study comparing media atti-
tudes of blacks and whites exists, some available data
agree. Allen found the same tendency to name people
as sources with his black respondents and the National
Advisory Commission on Civil Disorders noted that
blacks must more often go to non-institutionalized
sources for their information.[17]

2. In terms of media use, the most striking
finding was the sizable difference in amount of daily
TV viewing, the low-income sample averaging 5.2 hours
yesterday compared with 2.0 hours for the general population. The general population reported significantly
higher readership of newspapers and magazines and movie
attendance; the low-income population spent more time
listening to record players.
3. In media content preferences--both TV and
newspaper--the two samples were quite different. The
popularity rankings they gave to various TV programs
and sections of the newspaper were uncorrelated.
4. In media attitudes, the low-income adults
were far more favorable to TV. The low-income sample
more often rated TV as its most believed medium as
well as its preferred medium for world and local news.
Low-income adults also reported liking TV more than
did the general population. The low-income adults
were also more likely to cite people as a preferred
source of local news.

In contrast to the general pattern of mass communication differences between low-income and general
population adults, there were few differences between
low-income blacks and low-income whites. The two sub-
samples were similar in their ownership levels of both
TV and radio equipment. They had equal levels of TV
viewing, frequency of newspaper reading and number of
newspaper sections read regularly, amount of radio
listening, recency of magazine reading, and recency
of movie attendance. Their media content preferences
for both TV shows and newspaper sections were highly
correlated. Furthermore, their media attitudes were
quite similar in terms of the media preferred for
world news, the media considered most believable, and
a general liking for TV.

However, the two sub-samples did differ on a few
variables. Low-income whites were significantly more
likely to have newspapers delivered; blacks were significantly more likely to own phonographs and to own
more phonograph records. The uses of these two media--
newspapers and phonographs--agreed with the ownership
patterns: whites read more of the newspaper in general
and blacks reported significantly higher use of phonographs. Finally, when asked what sources they preferred for local news, blacks were more likely to cite
people.

CONCLUSIONS

The findings reported in this chapter give us a picture of the typical low-income media user. At least in the winter he is highly dependent on television in particular and the electronic media in general. He spends over one-third of his waking day on TV alone and almost one-half of his day on the electronic media. He not only uses TV a great deal, he prefers it as a source for his news and believes it more. He is unlike the typical general population adult in almost every one of his media behaviors. Whether he is black or white makes relatively little difference in how much he uses each medium, what he prefers to pay attention to in the media, and what he thinks about the media.

These findings indicate that our two working hypotheses served well.* The low-income sample was, indeed, considerably different from the general population and the low-income black was considerably like the low-income white in terms of mass media behaviors.

For the practitioner trying to reach low-income audiences, our findings suggest that use of either television or radio is his best means. The few differences found between the media behaviors of low-income whites and blacks also provide some guidelines for the poverty program practitioner as well as the researcher. We found that low-income whites use newspapers more, blacks use phonographs more, and blacks more often cite people as a preferred source of local news. These differences suggest that there are subcultural differences between low-income blacks and whites that were not fully tapped in this study but must be taken into account. We can reason that the low-income white has at least race in common with the majority society and so newspapers will be a more useful source of information for him. The black, does not have this similarity and must therefore locate

----

*However, we should note some limitations on the data reported in this chapter. Except for dividing the low-income sample into two racial groups no differentiation was made. Considerable recent work on poverty suggests that the poor are quite different among themselves, despite their apparent homogeneity.[18]

more specialized sources of information. The low-income blacks' greater use of phonographs may be a way
of hearing more black music than can be received
through the majority society media. Since the majority
media--television, radio, and newspapers--do not report on news within the black ghetto, other sources
of information must be found. The National Advisory
Commission on Civil Disorders agreed with this theory.
Their data searches indicated that blacks distrust the
"white press" and use sources other than establishment
media.19

Therefore, although this study generally suggests
that television and radio are the best means of reach-
ing low-income urban adults, the findings also suggest
that non-establishment media are needed to effectively
reach low-income blacks.

NOTES

1. See, for example: Elizabeth Herzog, "Some
Assumptions About the Poor," Social Service Review
XXXVIII, 4 (December, 1963), 389-402; Lola M. Irelan
and Arthur Besner, "Low Income Outlook on Life," Wel-
fare in Review III, 9 (September, 1965), 13-19; Oscar
Lewis, "The Culture of Poverty," Scientific American
CCXV, 4 (October, 1966), 19-25; National Advisory Com-
mission on Civil Disorders, Report on the National
Advisory Commission on Civil Disorders (New York:
Bantam Books, 1968).

2. See, for example, these classic studies of
media use: Merrill Samuelson, Richard F. Carter, and
Lee Ruggels, "Education, Available Time, and the Use
of the Mass Media," Journalism Quarterly XL, 3 (Fall,
1963), 491-496; Gary A. Steiner, The People Look at
Television (New York: Alfred A. Knopf, 1963); Bruce
H. Westley and Werner J. Severin, "Some Correlates
of Media Credibility," Journalism Quarterly XLI, 2
(Summer, 1964), 325-335.

3. See, for example, these studies specifically
on the poor: T. H. Allen, "Mass Media Use Patterns
and Functions in a Negro Ghetto" (Master's thesis,
University of West Virginia, 1967); Leslie W. Sargent
and Guido H. Stempel III, "Poverty, Alienation, and

Mass Media Use," Journalism Quarterly XLV, 2 (Summer, 1968), 324-326.

4.   Herzog, op. cit.

5.   See, particularly, these studies: Leonard Broom and Norval D. Glenn, "Negro-White Differences in Reported Attitudes and Behavior," Sociology and Social Research L, 2 (January, 1966), 187-200; Albert K. Cohen and Harold M. Hodge Jr., "Characteristics of the Lower Blue-Collar Class," Journal of Social Problems X, 4 (Spring, 1963), 103-134; Lenore A. Epstein, "Some Effects of Low-Income on Children and Their Families," Social Security Bulletin XXIV, 2 (February, 1961), 12-17; Walter M. Gerson, "Mass Media Socialization Behavior: Negro-White Differences," Social Forces XLV, 1 (September, 1966), 40-50; Susanne Keller, "The Social World of the Urban Slum Child: Some Early Findings," American Journal of Orthopsychiatry XXXIII, 5 (1963), 823-831.

6.   Studies available on the media behaviors of the poor include: Lewis Donohew and B. K. Singh, "Poverty 'Types' and Their Sources of Information About New Practices" (Paper presented at the International Communication Division, Association for Education in Journalism, Boulder, Colorado, August 27-31, 1967); Jack Lyle, "The Negro and the News Media," in Jack Lyle, The News in Megalopolis (San Francisco: The Chandler Press, 1967), Chapter 9, 163-182; James W. Carey, "Variations in Negro/White Television Preferences," Journal of Broadcasting X, 3 (1966), 199-211; Maxwell E. McCombs, "Negro Use of Television and Newspapers for Political Information, 1952-1964," Journal of Broadcasting XII, 3 (Summer, 1968), 261-266; Arnold M. Barban and Werner F. Grunbaum, "A Factor Analytic Study of Negro and White Responses to Advertising Stimuli," Journal of Applied Psychology XLIX, 4 (1965), 274-279; Gerson, op. cit.

7.   Guido H. Stempel III, "Increasing Reliability in Content Analysis," Journalism Quarterly XXXII, 4 (1955), 449-455.

8.   For example, see: Arthur Besner, "Economic Deprivation and Family Patterns," Welfare in Review III, 9 (September, 1965), 20-28; Epstein, op. cit.; Herzog, op. cit.; Keller, op. cit.; Lewis, op. cit.

9.   See, for example: Besner, op. cit.; Epstein, op. cit.; Herzog, op. cit.; Keller, op. cit.

10. U. S. Bureau of Census, <u>1960 U. S. Census of Population and Housing, Census Tracts, Final Report</u> (Washington, D. C.: Government Printing Office, 1961).

11. Allen, <u>op. cit.</u>; Sargent and Stempel III, <u>op. cit.</u>

12. McCombs, <u>op. cit.</u>; Sargent and Stempel III, <u>op. cit.</u>; Steiner, <u>op. cit.</u>; Westley and Severin, <u>op. cit.</u>

13. Carey, <u>op. cit.</u>

14. Allen, <u>op. cit.</u>

15. Samuelson, Carter, and Ruggels, <u>op. cit.</u>

16. Bradley S. Greenberg and Hideya Kumata, "National Sample Predictors of Mass Media Use," <u>Journalism Quarterly</u> XLV, 4 (Winter, 1968) 641-646, 705.

17. Allen, <u>op. cit.</u>; National Advisory Commission on Civil Disorders, <u>op. cit.</u>

18. Donohew and Singh, <u>op. cit.</u>; S. M. Miller, "The American Lower Classes: A Typological Approach," <u>Social Research</u> XXXI, 1 (Spring, 1964), 1-22.

19. National Advisory Commission on Civil Disorders, <u>op. cit.</u>

CHAPTER **2** MASS MEDIA FUNCTIONS
AMONG LOW-INCOME
ADOLESCENTS

Joseph R. Dominick and
Bradley S. Greenberg

INTRODUCTION

To understand the role of television in the lives
of low-income teen-agers, we must begin to identify
the overall patterns of television usage, attitudes,
and motivations. The present study had three purposes:

1. To describe the use of the major mass media
by urban teen-agers from low-income families, with a
more detailed analysis of their TV exposure.
2. To explore the attitudes of disadvantaged
teen-agers toward the mass media.
3. To examine their motivations for watching
television.

Prior studies of television among teen-agers have
not provided enough instances of low-income youths for
extended analysis.[1] Studies that have focused on this
age and economic grouping have been highly specific
in nature. Robert Blood examined family control over
TV viewing and found that middle-class families generally exercised more influence over viewing times and
program choices.[2] Walter Gerson investigated the ways
in which white and black teen-agers used all mass media to learn about dating behavior. Controlling for
income differences, he found that blacks were more
likely to use the media to learn dating information.[3]
Wilbur Schramm et al. found that among tenth graders,
those who fell in the low-socio-economic group were
more likely to use the media for what the researchers
labelled "fantasy seeking." Middle-class teen-agers
were more likely to be "reality-oriented." That is,

31

they were lower on TV use and higher on use of the
print media. They also were more likely to turn to
the media for information than for entertainment.[4]

HYPOTHESES

    Research among low-income groups has identified
certain relevant characteristics of their sub-culture.[5]
The poor participate in a more restricted range of activities, their workday rules are less complex, and
they less often assume public service roles. There
is also an emphasis on the concrete, the here-and-now
aspect of life. Television behavior would seem to
fit into this framework. TV watching is low-cost,
can be done at home, requires little effort, and emphasizes concrete, visual experiences. With these
facts in mind, two working hypotheses were developed:

    1. Teen-agers from low-income homes would spend
more of their media time with TV than middle-income
teen-agers and more absolute time with TV.
    2. More favorable attitudes toward television
offerings would exist among the less-advantaged teens.

    These hypotheses express differences in media
behaviors between income groups. Research also has
shown that there are differences between whites and
blacks within the low-income level. Blacks typically
earn less money than their white counterparts, are
more likely to live in an inner city ghetto, and are
more likely to engage in "fantasy" behaviors.[6] For
these reasons, further segmentation of the low-income
teen-agers into black and white sub-groups was expected
to accentuate the predicted differences.

    Moreover, a young person from a low-income family
can be thought of as living in a world where contacts
with the middle-class are infrequent and limited in
diversity. The Commission on Civil Disorders reported
a high degree of segregation between the poor and the
middle-class, regardless of race.[7] For example, a
low-income teen-ager would be more likely to attend
a school in a lower-class neighborhood where he would
have less direct contact with middle-class youngsters.
The amount and quality of information about the middle-class world generally would be minimal for a young
person from a lower-income environment. We therefore
expect he would turn to TV to find out about the middle-class environment that is so different from his

own. Since television would be his main source of
information about this outside environment, we would
expect that he would be more likely to believe in the
accuracy of TV portrayals of such life. This reasoning
led to three additional hypotheses:

1. Teen-agers from lower-income homes would
watch TV more often for learning reasons than would
middle-income teen-agers.
2. Lower-income teen-agers would be more likely
to believe that TV portrays real-life situations and
that the world outside their immediate environs cor-
responds to the world presented on TV.
3. Low-income teen-agers would be less likely
to prefer variety shows whose main purpose can be
classified as "entertainment" than would middle-class
youngsters.

Again, we expected to bring out these overall differences by dividing the low-income teen-agers into black
and white sub-groups.

METHODS

A self-administered questionnaire was presented
to eight classes of tenth and eleventh graders in a
Philadelphia high school on May 6, 1968, during regular 45-minute morning class periods. Classes in the
lowest ability level in the school were not interviewed
because the school people felt these students had in-
sufficient reading skills to handle the questionnaire.

The high school is located at the edge of a ghetto
from which it draws almost all its black students. It
is also near a low-income white residential area that
contributes a large proportion of its white enrollment.
The racial distribution in the school was about 60 percent white and 40 percent black. We obtained data from
206 teen-agers, 60 percent whites and 40 percent blacks.
On the next day, the same questionnaire was administered
to 100 middle-class, white teen-agers attending another
high school in North Philadelphia.* The student groups

_____

*The index of social status used in this study is
one developed by Verling Trohdahl to measure occupational prestige.[8] Using a 13-point scale with 12 indicating an occupation with the highest prestige and 0

consisted of approximately one-half boys and one-half
girls. Data were obtained for three major variable
categories: .

    1. Television usage: amount of television view-
ing; specific content or program choices; popularity
of TV versus other leisure-time activities; process
of selecting programs; presence of rules connected
with TV viewing; parental viewing habits; and other
mass media usage.
    2. Attitudes toward television: perceived real-
ity in TV programming; relative believability of TV
versus other media; and relative competence of TV versus other media.
    3. Motivations for watching television: reasons
given for TV watching.

    Data obtained from three sub-groups--lower-class
whites, lower-class blacks, and middle-class whites--
enabled a three-way analysis:

    1. The two lower-class groups were compared to
examine the influence of race on television behavior.
    2. The middle- and lower-class whites were com-
pared to examine the effects of economic background
on TV-related behaviors.
    3. All three groups were compared directly to
examine the linearity of differences among groups.

FINDINGS

    Both social class and racial differences were
found for many of the dependent variable behaviors.
Being poor prompted many differences. Being poor and
black usually served to extend those differences.

Time Spent Viewing TV

    Each respondent went through a TV log for Sunday,
May 5, 1968. Total time was obtained by summing the
lengths of shows watched. The middle-class teen-agers
watched an average of 3.7 hours of TV compared to 4.6
hours for the lower-class whites. The black teen-agers
watched most--6.3 hours. (See Table 7.)

---

the lowest prestige, the following were the average
prestige ratings for each of the groups: low-income
blacks = 4.18; low-income whites = 4.07; middle-income
whites = 6.54.

We also found racial and economic differences in
the time of day these teen-agers watched TV. Low-income teens were more likely to be in the TV audience
during the morning, afternoon, and after midnight.
Black teens were more likely than their white counterparts to be watching during the morning hours and in
the early and late evening. Black teen-agers were
also more apt to be watching the set after midnight.

Choice of Favorite Programs

Respondents were asked to name their three favorite TV shows. Several shows appealed to all teen-
agers, regardless of race or social class. "Mission
Impossible" was ranked first or second by all three
groups. Movies were also rated high by all. Two
shows, "Laugh In" and "The Smothers Brothers Show,"
appealed primarily to white audiences. "Laugh In"
was among the top three choices for both the middle-
and lower-income whites but only three blacks mentioned it as a favorite. In general, variety shows
were more preferred by white youngsters. Not one variety show made the top ten list of the low-income
black youngsters (See Table 9). Five shows appeared
in the black top twenty popularity rankings that did
not appear among the favorites of either white sample.
In four of these five shows, family units played a
central role in most episodes.

Popularity of TV Versus
Other Leisure Time Activities

Respondents indicated whether they would rather
watch TV or (separately) read a book, listen to radio,
do homework, or go out with friends. We found both
race and class differences in response patterns to
these items (see Table 10). When given a choice between reading a book or watching television, middle-
class youngsters split almost 50-50 in reporting what
they usually do. In contrast, 79 percent of the blacks
and 87 percent of the lower-class whites reported they
would choose TV. Black teen-agers reported that they
usually do homework instead of watching TV more often
than did white teen-agers, regardless of social class.
However, blacks also reported they usually watched TV
instead of going out with friends more often than
whites. Choice of radio versus TV was not different
by class or race.

TABLE 7

Sunday TV Viewing Among Teen-Agers

No. of Hours of TV Viewing	Low-Income		Middle-Income
	Blacks (N=84)	Whites (N=124)	Whites (N=98)
None	14%	25%	21%
½ to 3½ hours	15%	15%	29%
4 to 8 hours	35%	44%	43%
8½ or more hours	36%	16%	7%
Average number[a] of hours	6.3	4.6	3.7

[a]A t-test of uncorrelated means yielded a significant difference between middle- and low-income groups (t=3.27; df=305; p .01) as well as a significant difference between black and white low-income respondents (t=2.75; df=207; p .01).

TABLE 8

Percentage of Teen-Agers Watching TV,
by Time of Day[a]

Time of Day	Low-Income		Middle-Income
	Blacks (N=84)	Whites (N=124)	Whites (N=98)
6a.m.-noon	52	31	21
Noon-6p.m.	61	54	41
6p.m.-midnight	86	70	72
Midnight-3a.m.	26	14	3

[a]Chi=square tests indicated significant differences between middle- and low-income groups for all time periods with the exception of the 6 p.m. to midnight category. Significant differences between low-income black and white respondents were obtained for all time categories except the noon to 6 p.m. time period.

36

TABLE 9

Ten Favorite TV Shows Among Teen-Agers

Order of Preference	Program Name	Percent of Sample Naming Show
Low-Income Blacks		
1	Mission Impossible	30
2	Dark Shadows	29
3	It Takes a Thief	22
4	Movies	18
5	Big Valley	17
6	Garrison's Gorillas	11
7	Lost in Space	10
8	The Doctors	8
9	Star Trek	8
10	(Tie) Invaders Untouchables General Hospital	7
Low-Income Whites		
1	Mission Impossible	30
2	Dark Shadows	24
3	Laugh-In	18
4	It Takes a Thief	14
5	Movies	13
6	Star Trek	13
7	That Girl	11
8	Peyton Place	10
9	Carol Burnett	9
10	Smothers Brothers	6
Middle-Income Whites		
1	Laugh-In	46
2	Mission Impossible	33
3	Movies	18
4	Smothers Brothers	15
5	I Spy	14
6	Star Trek	14
7	It Takes a Thief	13
8	Carol Burnett	12
9	That Girl	10
10	Dark Shadows	7

TABLE 10

Popularity of TV Versus
Other Leisure Time Activities
Among Teen-Agers[a]

Percent Choosing TV in Preference to:	Low-Income		Middle-Income
	Blacks (N=84)	Whites (N=124)	Whites (N=98)
Reading a book	79	87	54
Listening to radio	45	36	43
Doing homework	45	62	57
Going out with friends	30	16	15

[a]Chi-square tests indicated significant differences between middle-income and low-income groups for the first three items. There were significant differences between black and white low-income respondents for the last two items.

Process of Selecting Programs

The three groups did not report different preparations for watching TV. Respondents were most likely to say that they read TV Guide or the TV listings in the newspapers to see if there was something they wanted to watch.

Presence of Household Rules
Concerning TV Viewing

Rules about TV watching exist in a minority of homes, without regard to social class or race. The most common rules is a late-night cut-off point after which TV viewing is not allowed (see Table 11). About 50 percent of the white students reported such a rule compared with 35 percent of the blacks.

Teen-Agers' Estimates of
Parents' TV Viewing

Class differences were obtained in the amount of time the three groups thought their parents spent watching TV. The black teen-agers reported that adults in their homes watched TV more than 3.5 hours

TABLE 11

Presence of Household Rules
Concerning TV Viewing[a]

	Low-Income		Middle-Income
	Blacks (N=84)	Whites (N=124)	Whites (N=98)
Are there rules in your house about how late you can stay up watching TV? (percent answering yes)	35	46	47
Does anyone in your home ever tell you there are some kinds of TV shows they wish you didn't watch? (percent answering yes)	30	18	27
Are you ever punished for something by not being allowed to watch TV? (percent answering yes)	20	18	19

[a] A Chi-square test yielded no significant differences between the middle-income and low-income respondents on any of the three items. There were also no significant differences between low-income blacks and whites.

per day; lower-class whites reported 3.3 hours per day; and middle-class youngsters, 2.4 hours (See Table 12).

Time Spent with Other Mass Media

Major differences were found in the use of radio, magazines, newspapers, and record players but not movies (see Table 13). A class difference was evident in both magazine and newspaper reading. The middle-class youngsters used these media more often than lower-class teens. Radio listening showed a race difference: the two white groups reported listening a half-hour longer than did the blacks. A race

TABLE 12

Teen-Agers' Estimates of
Parents' TV Viewing[a]

| No. of Hours[b] | Low-Income | | Middle-Income |
	Blacks (N=82)	Whites (N=124)	Whites (N=97)
6 or more	36%	26%	5%
5 to 6	8%	15%	3%
3 to 4	36%	39%	35%
1 to 2	17%	13%	42%
Less than one	2%	7%	15%
Average	3.60	3.34	2.37

[a]An analysis of variance showed a significant difference among the means of the three groups ($F = 27.33$; df = 2/300; p .0005). A t-test indicated a significant difference between the means of the low-income group and the middle-income group (t = 5.12; df = 302; p <.001).

[b]To compute the above averages the responses were coded as follows; 6 hours or more = 5; 5 to 6 hours = 4; 3 to 4 hours = 3; 1 to 2 hours = 2; less than an hour = 1.

TABLE 13

A Typical Media Day for Teen-Agers

| | Low-Income | | Middle-Income |
	Blacks	Whites	Whites
Television viewing	6 hours	4½ hours	3½ hours
Radio listening	2 hours	2½ hours	2½ hours
Newspaper reading	Maybe	Maybe	Yes
Magazine reading	2/week	2/week	3/week
Movies	1/month	2/month	2/month

difference was also present in phonograph use: the
black youngsters listened longer than the whites.
Table 13 summarizes the above findings and shows a
composite "media day" for these three groups of
teen-agers.

TABLE 14

Average Time Spent with
Mass Media Other than TV

	Low-Income		Middle-Income
	Blacks (N=84)	Whites (N=124)	Whites (N=98)
Radio Listening (hours)	1.95	2.54	2.50[a]
Record Player Use (hours)	1.57	1.03	1.14[a]
Newspaper reading (times per week)	5.70	6.10	6.93[b]
Magazine reading (number in past week)	2.61	2.23	2.99[b]
Movie attendance (number in past month)	1.37	1.76	1.71

[a]An analysis of variance of these means yielded a
difference significant at the .05 level.

[b]An analysis of variance of these means yielded a
difference significant at the .001 level.

Perceived Reality of TV Programs

Three questions indicated whether the respondents
perceived any similarity between the world they saw
portrayed on TV and the world they saw around them.
They were asked to agree or disagree with the following statements:

The people I see on TV are just like
people I meet in real life.

The programs I see on TV tell about
life the way it really is.

The same things that happen to people
on TV happen to me in real life.

Scores on these three items were summed, creating an index for each respondent. The results formed a statistically significant step-wise progression.* With total agreement indexed by a score of 9.0, the average score for the low-income blacks was 6.08; for the low-income whites, 5.08; and for the middle-class whites, 4.47. The average score of the middle-class youngsters can be interpreted as an answer of "I disagree" to the three statements cited above. Next came the lower-class whites. The black teen-agers were highest in perceived reality in TV. Their replies fell between "I'm not sure" and "I agree" on the index.

This step-wise progression of results persisted when six variables were used as controls. In all six comparisons, the low-income black teen-agers scored the highest on the reality items, followed by the low-income white teen-agers, and then the middle-income teens (see Table 15). Analysis of these data also revealed that both low- and middle-income females perceived more reality in TV content than did their male counterparts. Those among the middle-income teen-agers who belived TV was most credible also perceived a higher degree of reality in TV programs.

Credibility of TV

Three questions dealt with the perceived believability of television in comparison with radio and newspapers (see Table 16). If conflicting stories were received, the majority in each of the three groups would believe the TV version. Radio and newspapers were named by 15-18 percent of each lower-class group. The middle-class youngsters showed more belief in the newspaper: 35 percent named it as most believable. From two-thirds to three-fourths in each of the three groups reported that TV would be the one medium they would keep if they could have only one. Radio was second and hardly anyone named newspapers.

---

*An analysis of variance indicated a significant difference among the means of the three groups (F= 18.91; df=2/303; p <.0005). A t-test yielded significant differences between middle and low-income groups (t=4.69; df=305; p <.001). The same statistic also showed a significant difference between low-income blacks and whites (t=3.76; df=207; p .001).

TABLE 15

Index of Perceived Reality in TV Content,
by Six Control Variables

	Low-Income		Middle-Income	p(F)
	Blacks	Whites	Whites	
Males	5.97	4.68	4.10	<.0005
Females	6.19	5.45	4.87	<.005
TV most credible	6.33	5.26	4.92	<.0005
TV not most credible	5.65	4.71	4.00	<.0005
Read newspaper every day	6.15	4.90	4.50	<.0005
Don't read every day	6.02	5.32	4.40	<.001
0 or 1 movie in past month	6.02	4.77	4.32	<.0005
2 or more movies in past month	6.18	5.34	4.61	<.0005
Church every week	6.19	4.93	4.53	<.001
Church not every week	6.00	5.22	4.44	<.0005
Say-so over what is viewed:				
Myself	5.88	5.34	4.79	<.100
Someone else	6.17	4.93	4.25	<.0005

TABLE 16

Desirability and Believability
of Television Versus Other Media[a]

| | Low-Income | | Middle-Income |
	Blacks (N=84)	Whites (N=124)	Whites (N=98)
Suppose you got different stories about the same thing from radio, TV and the newspaper, which one would you believe? (percent choosing TV.)	63	66	51
Which do you think does his job the best: the reporter for the newspaper, the news announcer on TV, or the news announcer on the radio? (percent choosing TV announcer.)	65	55	45
Let's say you could keep only one of these: radio, TV, newspaper. Which one would you keep? (percent choosing TV.)	76	69	66

[a]A Chi-square test indicated differences significant at the .05 level between the low- and middle-income groups for the first two items.

Newspapers did better, but still not well, when the respondents named the person who did his job best-- the newspaper reporter or the radio or TV news announcer. In the black sample, 65 percent named the TV announcer; the radio announcer was second with 17 percent. Among lower-class whites, 55 percent thought that the TV announcer did the best job; 29 percent felt the newspaper reporter did the best job. Middle-class teen-agers showed more ambivalence. The newspaper reporter and the television news announcer were named with almost equal frequency, 42 percent and 45 percent respectively.

Reasons for Viewing TV

The youngsters responded to 34 possible reasons why they might watch television.* These reasons were derived from a content analysis of 75 essays written by different groups of low- and middle-income high school students on the topic "Why I Watch Television." The questionnaire used those statements that represented as wide as possible a range of reasons. Many reasons were mentioned with equal frequency across the groups; other reasons differed with race and social class. These results indicate that TV serves some general functions for all teen-agers but also serves some specific functions that vary with social class and/or race.

There were substantial racial and/or social class differences on 18 of the 34 items. Twelve of these 18 reasons referred to ways in which TV serves an informal "learning-about-life" function. The degree to which TV is used as this kind of learning device depends on both social class and race. Black teen-agers had the greatest tendency to use TV for such information; middle-class white teen-agers had the least tendency. The 12 items were:

I watch TV because . . .

. . . I can learn from the mistakes of
        others.
. . . I can learn a lot without working
        very hard.
. . . it shows how other solve the same
        problems I have.
. . . it shows what life is really like.
. . . it helps me learn about myself as a
        human being.
. . . I get to know all about people in all
        walks of life.
. . . I want to know what's going on in the
        world.
. . . I can understand things better when I
        can see them as well as hear them.
. . . without it I wouldn't know much about
        the world.

---

*The complete set of statements and the means obtained for the respondent groups are available from the authors.

        . . . the programs give lessons for life.
        . . . I learn things on TV I don't learn
              in school.
        . . . I get to see what people are like.

     The six other items showing significant racial
and/or class differences deal with use of TV for
stimulation. The items were:

     I watch TV because . . .

        . . . it excites me.
        . . . it gives me a thrill.
        . . . it keeps my mind off other things.
        . . . it keeps me out of trouble.
        . . . it's almost like a human companion.
        . . . it brings my family together.

Low-income teens were more likely to agree with these
statements. Among the low-income sample, blacks were
more likely than whites to agree. Thus, our data suggest that the more disadvantaged have a greater tendency to seek excitement and thrills from TV.

     Functional differences were not found by social
class or race for such motivations for TV watching as
relaxation, low cost and easy access, escape, and for-
getting.

                          SUMMARY

     This study was designed to obtain information
on the extent to which television is used among teen-
agers from low-income homes in comparison with youngsters from middle-class environments. We also explored
the comparative attitudes toward TV of these two groups
and the motivations they bring to the viewing situation. Data were obtained from 206 teen-agers from
low-income urban areas (60 percent white and 40 percent black) and from 100 teen-agers of at least middle-class, urban backgrounds.

     Teens from low-income homes watched more TV than
did middle-class teens. The black teen-agers watched
more than did the whites from the same economic setting. Teen-agers from lower-income families also reported more parental TV viewing than did middle-class
youngsters.

On program preferences, comedy shows and general variety shows were more preferred by the white teen-agers. There were no differences in how these subgroups decided to watch a show. Little consistent difference among the groups was evident concerning household rules on TV watching. However, black youngsters were less likely to have a deadline on how late they could watch. Twenty-five percent of the black youngsters did some watching after midnight compared with 14 percent of the lower-class whites and 3 percent of the middle-class whites. In all homes, the predominant say-so about what programs were watched was made by the teen-ager himself. In black homes, the second dominant program chooser was the mother; in white homes, it was the father.

In a hypothetical choice between watching television or reading a book, the lower-income teen-agers chose TV more frequently. In a hypothetical choice between watching TV or going out with friends, the black youngsters were more likely to choose TV.

As for time spent with media other than TV, whites from both income levels did more radio listening and less record playing. Lower-class youngsters, both black and white, were less likely to have gone to a movie in the past month or to have read as many magazines. Middle-income teens were more likely to report some newspaper reading every day.

The major finding on attitudes toward the media was that lower-class teen-agers were more likely than their middle-class counterparts to think that TV depicted life the way it is. The black youngsters from lower-income homes believed in TV's reality more than did disadvantaged whites. A majority of each group was more inclined to believe the TV version of a news story than the radio or newspaper version; this majority was larger among the lower-income groups. Similarly, the TV news announcer was rated better at his job than his radio or newspaper counterpart.

Lower-class respondents were more likely to use TV as a means of finding out what life is about; low-income black teen-agers were more likely to do so than their white counterparts. The lower-class respondents were also more likely to use TV to get excitement and thrills; again, the lower-class were more likely to do so than the lower-class whites.

IMPLICATIONS

    The young man or woman emerging from an environ-
ment that is below standard in economic and social
terms has been greatly dependent on a single mass
medium--television--for his information and attitudes
about the world outside his own neighborhood. He has
spent more time with TV, has different favorite programs, has more positive attitudes toward TV, and is
less critical of TV than the youngster in the suburbs
or in better-off urban homes. The low-income youngster thinks that much of what he is seeing in entertainment programs portrays life as other people are
living it, and perhaps as he wishes he could.

NOTES

    1.   See for example, Jack Lyle "Immediate vs.
Delayed Reward Use of Newspapers by Adolescents,"
Journalism Quarterly XXXIX (Winter, 1962), 83-85;
Irving Merrill, "Broadcast Viewing and Listening by
Children," Public Opinion Quarterly XXV (Summer,
1961), 262-276.

    2.   Robert O. Blood, Jr., "Social Class and
Family Control of Television Viewing," Merrill-Palmer
Quarterly VII, 3 (July, 1961), 205-222.

    3.   Walter Gerson, "Mass Media Socialization
Behavior: Negro-White Differences," Social Forces
XLV, 1 (September, 1966), 40-50.

    4.   Wilbur Schramm et al., Television in the
Lives of Our Children (Stanford, Calif.: Stanford
University Press, 1961).

    5.   Albert K. Cohen and Harold M. Hodge, Jr.,
"Characteristics of the Lower Blue-Collar Class,"
Journal of Social Problems X, 4 (Spring, 1963),
103-134; Catherine S. Chilman, Growing up Poor
(Washington, D.C.: Government Printing Office, May,
1966).

    6.   Kenneth B. Clark, Dark Ghetto: Dilemmas of
Social Power (New York: Harper, 1967); Jules Henry,

"White People's Time, Colored People's Time" Trans-Action II, 3 (March-April, 1965), 31, 34; National Commission on Civil Disorders, Report of the National Commission on Civil Disorders (New York: Bantam Books, 1968).

7. National Commission on Civil Disorders, op. cit. p. 253.

8. Verling Troldahl, "Occupational Prestige Scale," (mimeographed) (East Lansing: Department of Communication, Michigan State University, 1967).

CHAPTER **3** TELEVISION BEHAVIOR
AMONG DISADVANTAGED
CHILDREN

Bradley S. Greenberg
and Joseph R. Dominick

INTRODUCTION

The use that a child or a group of children makes
of television varies with the individual's life style.
Researchers have identified some variables that influence the way a child uses the mass media. Among these
are social class, race, age, and how a child gets along
with his parents and peers.[1] This study elaborates on
the functions of television for young children of different race and social class.

Our own work (see Chapter 2) indicated that
social class and race were key variables among teen-
agers in detecting differences in mass media use,
attitudes toward the media, and motivations for
watching TV. This chapter examines parallel media
behaviors for a younger age group--fourth and fifth
graders.

Data for this particular age group are scarce.
Wilbur Schramm et al. found sixth graders from lower-
class families were more prone to use the media, especially TV, in a "fantasy-oriented" way than were
middle-class youngsters. They also tended to be
heavier TV users.[2] Friedman reported that lower-income eleven-year olds viewed more television per week
than did upper- or middle-class ones. Parental censorship of viewing was found in only a few instances.[3]

The basic rationale for our research is the notion that the low-income child is more dependent on
the mass media, particularly television, as a means
of contact with and information about the world

outside his immediate grasp. Because he has fewer direct contacts with the "real" world and greater frustrations in his own life, the low-income child gives
more of himself to television, believes its messages
more readily, and is more inclined to perceive that
it does more for him. The Violence Commission subscribed to this theory: "Moreover, television is a
particularly potent force in families where parental
influence and primary group ties are weak or completely
lacking, notably in low-income areas or where violent
life-styles are common. In these instances, television does not displace parental influence: it fills a
vacuum".[4] In such families, the social impact of television should be most evident.

METHODS

Questionnaires were administered to fourth and
fifth grade students in four East Cleveland, Ohio,
elementary schools on April 22-23, 1969, during regular class periods. Three schools were located in an
area populated by a large number of black and white
families of varying income levels. The fourth school
was in a white, middle-class, residential area. Data
were obtained from 392 youngsters, two-thirds of whom
were black. Both black and white groups were subdivided into three groups according to the occupation
of the main wage earner in the family. Occupations
were rated by the Troldahl occupational prestige
scale.* Six groups of children were formed of the
following sizes and occupational prestige ratings:

Occupational Prestige

	Low	Medium	High
Whites	2.96 (n=47)	4.30 (n=49)	8.00 (n=38)
Blacks	2.74 (n=142)	4.00 (n=54)	5.70 (n=62)

---

*For elaboration of this scale, see Chapter 2,
pages 33-34. With 12 representing the highest occupational prestige and 0 representing the lowest, all
respondents were grouped into three prestige levels.
For whites, high-income respondents were those whose

Low-prestige occupations for blacks included
night watchman and gas station attendant; for whites,
assembly-line worker and waitress. Examples of medium-
prestige occupations for blacks were auto mechanic and
secretary in a real estate office; for whites, sales-
man in a department store and clerk in a furniture
company. High-prestige occupations for blacks included grade school teacher and police detective; for
whites, district manager for an insurance company and
chemical engineer.

Data were obtained for four kinds of media behaviors: (1) television use; (2) use of other mass
media; (3) parental and personal influence over TV
viewing; and, (4) some functions of television. The
specific variables examined for each of these behaviors
were:

1. Television usage; amount of TV viewing; TV
viewing by time of day; TV set ownership; and content
preferences.

2. Use of other mass media; newspaper reading;
radio listening; record player use; and movie going.

3. Influence over television viewing; family
rules about viewing; amount of personal choice in programs watched; and perceived parental viewing.

4. Functions of television; perceived reality
in TV content; reasons for watching TV; learning about
preferred occupation; learning about preferred place
to live; identification with TV characters; and TV as
a topic of conversation.

RESULTS

TV Usage

TV Set Ownership

A working television set was available in the
homes of virtually all the children on the sample.

---

prestige ratings were six or above; medium-income respondents, four or five; low-income respondents, three
or below. The lack of a comparable group of high-income blacks led to the following divisions among this
group: high-income respondents were those coded five
or above; medium-income, those in level four; low-income, those coded three or below. The percentage of
males in the six sub-group ranged from 39-53 percent.

In fact, the modal number of working sets for all sub-
programs was two per family. Black children reported
a higher average number of sets across all occupational
levels.*

Amount of TV Viewing

The results of the overall analysis of variance
indicated a significant interaction effect (see Table
17). Viewing time among whites decreased as income
increased but among blacks the trend was less clear.
Specific comparisons of individual means showed:

1.   High-income whites averaged significantly
less viewing time than low- or medium-income whites.
2.   Low-income blacks watched significantly more
TV than medium- or high-income blacks.
3.   Blacks at low-income and high-income levels
watched significantly more TV than whites at those
levels.

TABLE 17

Average Hours of Weekday TV Viewing
Among Disadvantaged Children[a]

	Family Income		
	Low	Medium	High
Whites	5.73	5.19	3.82
Blacks	6.85	5.90	6.29

Variable	Analysis Results	
	F	P
Income	7.83	<.0005
Race	28.82	<.0005
Income X Race	3.63	<.03

[a]Amount of television viewing was calculated for
these samples by totaling the length of each show the
respondents had circled on a TV schedule for the day
before the interview. Times were rounded to the
nearest half-hour.

_____

*An analysis of variance of this data indicated
a racial difference significant at the .005 level.

Low-income black youngsters reported the most viewing time on a given weekday, nearly seven hours; high-income whites watched for four hours.

Time-of-Day Viewing Differences

Two sets of items examined differential viewing patterns throughout the day. The first consisted of two questions that asked the youngsters how often they watched TV before or after school. Possible responses were "all the time," "sometimes," and "never". Both income and racial differences were found in the frequency of watching before school. Blacks in the medium- and high-income levels reported more watching than whites; low-income whites reported significantly more viewing than high-income whites. After-school viewing was significantly higher among blacks than whites, particularly within the medium-and high-income groups.

The second measure of time-of-day viewing was derived from the children's report of their actual TV watching on the day before these data were gathered. Significant differences were found between income groups in the proportion who were watching TV at any given time (see Table 18). Viewing times were divided into five periods--before school, during the noon hour, from 3 to 7:30 p.m., from 7:30 to 11 p.m., and after 11 p.m. Low-income youngsters of both races were more likely to be watching the set during the first four of these five periods.

Content Preferences

Two shows, "Mod Squad" and "Bewitched," were among the children's favorite shows, regardless of race and social class (see Table 19). Other shows were primarily favored by one racial group but not the other. "Julia" and the cartoon show "Speed Racer" were chosen more often by blacks than by whites. "Dark Shadows," "Laugh-In," and "Here Come the Brides" were favorites among whites, that did not appeal to blacks. Black youngsters of different income groups were more likely to have the same favorite programs than whites of different income. Black youngsters also reported that they paid more attention to TV commercials than did whites.* No differences were found in the regularity of watching TV newscasts.

----

*An analysis of variance of these data indicated a racial difference significant at the .004 level.

TABLE 18

Time-of-Day Differences in Children's
TV Viewing[a] (Percent of Sample
Who Watched During Given
Time Period)

	Family Income		
	Low	Medium	High
Before School			
Whites	61	51	37
Blacks	67	54	32
During the noon hour			
Whites	80	71	42
Blacks	81	63	53
3-7:30 p.m.			
Whites	90	87	74
Blacks	95	95	71
7:30-11 p.m.			
Whites	90	89	74
Blacks	95	90	68
After 11 p.m.			
Whites	14	12	6
Blacks	20	17	9

[a]Chi-square analysis of the above indicated significant income differences in the first four viewing periods.

Use of Other Mass Media

Newspaper Reading

Most of the children indicated that they read the comics almost every day. There was a racial difference, however, with regard to reading parts of the paper other than the comics (see Table 20). In general, whites averaged more newspaper reading than blacks at all income levels, with the difference most pronounced between high-income blacks and whites. Whites reported reading a newspaper three or four times a week; blacks reported some reading less than three times a week.

TABLE 19

Children's Five Favorite TV Shows

Blacks

	Percent of Sample Naming Show
Low-Income	
1. Mod Squad	49
2. Julia	35
3. Speed Racer	15
4. Gilligan's Island	14
5. Patty Duke	13
Middle-Income	
1. Mod Squad	58
2. Julia	40
3. Speed Racer	18
4. Bewitched	16
5. Dark Shadows	14
High-Income	
1. Mod Squad	45
2. Julia	43
3. Speed Racer	21
4. (Tie) Bewitched and Gidget	13
5. (Tie) Patty Duke and Gilligan's Island	12

Whites

	Percent of Sample Naming Show
Low-Income	
1. Mod Squad	27
2. Bewitched	23
3. Dark Shadows	19
4. Gilligan's Island	17
5. (Tie) Wild, Wild West and Here Come the Brides	15
Middle-Income	
1. Bewitched	24
2. Mod Squad	22
3. Here Come the Brides	18
4. Dark Shadows	16
5. Laugh In	14
High-Income	
1. Dark Shadows	21
2. Mod Squad	18
3. Laugh In	16
4. Here Come the Brides	13
5. (Tie) Jerry Lewis and Gilligan's Island	11

TABLE 20

Average Number of Times Newspaper
Is Read Per Week

	Family Income		
	Low	Medium	High
Whites	3.40	3.65	3.92
Blacks	2.92	2.83	2.60
Variable	Analysis Results		
	F	P	
Income	.03	–	
Race	6.54	<.02	
Income X Race	.53	–	

Radio Listening

There was no difference among the groups in the
amount of time they had listened to the radio on a
particular weekday (see Table 21). Most had listened
about one hour. However, whites, listened more frequently to radio newscasts than did blacks, especially
in the high-income level (see Table 22).

Record Player Use

At all income levels, black children listened
more often to a record player than did whites (see
Table 23). The greatest differences were between
blacks and whites in the medium- and high-income
groups. In general, whites listened to records about
45 minutes on the weekday before the interview and
black youngsters spent more than 80 minutes listening
to records.

Movie attendance

Blacks at all income levels reported significantly more movie attendance in the past month than
did whites, as seen in Table 24. Across all income
levels, whites averaged less than one movie per month
whereas black youngsters averaged nearly two movies.

TABLE 21

Average Number of Hours of Weekday
Radio Listening

| | Family Income | | |
	Low	Medium	High
Whites	1.12	1.43	1.39
Blacks	1.20	0.96	1.10

| Variable | Analysis Results | |
	F	P
Income	.08	--
Race	1.85	--
Income X Race	.97	--

TABLE 22

Frequency of Listening to Radio News[a]

| | Family Income | | |
	Low	Medium	High
Whites	2.15	2.37	2.42
Blacks	2.10	2.11	2.08

| Variable | Analysis Results | |
	F	P
Income	.60	-
Race	3.89	<.05
Income X Race	.73	-

[a]The question asked was: "How often do you listen to the news on radio?" The response categories were coded as follows to compute the above means: never = 1; sometimes = 2; quite a bit = 3; all the time = 4.

59

TABLE 23

Average Number of Hours Spent
Listening to Record Player

	Family Income		
	Low	Medium	High
Whites	1.06	0.55	0.60
Blacks	1.43	1.11	1.40

Variable	Analysis Results	
	F	P
Income	2.55	<.08
Race	12.93	<.0005
Income X Race	.60	—

TABLE 24

Average Number of Movies Seen
in the Past Month

	Family Income		
	Low	Medium	High
Whites	1.15	0.56	0.74
Blacks	1.82	1.89	2.11

Variable	Analysis Results	
	F	P
Income	0.87	—
Race	41.73	<.0005
Income X Race	1.90	<.15

Influence over TV Viewing

The children were asked whether or not three specific rules about TV watching existed in their homes:

1. Is there a rule about how late you can stay up watching TV?
2. Does anyone in your house tell you there are certain shows they'd rather you didn't watch?
3. Are you ever punished by not being allowed to watch TV?

A control index was computed for each child by summing his yes responses to these three items. Analysis of this index showed that income was the important differentiator: both whites and blacks in the low-income level reported significantly fewer rules than did youngsters in the medium- and high-income groups (see Table 25).

The late-night cut-off rule was prevalent with about 70 percent of all children reporting such a rule. Attempts at censorship were also widespread, reported by 60 percent of the youngsters. Punishment by having TV privileges withheld was reported by about 40 percent of all youngsters.

Amount of Personal Control over Viewing

The youngsters were asked to name the person in their family who had the most say-so over what was watched on TV. For all groups except the high-income whites, "myself" was the answer most often given with about one-third of the youngsters making this response. The father, the most influential figure among the high-income whites, was named by 30 percent; 18 percent cited themselves. Among the other two groups of whites, the father ranked second. In contrast, among black children at all income levels the second most influential person was the mother. Other responses were divided among "my brothers and sisters" and "someone else in my family."

Children's Perceptions of Parental Viewing

Black children of low- and medium-income families said that their parents spent more time viewing TV but not significantly more (See Table 26). But high-income blacks indicated that their parents spent

TABLE 25

Prevalence of Family Rules about TV
Watching (Control Index)[a]

	Family Income		
	Low	Medium	High
Whites	1.66	2.02	2.00
Blacks	1.50	1.94	1.82
Variables	Analysis Results		
	F	P	
Income	7.52	<.001	
Race	2.05	<.15	
Income X Race	.10	-	

[a]This index was formed by summing the number of yes answers given by respondents to each of the three items listed in the text.

TABLE 26

Children's Perceptions of
Parental Viewing[a]

	Family Income		
	Low	Medium	High
Whites	3.26	3.24	2.74
Blacks	3.43	3.48	3.58
Variables	Analysis Results		
	F	P	
Income	0.72	-	
Race	8.11	<.005	
Income X Race	2.00	<.14	

[a]The question asked was: "On an average day, how much time do the adults in your family watch TV?" The above averages were computed by assigning the following scores to the response categories: 5 = 6 or more hours; 4 = 5 to 6 hours; 3 = 3 to 4 hours; 2 = 1 to 2 hours; 1 = an hour or less.

significantly more time (3-4 hours) viewing than did
the parents of the high-income white children (less
than 3 hours).

Functions Performed by TV

Perceived Reality in TV Content

The youngsters were asked whether or not they
perceived some similarity between the world portrayed
on TV and the world they lived in. Five agree-dis-
agree items were used, including the following:

> The people I see on TV are just like
> people I know in real life.

> Families I see on TV are like my family.

> The programs I see on TV tell about life
> the way it really is.

Response scores to the five items were summed.*
Both income and race differences were evident in the
results (see Tables 27 and 28). In general, the
blacks perceived TV as being more realistic than did
the whites. The high-income group perceived the least
realism and the low-income group perceived the most
realism in TV presentations. Other comparisons with
the reality index showed:

----

*To check on the possibility that an acquiescent
response set might be in operation among the low-income and black sub-groups on these items, a two-item
scale consisting of two of the reality index items
using negative wording was also included in the questionnaire. Analysis of this second index showed that
wording the items negatively decreased the overall
level of agreement with the statement for five of the
six sub-groups. For high-income blacks, there was
more disagreement with the negative items than there
was agreement with the positive items. However, none
of the differences between total scores using posi-
tively- and negatively-worded items was significant.
Although the above comparison is not conclusive, it
indicates that the suspected acquiescent set was not
operating differently across the groups.

1.   Whites in the low-income group perceived
more reality than high-income youngsters but did not
differ significantly from the medium-income group.
2.   Among blacks, the low- and medium-income
groups were not significantly different. Medium-income youngsters did score significantly higher than
those in the high-income category.

TABLE 27

Index of Perceived Reality
in TV Programs[a]

	Family Income		
	Low	Medium	High
Whites	9.9	9.7	8.8
Blacks	10.3	10.5	9.5

Variable	Analysis Results	
	F	P
Income	6.24	<.002
Race	7.67	<.006
Income X Race	.43	-

[a]This index was formed by summing the scores for
the five items in Table 28. The greater the perceived
reality the higher the score.

Reasons for Watching TV

Each group received a list of 19 reasons why they
might watch television. Eleven referred to ways in
which TV was used as a learning device, including the
following:

I watch TV because I can learn a lot from
it.

I watch TV because it teaches me things I
don't learn in school.

I watch TV because I learn how to do new
things I've never done before.

Analysis showed consistent inter-correlations among
the 11 items and scores were summed across the items
to form a single learning index for each respondent.

TABLE 28

Perceived Reality in TV Programs:
Individual Item Results[a]

	Family Income			Analysis Results (p values)	
	Low	Medium	High	Income	Race
1. The people I see on TV shows are just like people I know in real life.					
Whites	1.83	1.84	1.60	–	<.0005
Blacks	2.02	2.19	2.05		
2. The same things that happen to people on TV often happen to me in real life.					
Whites	2.04	1.96	1.82	<.06	–
Blacks	1.96	2.13	1.73		
3. Families I see on TV are like my family.					
Whites	1.83	1.90	1.74	<.05	–
Blacks	1.87	1.81	1.47		
4. The people I see on TV are just like I want to be when I grow up.					
Whites	2.10	2.20	2.07	–	<.06
Blacks	2.30	2.35	2.22		
5. The programs on TV tell about life the way it really is.					
Whites	2.10	1.76	2.07	<.02	<.003
Blacks	2.30	2.06	2.06		

[a]The above means were computed by assigning the following scores to the response categories: 3 = I agree; 2 = I'm not sure; 1 = I don't agree.

Analysis of this index indicated that the degree
to which TV yields a learning function is dependent
on both race and occupational level (see Tables 29
and 30). At all levels, blacks reported more use of
TV for this purpose than did whites although no single
pair of means differed significantly. The following
comparisons were statistically significant:

1.   Among whites, the high-income group scored
significantly lower on the learning index than did
low- and medium-income groups.
2.   Among blacks, the same pattern emerged.
High-income blacks reported less usage for this
purpose than did the low- and medium-income groups.

A second index of two items gauged the extent
to which television served as a source of excitation, e.g., "I watch TV because it excites me" and
"I watch TV because it gives me a thrill." This
index resulted in an interaction effect (see Table
31).

1.   High-income whites scored significantly
higher on the index than did the middle-income
category.
2.   Among blacks, there were no significant
differences in the scores across income groups.
3.   Blacks at the medium level reported more usage of TV as a source of stimulation than did whites
at the same income level. However, this finding
was reversed at the high-income level. High-income
whites were more likely to report greater usage for
this reason than were high-income blacks. These two
comparisons were statistically significant.

Four other items showed significant race differences. Blacks reported more TV usage for the
following reasons:

I watched TV because I want to be like some
of the people I see on TV.

I watch TV because it keeps me out of
trouble.

I watch TV because I have nothing better
to do.

I watch TV because I don't have to think
of work while watching TV.

TABLE 29

Reasons for Watching TV:
Individual Item Results for the Learning Index[a]

	Analysis Results	
	Income	Race
1. I watch TV because I can learn a lot from it.	<.10	-
2. I watch TV because it shows how other people solve the same problems I have.	<.04	<.08
3. I watch TV because I get to know about all kinds of people.	<.10	-
4. I watch TV because I can understand things better when I can see them as well as hear them.	-	-
5. I watch TV because it teaches me things I don't learn in school.	-	-
6. I watch TV because it helps me learn things about myself.	<.09	<.0005
7. I watch TV because I learn how to do new things I've never done before.	-	<.001
8. I watch TV because it shows what life is really like.	<.12	-
9. I watch TV because I want to know what's going on in the world.	-	-
10. I watch TV because you can learn from the mistakes of others.	-	-
11. I watch TV so I can learn how I'm supposed to act.	<.04	-

[a]The response categories to the above 11 items were coded as follows: 4 = a lot like me; 3 = a little like me; 2 = not much like me; 1 = not at all like me. The responses were summed across the items per respondent. The means reported in Table 30 are based on these summed scores.

TABLE 30

Reasons for Watching TV: Learning Index[a]

	Family Income		
	Low	Medium	High
Whites	30.62	30.67	28.42
Blacks	32.19	31.89	29.63

Variable	Analysis Results	
	F	P
Income	5.04	<.007
Race	3.98	<.05
Income X Race	.03	-

[a]The more TV is used for learning purposes, the higher the score.

TABLE 31

Index of the Degree TV is Used
as a Source of Excitation[a]

	Family Income		
	Low	Medium	High
Whites	6.47	6.31	7.05
Blacks	6.82	7.00	6.69

Variable	Analysis Results	
	F	P
Income	0.61	-
Race	1.43	-
Income X Race	3.16	<.05

[a]The more television is used for excitation, the higher the score.

Learning about Preferred Occupation

Respondents named the kind of a job they wanted to have when they grew up and indicated the source from which they had received the most information about this occupation. The sources of information most often given were "from someone I know" and "from television." There were no racial or income differences among the children who named TV as their chief learning source.

Learning about Preferred Place to Live

There were no racial or income differences among children who named TV as their chief source of information about the place they would like to live. In all, TV was named by about 26 percent of the respondents, ranking second in frequency to the response "I have been there myself."

Identification with Television Characters

Each child was asked to choose the person on TV that he would most like to be. Responses were coded according to the race of the chosen identification figure. Every white youngster chose to identify with a white. In addition, 31 percent of the black children identified a white as the person they would most like to be. This percentage is roughly equivalent to that found in earlier studies of the race of black children's identification choices.[5] The fact that this percentage has remained at the same level may be somewhat surprising in view of the current emphasis on black culture and racial pride. The black children who identified with whites did not differ in social status and consisted of almost equal numbers of boys and girls.

Television as a Topic of Conversation

There were no significant racial or social class differences in the frequency with which the children talked about TV shows with their friends and family. In general, youngsters reported that they talked about TV shows "quite often" with their friends and "sometimes" with their families.

SUMMARY

The children in the sample were 392 fourth and fifth graders subdivided by race and occupational status of family. Questionnaires were administered in classrooms in East Cleveland, Ohio, during April, 1969.

The average number of working TV sets was two
per family for all race and income groups. Black
youngsters reported a higher average number of sets
and more television viewing. Low-income children
watched longer than high-income children. Black
children from low-income families averaged almost
7 hours of viewing on a given weekday in comparison
to 4 hours for white youngsters from high-income
families. Low-income children were more likely than
high-income children to watch TV before school, during
the noon hour, from 3-7:30 p.m., and from 7:30-11 p.m.
There was more consensus among the favorite program
choices of black youngsters than among whites. Blacks
reported giving more attention to TV commercials.

White children were more likely to read newspapers and listen to radio newscasts than were black
children. There were no differences in general radio
listening time. Black children at all income levels
reported more frequent attendance at movies in the
past month as well as significantly more time listening to records.

Children from poorer homes reported less parental
control over their viewing habits. Among all the
youngsters, 70 percent reported a late-night cut-off
time; 60 percent reported being told not to watch
certain shows; and, 40 percent said a form of punishment used in their homes was withholding TV privileges. All children reported that they themselves
controlled what they watched except for the white
children from high-income homes where the father
exercised more control over the TV set. Black children reported more average parental TV watching than
did white children.

Children from low-income families were more
likely to believe that TV content was true-to-life
than children from higher-income homes. Black children were more likely than white children to indicate
that television was realistic. Lower-income children
were more likely than the upper-income children to
state that they watched television to learn--about
things not taught in school, about new things, about
how to solve problems, and about how to act. Black
children were more likely to state such reasons than
white youngsters.

Watching television for excitement interacted
with race and income; high-income white children were
more likely to seek excitement through TV than other
whites. The black income groupings did not differ.

When asked what person on TV they would most like to be, 100 percent of the white youngsters named a white character as did 31 percent of the black youngsters.

No race or social class differences were found in the extent to which the children used TV as a source of information about a preferred occupation or place to live. There was also no difference in the frequency with which the youngsters talked about TV programs with friends or members of their families.

IMPLICATIONS

Let us for a moment reverse the emphasis of the findings. There is a surprisingly high level of media use not only among low-income and black youngsters but among high-income and white children. For example, a white child of 9 or 10 from a well-off family spends some 5 hours and 48 minutes with TV, records, and radio each day. If he sleeps for 8 hours, goes to school for 6 (including travel time), and spends an hour at his morning and evening meals, he has about 3 hours left in his 24-hour day. Media behavior for a black child from a disadvantaged home totals 9 hours and 30 minutes on a given weekday. Of course we do not assume that media behaviors are exclusive ones, i.e., preclude accompaning activities; we do not know what combination of things occur at the same time.

The effects of this media exposure are unknown. What specifically do these youngsters get from the media? When children watch television to learn, we know virtually nothing of the content that is learned or the specific sources of learning. From what kinds of shows, with what kinds of thematic emphases, does learning occur? What exactly is retained?

NOTES

1. See for example, John and Matilda Riley, "A Sociological Approach to Communication Research," in The Process and Effects of Mass Communication, edited by Wilbur Schramm (Urbana, Ill.: University of

Illinois Press, 1954), pp. 389-402; Robert D. Hess
and Harriet Goldman, "Parents' Views of the Effect
of Television on Their Children," Child Development
XXXIII (June, 1962), 411-426; Herbert Gans, The Urban
Villagers (Glencoe, Ill.: The Free Press, 1962).

2. Wilbur Schramm et al., Television in the
Lives of Our Children (Stanford, Calif.: Stanford
University Press, 1961).

3. M. Friedman, "Television Program Preferences
and Televiewing Habits of Children Related to Their
Socio-Economic Status" (Ph. D. dissertation, Yeshiva
University, 1957).

4. National Commission on the Causes and Prevention of Violence, "Statement on Violence in Television Entertainment Programs" (Washington, D. C.:
Government Printing Office, 1969) p. 7.

5. Kenneth and M. P. Clark, "Racial Identification and Preferences in Negro Children," in Readings
in Social Psychology edited by Theodore Newcomb and
E. L. Hartley (New York: Holt, Rinehart and Winston,
1947), pp. 169-178; Kenneth and M. P. Clark, "Emotional Factors in Racial Identification and Preference in
Negro Children," Journal of Negro Education XIX, 2
(1950), 341-350; J. K. Morland, "Racial Recognition
by Nursery School Children in Lynchburg, Virginia,"
Social Forces XXXVII, 1 (1958), 132-137; H. W. Steven-
son and E. C. Stewart, "A Developmental Study of Race
Awareness in Young Children" Child Development XXIX,
3 (1958), 399-410.

CHAPTER **4** SUMMARY OF FINDINGS
AND FUTURE RESEARCH
DIRECTIONS

Bradley S. Greenberg

BACKGROUND

The 1960's are described as the decade of be-
ginning action against poverty and race problems.
Large-scale programs for education, social reform,
and welfare were created for and are still being
directed at the poor. Communicating with potential
and actual recipients has been the main problem found
by staff people in such programs. How does one obtain
awareness of such programs? How does one increase
understanding of the programs? How does one get
participation?

The research reported in the preceding chapters
was designed and carried out in the context of such
questions. We could find little empirical data on
the mass communication behaviors of the poor and decided to collect fresh data. Our data do little to
answer in detail the questions of poverty program
planners. But they do much, we think, to describe
the mass communication context in which information
about poverty programs is typically disseminated. In
our continuing research program, efforts are turning
to the non-mass communication context--person-to-
person communication among the urban poor. The interface of these two modes of communication--mass and
interpersonal--appears to be a critical juncture.
If we wish to penetrate the environment of the disadvantaged with useful and desired information, it
can be done only with a thorough understanding of
their communication behaviors.

This summary gives a panoramic portrayal of the
use and some functions of mass communication for the

urban poor as they progress from childhood through
adolescence to adulthood. The data derived from our
three studies permit us to talk about three different
age groups, or perhaps three different generations,
not about developmental phenomena. However, it is
striking that the mass media behaviors of child, teen-
ager, and adult are so very much alike.

RESULTS OF THE THREE STUDIES

In this research, we focused on four major
aspects of mass communication behavior:

1. Ownership or access to the mass media;
2. Use of the mass media;
3. Attitudes toward the mass media;
    and
4. Functions of the mass media

Ohio Study of Children

Let us begin with the mass communication behaviors of some 400 fourth and fifth graders in Ohio.
At this age level, to the surprise of no one, the
predominant mass medium is television. On the average, children from poor families had two working
television sets in their homes as did children from
better-off homes. Children from low-income homes
were spending from 6-7 hours each and every weekday
watching TV in comparison to 4 to 5 hours for those
from middle-class homes. The former were more likely
to watch television before going to school in the
morning, during their lunch hour, after school, and
in the late evening. If there is an "addiction" to
TV, it occurs early and frequently for lower-class
children. The children also spent about an hour each
day listening to the radio and about an hour playing
records. Both the disadvantaged children and their
middle-class counterparts looked at newspapers 3-4
times per week.

Thus, television predominates in terms of potential impact; watching television consumed virtually
the same amount of time for fourth and fifth graders
as the school day. Consequently, further analysis
of the communication behavior of this group concen-
trated on TV.

Given this devotion to TV, what kinds of controls exist on the children's viewing habits? Children from poorer homes reported less control. They were less likely to have a rule about how late they could watch at night, less likely to be told by anyone that there were certain shows they should not watch, and less likely to be punished by not being allowed to watch television. When asked who in their family had the most control over what was watched, a child from a low-income home was more likely to answer "myself." The low-income children also made higher estimates of viewing time by their parents.

Perhaps more important are the results that describe certain functions of television for low-income children. These are reflected by the extent to which the youngsters perceive television as true-to-life in its portrayal of people and events. The children were given a series of statements with which to agree or disagree, including the following:

The people I see on TV shows are just like people I know in real life.

The same things that happen to people on TV often happen to me in real life.

Families I see on TV are like my family.

The programs on TV tell about life the way it really is.

Children raised in disadvantaged environments were far more likely to say, "Yes, TV shows it like it is," TV is true-to-life. Low-income youngsters said this more often than middle-income children and black children were more likely to agree than their white counterparts. This finding is significant; belief in the reality of television content correlates with socio-economic background and/or race. A possible explanation for this correlation might be that a disadvantaged child seldom gets outside his home except to go to school and watch television. His school is often an educational relic filled with children whose backgrounds are similar to his. Few school activities take place outside the school grounds. He has limited direct contact with the outside world. His primary contacts with the outside world are mediated by television and he has virtually no standards of comparison against which to check the reality of the TV world. Thus, he is more inclined to believe that what he sees is representative of the "real world." Such speculation demands more rigorous study than we have yet done.

Let us turn to the question of why he watches so much television. Agreement or disagreement was obtained to such items as these:

I watch TV because I can learn a lot from it.

I watch TV because I have nothing better to do.

I watch TV because it excites me.

I watch TV because it keeps me out of trouble.

I watch TV because you can learn from the mistakes of others.

Youngsters from lower-class families were more likely than their better-off counterparts to say that they watched television to learn about things not in school, new things, how to solve problems, and how to act. Black children were more likely to give these learning reasons than were white youngsters. For these children, television fulfilled a school-of-life function.

Pennsylvania Study of Teen-agers

Moving east several hundred miles to Pennsylvania, we obtained data from 300 ghetto and suburban teen-agers representing low-income whites and blacks and middle-income whites. The critical findings are basically similar to those summarized for children six to eight years younger.

Both social class and racial differences were found in many of the communication behaviors studied. Being poor was sufficient to elicit many differences from the middle-class teen-agers. Being poor and black usually served to intensify these differences.

We shall summarize these findings by describing a composite media day for our three groups of teen-agers. That day was a Sunday. The media effort of the middle-class white teen-ager included 3½ hours

with television, 2½ hours with a radio, an hour playing records, and definitely some newspaper reading.
In the past week, he had looked at 3 magazines and
in the past month, he had seen 2 movies. The lower-
class white teen-ager watched one more hour of TV (a
total of 4½ hours) and had the same amount of radio
listening and record playing but was less likely to
have done any newspaper reading. He had looked at 2
magazines in the past week and had seen 2 movies in
the past month. The black teen-ager spent more than
6 hours with TV, 2 hours with the radio, 1½ hours
listening to records, and was even less likely to
read the newspaper. He also read fewer magazines
and saw fewer movies. Media days, from electronic
stimulation alone, ranged from 7-10 hours.

These teen-agers were asked the same questions
about the reality of television content as the younger
children. The results were the same. Teen-agers from
poorer environments were far more likely to believe
that television "tells it like it is."

We gathered some additional information from the
teen-agers about their attitudes toward the mass
media. We asked whether they would believe television, radio, or the newspaper if they got conflicting reports from each, which they would keep if they
could only keep one, and which news staff on which
medium was doing the best job.

If conflicting reports were received, the majority would believe the TV version, with this response
even more prevalent among the lower-income teen-agers.
If they could only keep one, two-thirds to three-
fourths would keep TV. The TV news reporter was seen
as doing his job the best by 65 percent of the black
youngsters, 55 percent of the lower-class whites, and
45 percent of the middle-class whites.

Given this level of usage and these attitudes,
what are the functions of television for teen-agers?
Use of television as a means of finding out what
life is about was a more important function among the
lower-class respondents than among those in the middle-class. This was even more true for the black
teen-agers than the white lower-income teens. Like
the children we studied, these teens were identifying
the school-of-life function:

I watch TV because I can learn from the
mistakes of others.

I watch TV because I get to know all about
people in all walks of life.

I watch TV because I want to know what's
going on in the world.

I watch TV because it shows how others
solve the same problems I have.

A second function more dominant among the low-
income teens was a "kicks" function. They were more
likely to agree that watching television gave them
thrills and excitement.

Michigan Study of Adults

Our portrait of mass communication activities
among the poor concludes with an examination of adult
behavior. As a take-off point, we shall specify the
mass media habits of the average American as a basis
for comparing the behavior of other Americans. Tom
Green has a middle-range job and income. He gives
about 5 hours--one-fourth to one-third of the 16
hours that he is awake--to the mass media. His most
popular medium is television; his TV set is in use
for 6 hours a day. He himself watches 2-2½ hours
each weekday. He also listens to the radio two hours
a day, typically outside his home. His wife listens
and watches at least as much while at home. Green
has one newspaper delivered; he reads it for about
one-half hour and concentrates on the front page,
sports section and comics. Green reads one magazine
regularly and has probably read or looked through a
magazine in the past week but not enough on any given
day to increase the daily total of 5 hours he gives
to the other mass media. Movie going is also a negligible consumer of time: Green goes to a movie about
every three months.

What about his attitudes toward the media? They
follow a trend that is consistent with usage. When
asked where he gets most of his news about what's going on in the world today, Green replies, "television."
When asked which of the media he would be most inclined to believe, he says, "television." When asked
which of the media he would choose if there were only
one available, he answers, "television."

Tom Green depends on television for news, for
entertainment, for information about the outside

world. However, according to our research, despite
the pervasiveness of Green's dependency on television,
the economically-disadvantaged citizen is significantly more dependent on that medium for the same as
well as other purposes.

Let us quickly dispose of the question of mass
media access or ownership among the population. Some
95 percent of the general public owns at least one
working black-and-white TV set; among those whose
incomes qualify them for OEO assistance in urban
areas, the same percentage own at least one working
black-and-white TV set. In fact, more than a third
among these groups have more than one working set.
TV is equally accessible to all.

Similarly, there is no great difference between
more- and less-advantaged citizens in terms of access
to the other major mass media. Newspapers are delivered daily to 66-75 percent of low-income homes
(compared to 86 percent of the general public). The
poor are not media-poor. The media have their potential impact not in terms of access but in terms of
usage.

For the low-income American, television is the
preponderant if not the only source of mass media
stimulation. It is apparently his critical link to
the outside world of the "haves." He is far less
likely than the middle-class citizen to have done any
recent magazine reading. He reads the newspaper less
frequently and when he does read it, he reads it less
intensively (focusing on the "headlines" and ads).
There's a better than even chance that he hasn't been
to a movie in the past 6 months.

Tom Green and his wife watch television about
two hours on a weekday. Adults in the low-income
homes in our study watch TV for five hours each day.

Let us illustrate this quantity of television
exposure in another way. For most Americans, 8 hours
is a typical workday. Among the low-income adults
interviewed, one-fourth spent 8 hours each day with
TV compared to 5 percent of those in the general
population. Tom Green gives about one-quarter of
his waking day to the mass media. The low-income
American spends about half his day with the media
and three-quarters of that is TV time.

How people use the media may be related to the
attitudes that Americans have about the media. These
attitudes are generally predictable from the relative
exposure patterns just described.

For the general public, TV is regarded as the
principal information source for general news, world
news, and political news. At the same time, it is
far and away favored as the most credible media
source of information. TV is regarded even more
favorably by low-income Americans. For example, 40
percent of the general public say they get most of
their world news from TV compared with 70 percent of
the low-income citizens. A majority of the general
public would believe what they get from television
over what they get from the newspaper. An even
larger majority of low-income citizens hold that view.

So far, these research findings pinpoint the
relative dependence of the low-income adult on a
single mass medium. They also indicate the relative
non-use by the poor of alternative sources of information about the world outside their homes and
neighborhoods.

Let us now consider the general media content
preferences of these adults. In terms of newspaper
reading, low-income Americans differ from their
better-off counterparts in that they appear to use
the newspaper as a substitute bulletin board. They
focus on the newspaper headlines, advertisements,
and such things as obituaries, and weather. Television shows of adventure, excitement, action, and
violence are regularly viewed by a much larger proportion of low-income adults than the general public.
This fact must be tempered by the reminder that the
disadvantaged watch more of virtually any category
of TV fare. The TV viewing preferences and program
choices of low-income white citizens are extremely
similar to those of low-income black Americans and
markedly different from those of the general public.

These studies are, of course, more suggestive
than definitive. However, the few mass media studies
that have been done show more similarities than contradictions. The mass medium of the poor is television. It is a preferred and almost exclusive source
of information about the outside world. Without competing information, people from low-income backgrounds
think the world is similar to what they see on TV;
they would question competing information from other

media.   The poor prefer media content that provides
excitement.   Their relatively greater social isolation (fewer close friends, fewer people to talk to
regularly) may find a compatible substitute in television.

LIMITATIONS

There are some major limitations to these studies
that should be specified, both to avoid over-generali-
zation of the findings and to acknowledge admitted
flaws.

The data come from three different areas of the
country and three different age groups, at one point
in time, at one season of the year.   Adults in Lansing, Michigan, may be quite different from adult poor
in Watts, Harlem, St. Louis, or Atlanta by many criteria.   In Lansing, communication behavior may be
very different in the dead of winter and in the full
steam of summer but our data were gathered during the
winter only.   Data gathered in 1968 may not be fully
replicable in 1970 or 1971.   Indeed, our data are
limited to the specific groups, the cities identified,
and the seasonal characteristics that may confound
attempted generalizations.

Even the suggestion that these data serve as
baseline data must be qualified.   We can only legiti-
mately apply the term "sampling" to our study of
adult poor.   And the less-than-adeuate response rate
in that study has been specified.   We are over-sampling willing respondents.   For the studies of children and teen-agers, we coordinated with cooperative
school districts in choosing schools that purposively
met income and race criteria and then worked with
intact classrooms.   Not ideal, but nonetheless as
representative as could be accomplished for the
facilitative collection of data.

Consequently, the notion that parameters could
be derived for this segment of the population must
remain qualified.   We have established parameters of
communication behaviors under the conditions of data-
gathering described.   The adult data exclude a significant number of respondents unwilling to open their
doors to us; the teen-age data exclude young drop-outs
and absentees; data from the youngest group may be the
most representative.

A final methodological point deals with the sizes
of our respondent groups. We could be more definitive
and have better parameter estimates had our groups
been of the size of 1,200-1,600. They are one-fourth
that size, which is again a caveat to our attempts to
generalize. Because of such methodological limitations, our data await subsequent verification, repli-
cation, and validation.

We wish also to point out a tenuous theoretical
implication we have made. Throughout this summary,
for example, we emphasize the time that was given to
each communication activity. Time, as we talk about
it, begins to sound as if it were isomorphic with
impact and we cannot advocate that proposition. Six
hours with a television set may not be equal to--in-
deed, is not equal to--six hours of effect, impact,
or anything so grand as these functional terms would
indicate. We do not know what time represents beyond
an allocation of some psychic energy. The impact of
these mass communication behaviors has yet to be assessed. We have implied, not demonstrated, certain
effects.

Time data are misleading in another way as well.
Some activities are concurrent. For example, virtually no one plops down in front of a radio and does
nothing but listen. People may cook, read, sew, baby-
sit, do homework, or dance. There are no reliable
data on the extent to which alternative activities
occur while watching television; this would seem a
necessary adjunct to subsequent research.

Nevertheless, we do indeed propose that X number
of hours on a given communication activity represents
X hours that cannot be allocated to some alternative
activity; this seems to be the brunt of the argument
we have been making. These communication behaviors
are extensive in terms of time and they preclude alternative learning or social activities, though in
fact, they may serve to focus the content and form
of such other activities.

RESEARCH EXTENSIONS

Let us now turn to a more thorough outline of
the research that these three studies suggest be done.
We propose four overlapping areas of research that
appear to be most meaningful in terms of theoretical

utility and practical significance. These choices
represent, of course, our own predispositions and
training and will undoubtedly be amended by those with
differing preferences. The four areas of key interest
to us deal with the inter-personal communication behaviors of the poor, social diffusion of media information, racial differences in the impact of the mass
media, and social learning from the mass media, especially television.

Inter-Personal Communication

In particular, a thorough study of the face-to-
face communication activity of the poor is in order.
What is the intersection between the mass communication behaviors we have described and peer and family
communication patterns? The more time given to the
media, the less time presumably available for such
interaction. Other research points to the greater
social isolation of the poor. We know little of the
scope, frequency, variety or content of such inter-
personal exposures. Presumably, at some point there
is direct conflict between media suggestions and suggestions from extra-media sources. When advice from
peer or parent conflicts with media advice, which
path is followed?

One expects other people and the media to serve
different functions as communication sources. What
functional distinctions exist? What is the relative
credibility of other people in comparison to the
media? Who, in particular, serve as critical links
between communication message and action?

Social Dissemination

Social diffusion of information is an extension
of inter-personal communication. Given the fact
that certain information originates with the mass
media, to what extent is there reliance on other
people for interpretation and/or approval prior to
the acceptance of such information? The entertainment fare of television is discussed in social groups.
What is the nature of such discussions and the composition of the groups themselves? What is the relative importance of different issues for the poor and
the non-poor? These diffusion variables come readily
to mind:

1. Initial sources of information;
2. Subsequent sources of information and verification about some issue;
3. Location of diffusion process;
4. Timing of dissemination;
5. Coverage, and span of dissemination; and
6. Message retention, distortion and omission.

One might propose that an experimental research design done in field settings begins to amend existing knowledge about dissemination patterns in the general public. In this manner, it would be possible to begin to manipulate the originating sources of information and certain content characteristics of the messages themselves. These two factors would appear to have the largest pay-off for those attempting to disseminate information among the disadvantaged.

Race and the Media

Race appears to interact with many of the communication variables examined. Being poor leads to communication differences from non-poor counterparts; being black and poor intensifies such differences. For example, the black adults in our study were heavier users of records and record players. Perhaps this is their source of cultural referent because the white media are inadequate suppliers. These same adults were more likely to refer to other people as the best source of local information. Again, the explanation most available is that the white press or media do not deal heavily enough with the black community.

For practitioners, the black community may be more reachable through non-establishment media--such as records, billboards, and telephones--or unreachable save through direct personal contact. One should also cite the need for further study of differentiation among the poor. That is, no attempt has been made in our studies or elsewhere to examine typologies of the poor. One such study might attempt to look at subsets of poor blacks and subsets of poor whites along relevant criteria.

For the white community, what is the impact of the increasing appearance of blacks in all the media from Playboy to soap operas?

Social Learning

Although the research area of social learning is
applicable at all age levels, it is among the youngest
that one anticipates maximum opportunity for social
learning. Among the older, un-learning may be a more
pertinent label.

What is the nature of attention given to television? If a child watches TV for 6-7 hours, what
can be the degree of attentiveness and to what inputs?
What then are the outputs? For example, television
spokesmen have argued that programs depicting criminal
acts discourage children from imitating what is shown
because the final message of the show is that "crime
doesn't pay." However, it might be argued, that
children who view heavily pay different amounts of
attention to the various segments of a program. They
may be more likely to notice and retain criminal and
violent acts since such scenes have more visual action
and more distinctive sound. Such scenes may be watched
very closely by the child. He may miss the "lesson"
of the program if the ending is less stimulating to
the senses.

What specifically do these youngsters get from
the media? Some children say they watch television
to learn but we know virtually nothing of the content
that is learned or the specific sources of learning.
From what kinds of shows, with what thematic emphases,
does learning occur? What is learned? For example,
is a young child learning about theme, plot, individual characters, or something else? Recent studies
show that record listeners are responding to rhythm
and beat and know very little of the "message" contained.

When there is greater perceived realism, what
content contributes to and enhances such perceived
reality? What check against reality does the youngster make? Does he believe, for example, that the
principal way of solving individual problems is the
technique shown in a preponderance of TV drama--direct
aggression against the problem source? We would
predict less evidence of perceived reality of TV content among those people who have other sources of
information about middle-class life. Such reasoning
would predict that there would be less tendency to
see TV as an accurate portrayal of life among those

low-income teen-agers who have more exposure to middle-
class people or middle-class experiences.

One might approach social learning issues by first
identifying a small subset of programs that most youngsters watch regularly. Having analyzed the themes of
those programs, one might determine to what extent
these themes had been learned, the behaviors imitated,
and the general extent of incidental and non-inciden-
tal learning. Within such programs, with whom does
the youngster chiefly identify? With which attributes
is he identifying, and why?

What effect does the increased frequency with
which blacks now appear on TV have on these variables?
Does this new trend increase the believability TV has
for the lower-class black teen-ager or does it serve
to decrease it? To what extent can a young black girl
identify with "Julia"? Further, what is the white
reaction to the same trend? Do whites tend to think
that TV accurately portrays the way most blacks live?
We would expect, for example, that whites would consider TV's depiction of blacks to be more accurate
than would blacks themselves and that they would think
many more blacks appear on TV than objectively do or
than black viewers say there are.

Perhaps a new stereotype of blacks is replacing
the old one for youth in this country. To the extent
that blacks did not exist in the media or were consistently presented in subservient roles emitting
attributes of laziness, and foolishness, the new
portrayal is at least different. Its impact is unknown but one would reasonably expect maximum impact
among the young. In fact, for middle-class youngsters, this medium may well be the primary contact
and principal learning source about race.

All these critical issues are unsettled. Many
are unsettling. We have asked some minor questions
and partly answered them. Those answers increase
the scientist's frustration in recognizing the
larger-order questions barely asked and certainly
unanswered.

PART **II**

RELATED RESEARCH ON
COMMUNICATION BEHAVIORS OF THE POOR

CHAPTER **5** SUMMARY OF RELATED
RESEARCH FINDINGS

Brenda Dervin,
Bradley S. Greenberg,
John Bowes, and
Margaret Curley

INTRODUCTION

For the most part, sociological literature has
ignored communication behaviors of the poor. Likewise, few empirical studies in communication have
specifically examined the poor or the ghetto black.
A search of approximately 3,000 articles, books, and
papers yielded comparatively few studies based on
theory and empirical data that discussed communication behavior among the poor. The works synthesized
in this chapter and the next were chosen for their
bearing on the issues of both communication and poverty, particularly if they contrasted the communication behavior of the poor with the less poor or of
black people with whites.

This chapter summarizes the works that are annotated in Chapter 6. As a summary, this chapter is
intended to be more representative than exhaustive of
theoretical findings and concerns detailed in the
poverty literature. Expansion on summarized material
is easily accomplished by a follow-up of the biblio-
graphical references.

Chapter 5 has three sections. Each covers a
major domain of communication behavior: intra-family
or communication among family members, extra-family
or social communication, and mass communication behavior. Abstracts found in Chapter 6 are arranged
alphabetically by author. Chapter 6 concludes with
a summary listing of authors and publications and
an index by major subject matter areas. In general,

the abstracts are divided into sections describing
the study's purpose, methods of investigation and
analysis, and results.

INTRA-FAMILY PATTERNS

This section examines family interaction patterns
and child rearing practices of the urban poor. Specifically, how is family interaction in the poor family different from that in the middle-class family?
What effect does this have on the family partners and
on certain aspects of the child's development? Besner
characterizes the overall differences between middle-
and lower-class families as one of degree.[1] Loose
family ties, conflicts stemming from disagreement on
expectations in a matriarchial household, and rigid
discipline make the poorer household a more difficult
place for child development. This section summarizes
the research on husband-wife interactions and then
turns to parent-child practices.

Husband-Wife Relationships

Establishment of the Partnership

The lower class is more influenced by proximity--
the girl next door--in choosing a mate than is the
middle class. There is a relative absence of strong
feeling about whom to marry. This lack of emotional
involvement stems from the general poverty cycle,
fear of failure in marriage, and the fact that men
value marriage more for its social acceptability than
its emotional components. Chilman[2] and Herzog[3] observed that courtships are short and marriages often
occur because of pregnancy. Although marriage due
to pregnancy is considered unfortunate by the poor,
it is not particularly unacceptable. From the begin-
ning, the lower-class marriage relationship is less
emotional and less involved. This probably contributes heavily to the observed unstable family
life and child development patterns of the poor.

Physical and Emotional Roles and Responsibilities

Men and women in lower-class families share
few duties.[4] The man is the breadwinner; the woman
takes care of home and children. The partnership
we find in middle-class families does not exist.

In one-parent families, which exist in much larger
numbers among the poor, the woman takes on both sets
of responsibilities.

There is a careful distinction between marriage
and consensual unions. Consensual unions have rights
and duties patterned after legal marriage, but they
are much more ambiguous. Liebow's respondents reported that marriage denotes exclusive sexual access
to one's spouse but this is not necessarily the case
in a consensual union.[5] Consensual unions also have
less public force behind them. That is, neither
society in general nor the particular social clime
of the urban poor has established a set of responsibilities for a consensual union (such as providing
for physical and psychological needs of mate and
children). Therefore, the failure to meet such responsibilities is less subject to public criticism
than is the case in legal unions.

The lower-class family is more loosely knit.
Spouses are emotionally isolated from each other.
The male is dominant--he places primary value on physical satisfaction from his wife and the work she
does.[6] However, Liebow claims that although the man's
exploitation of the woman is the major verbalized
theme, the practiced male-female relationship is not
only physical. The men often find that they are
lovers as much as users.[7]

Rainwater reports that a working-class woman
believes her, relationship with her husband is vi-
tally important to her emotional well-being.[8] She
is shy, acquiescent, retreating, and admiring but
feels the lack of openly-expressed affection. This
is reflected in her harsh discipline practices and
her lack of patience with her husband and children.
She reverts to violence and quarrelling techniques
as alternatives to regression and withdrawal.[9]

Because the men think of themselves as dominant
and exploitive, unemployment intensifies marital
difficulties. As more wives work, masculinity is
threatened and marital quarrels increase.[10]

Divorce and Separation

Divorce and separation rates are very high
among the poor.[11] Divorce rates are lowest for women
with 1-4 years of college and highest for women with
1-3 years of high school.[12] Different reasons are

given for marital failure. McCabe says that most
women hope for a permanent relationship but large-
scale economic and emotional deprivations cause them
to make poor judgments, leading to a series of unsatisfactory relationships.[13] Although he valued marriage, Liebow's streetcorner man feared it, believing
that he would not be able to carry out the responsibilities of marriage. For him, marriage, as experienced daily, did not work. It didn't work for his
parents, and it wasn't working for his friends. The
demands of the outside world were often too pressing
for the close and fragile relationship of the marriage
bond. Because he was unskilled, he had trouble finding and keeping work. Thus, he failed as a provider.
Because his wife was accustomed to the failure of
men, she expected little of him, thereby reinforcing
his sense of failure.

     These husband-wife problems focus around the
lack of interpersonal emotional consideration. The
male needs to feel dominant but he is threatened by
unemployment; the woman wants to be dependent and
loved but she is frustrated by the lack of affection
and communication. This family instability tends
to produce violent and aggressive methods of problem
solving. Let us now examine the effect of this family style on the children.

Parent-Child Relationships

One-Parent Families

     Between 25 and 40 percent of lower-class families
have only one parent.[14] At all income levels, female
heads are more prevalent among blacks than whites and
considerable research demonstrates that this situation
is a cause of emotional instability in the children.
In fact, Minuchin links it directly to delinquency.[15]
There is no stable father figure, and the mother often
works. Thus, the child spends much of his time in
the streets, in a criminal, impoverished, violent
environment. The child becomes acutely conscious of
a system that appears to reward those who illegally
exploit others and fails those who work in a traditional middle-class way.

Parent-Child Interaction

     When the father lives with his family, his main
function is discipline.[16] He takes little pleasure in

his children and gives them little time or attention.
Liebow suggests that often after the father has been
separated from his children for a time, they develop
a warmer, more affectionate relationship.[17] The separated father can afford to be attentive and affectionate because he is not charged with the day-to-day
responsibilities.

The mother is forced to establish a closer
relationship with her children. Often she feels
emotionally removed from her spouse and seeks recip-
rocal affection from her children. The father is
usually the discipliner and in his absence the mother
feels powerless and overwhelmed by her children's
demands. She gives little guidance; the children seek
guidance from their peers. As a result, the "gang"
value system thrives.[18]

Development of Values and Emotional Stability

Research shows that the lack of verbal and emotional communication between husband and wife is
carried over to their relations with their children.
Minuchin reports that these communication patterns
cause severe delay in child development and related
difficulties.[19] The child is handicapped in language, and verbal and perceptual skills in school.
Aggressive rather than verbal methods are used to relate to others. Since little attention is paid to the
child's requests at home, he assumes that he will not
be heard. He learns that intensity of sound is more
important than message content and that assertion by
force is more important than knowledge. The absence
of verbal interaction inhibits general development.[20]

In the adult-centered, lower-class family, children are expected to act like adults.[21] Childhood
ends at age ten. "Staying out of trouble" is the criterion for judging behavior.

Middle- and lower-class parents agree on some
values for their children--honesty, happiness, obedience, and dependability. However, parents of each
class emphasize the values they consider the most
important and difficult to achieve in their society
and whose absence would bring the most adverse consequences to their children. For example, working-
class parents stress honesty, obedience, and neatness
because they believe these attributes are most necessary to rise above their present social class or
at least to stay above the lowest class. They see

the lowest class as characterized by dishonesty and
dirt so they stress discipline and pragmatic values
to insure that their children will not be categorized
in that group. Middle-class parents emphasize values
that act as internal rather than external standards,
values for governing relationships with other people
and oneself. Such values include independence, cre-
ativity, consideration, and curiosity. The social
status and economic advantages of the middle class
enable their children to be less dependent on pragmatic values and discipline in order to be considered
successful. The middle-class parent has more time
and money to develop such internal guidance criteria
for their children.[22]

Negro mothers can be differentiated by educational level as to the aspirations they hold for their
children. The more educated the Negro mother, the
more she wants an education for her children, the
later she wants them to marry, the more importance
she assigns to a professional job, and the more she
believes that hard work and ambition are necessary
for success.[23]

The explosive, physical, unpredictable method
of handling anxiety in the lower class is in contrast
to the more optimistic, verbal, psychological method
in the middle class. The former causes severe emotional and behavioral problems in the children. Discipline is mostly "don'ts"--rarely an emphasis on the
positive. This method of child rearing is not purposive but impulsive, based largely on punishment and
reward. The children have little freedom for exploration and receive minimal guidance. Instead, they
receive harsh and inconsistent physical discipline
based on the extent to which any given behavior annoys
a parent. Discipline is authoritarian and low-verbal
in nature.[24] Walters finds that middle-class mothers
exhibit much more directing, teaching, helping, and
playing interaction with their children than lower-
class mothers.[25]

McCabe concludes that lower-class children are
a distinct product of their environment. They are
wistful and lack impulse control. They also exhibit
pervasive anxiety, unsatisfactory and fragmented
inter-personal relationships, and diminished capacity
for learning. They lack the self-identity to cope
with their environment in ways necessary for survival.
Their devotion to family is based on the family as
a defense against a hostile world.[26]

EXTRA-FAMILY RELATIONSHIPS

The focus of this section is the social matrix
of the low-income community--the relationship of the
low-income person to the world outside his family.
This is the world of friends, neighbors, school, job,
merchants, social welfare agencies, and the establishment. Much of the literature is contradictory, particularly when attempts are made to mesh findings
from different geographic regions. Nevertheless, a
number of generalizations emerge. They suggest that
the social world of low-income people is more alike
than different, despite racial, ethnic, or regional
characteristics. This section highlights the generalizations that appear to hold despite sub-group differences.

A major problem in describing the social matrix
of the poor is determining what is cause and what is
effect. The some 40 studies summarized in this section intersect on one major conclusion: the social
relationships of the ghetto are part of a vicious
poverty cycle. Lack of achievement in the majority
society is related to life styles and social relationships that in turn are related to lack of achievement.

The descriptive characteristics of the ghetto
world seem well documented. It is a highly mobile
world with people moving in and out constantly. It
is populated by the underdogs of society--the minority
groups, the aged, the unskilled. Its houses are often
dilapidated, its residents crowded. Life expectancies
are lower than elsewhere and health needs go uncared
for. Its school systems often lack the resources to
give more than custodial care. Indeed, the literature
suggests that ghetto conditions prevent the poor from
escaping poverty or succeeding in any individual way
that might increase motivation.[27]

The picture that emerges is of frustration, deprivation, and hopelessness. Most studies point to
a fairly common set of life views about self, others,
and society that characterize the poor. The researchers suggest that this syndrome is both cause
and effect of the social life style in the ghetto.
In intersecting the findings from some 14 studies,[28]
we find that the following attitudes emerge as most
characteristic of the poor.

1. <u>Alienation</u>. As a conceptual term, alienation refers to a complex set of attitudes--feelings that leaders are indifferent to the people's needs, that one cannot control or direct one's own life, that goals cannot be attained, that personal ties are no longer meaningful, that nothing can be done to change the flow of events, that the world is unpredictable and chaotic. These beliefs are compounded by the fact that the poor lack the resources and knowledge that would give them more control over their environment.

2. <u>Lack of belief in achievement</u>. Research shows that low-income persons lower their expectations because of the apparent discrepancy between their own achievements and those of the rest of society. But lowered expectations, do not deter feelings of frustration or deprivation.

3. <u>Low self-esteem</u>. A pervasive sense of inferiority is characteristic of the poor and is related to the use of fantasy as a defense. The poor present themselves as tough and aggressive. They maintain illusions about phantom successes and accomplishments. These illusions become part of the inter-personal life of the ghetto.

4. <u>Aspiration-expectation discrepancy</u>. Unlike peasant societies in underdeveloped countries where the peasant may be isolated from the majority society, the American urban poor are very much in touch with the majority society. They are aware of the value placed on achievement and of their own failures. They are aware of the material well-being of the majority society. Thus, although their goals are not very different from those of the general population, their expectations for achieving them are far different. For the middle class, expectations often equal aspirations. For the lower class, expectations are usually considerably lower than aspirations.

5. <u>Present time orientation</u>. Since the life view of the ghetto suggests that the individual cannot control his life, planning for the future is unrewarding. Immediate rewards are preferred and time, in the middle-class sense of appointment-keeping and scheduling, has little meaning.

6. <u>Simplification of the experience world</u>. Because of their limited education and few contacts with the world outside the ghetto, the poor have a highly simplified and concrete view of the world.

With this brief picture of the poverty worldview as background, the research on the ghetto social matrix is summarized below. First we consider the relationships most central to the ghetto--the peer

and friendship nets; then voluntary organizations,
leadership, and social service agencies; and finally,
attitudes and behaviors in three sectors of social ac-
tivity--education, employment, and consumer behavior.

Peers and Friends: The
Inter-Personal Network

The poor see little possibility for individual
gain or improvement. Therefore, energy is not focused
on individual activities. The social core of the low-
income society is composed of the kinship and peer
network and group life. This generalization appears
to hold whether the low-income person is black, Puerto
Rican, Spanish American, or white.[29]

Study after study shows that visiting family and
friends, gossiping, and talking about neigborhood and
family events are among the major activities in the
low-income community. Although contacts extend to
employer, landlord, teacher, policeman, and so on,
kinship and peer contacts form the major portion of
the low-income person's inter-personal ties. Within
these informal limits, gregariousness is high. Self-
esteem, beaten down by lack of success in the majority society, is raised by neighborhood ties. Although
individual achievement may be the criterion for
success in the middle-class society, the low-income
kinship and peer network is a strong mutual-aid
society in which the criterion for success is no
longer achievement.

The literature suggests that these ties are more
casual, spontaneous, and cooperative than middle-class
inter-personal relations. The middle-class person
helps another person and expects to be repaid; favors
are given as if the exchange was a financial trans-
action. In contrast, the lower-class society accepts
a "give back when you're able" norm. Entertaining
for personal gain as it occurs in the middle-class is
foreign.

Despite the strength of this kinship and peer
network, several researchers agree on an underlying
layer of weakness. In ghetto life, emergencies are
frequent and inter-personal mistrust is high. The
idealized image of a tight-knit lower-class community
may have applied to communities of several decades
ago. Contemporary lower-class communities have high
mobility due to job lay-offs, home repossession, and

other frequent economic crises. Friendships have
little depth or history and are frequently uprooted.
The mutual-aid norm seems to operate primarily for
male-male and female-female relationships. Between
the sexes, a norm of public exploitation exists. Much
daily conversation is based on illusion: men talk of
fantasy successes with women, women talk of husbands
they don't have, both talk of money that is non-exist-
ent. Although such emphasis on illusion and fantasy
is characteristic of low-income communities of various
ethnic and racial groups, the description has been
applied most often to low-income blacks.[30]

Unfortunately, the strength of the inter-personal
network in the low-income community also provides
a base for exploitation of the poor by outsiders.
Caplovitz documents well how the seller of shoddy
merchandise on high credit terms uses the strong inter-personal net to his advantage. Caplovitz also
suggests that peddlers are passed from family member
to family member and from friend to friend.[31]

Researchers therefore point to the low-income
inter-personal net, as part of the poverty cycle.
Lack of individual success means greater emphasis on
group life. This in turn means that the low-income
person places less importance on individual achievement and has less opportunity to develop an expansive
repertoire of role behaviors and more flexible social
skills. Several studies have suggested that this
lack of role flexibility leaves the low-income person
unprepared to function in the primarily middle-class-
oriented job world.[32]

The high emphasis in the low-income community
on the inter-personal network is related to the communication style used and reinforced there. For
various reasons, several studies agree that the low-
income communication skill is verbally concrete. Low-
income persons use highly subjective and personal
verbal terms.[33]

In describing his world, the low-income person
is often unable to take the role or view of another
person or, particularly, the view of people of other
classes. The world is described in present-oriented
terms and objects and events are seen as "one-of-a-
kind." Research also suggests that communication
is much more non-verbal for low-income persons than
it is for middle-class persons. Non-verbal acts
(such as nods and grunts) are more often given as

responses and cues. In one study in which welfare
mothers were asked to describe their caseworkers, they
frequently referred to non-verbal cues as the basis
for their judgments.[34]

Memberships in Voluntary Organizations
and Indigenous Leadership

The research agrees that low-income communities
show little organization beyond the informal kinship-
peer system. Participation in voluntary organizations
is low, club-going is considered a middle-class and
often snobbish activity.[35] This generalization cuts
across ethnic and racial groups.

Because participation in voluntary organizations
is low, indigenous formal leadership is also weak.
Informal leaders who maintain their influence within
the community often lack power in dealing with the
majority society. The research suggests that this
is particularly true of black communities.[36] On the
other hand, leaders who gain influence in the majority society do so at the cost of losing influence
within the low-income community.

Despite this picture of low participation, recent
studies suggest potential for involvement and leadership. In his cluster analysis of sources serving one
Spanish-American community, Kurtz found a cluster of
poor people actively serving the community with information for solving housing, health, and other
problems.[37] A recent nationwide study by O'Shea and
Gray supports the general picture of low involvement
for low-income adults. But they found that 16 percent of their lowest-income respondents considered
themselves leaders or active non-leaders in community
activities and 30 percent indicated that they had
been involved in some type of community activity, such
as signing petitions or collecting money.[38] These
data indicate a core of potential leadership.

The strength of the family and peer groups seem
to be the key to community involvement by the poor.
Participation in non-family and peer-connected organizations (such as labor unions and political parties)
is low across all studies; participation in organizations based on the family-peer linkage is higher.
Thus, the church, fraternal organizations, and school
organizations receive stronger support in low-income
communities and particularly in low-income black

communities.[39] Kurtz, for example, found that the
people in one of the clusters serving as information-
givers in a Spanish-American community were all
connected with the local church;[40] Gans found church-
connected people among the most frequently named
sources in his study of an Italian-American community;[41] Frazier named the church as one of the traditional organization foci of the black community.[42]

Professionals in Social
Service Agencies

The strength of the family-peer network also
seems to be behind low-income attitudes toward social
service and welfare agencies--the "caretakers" as
Gans calls them.[43] When asked to whom they go for
information and help, low-income respondents most
frequently mention family, friends, and neighbors.
Next they mention people connected to their local
churches and stores or politicians whose roots are
in the community. The professional outsider who has
come into the community to be a caretaker (whether
minister, caseworker, teacher, or lawyer) is rarely
mentioned.[44]

The professional caretaker and the establishment
to which he is attached are often viewed with suspicion and hostility. It is believed that the social
service agencies simply attempt to get their clients
to adjust to the status quo.[45] The law, police, and
government agencies are viewed as exploiters of the
low-income community.[46] Welfare recipients in one
study had only a vague idea of the purpose of regular
caseworker visits. The most usual explanation was
that caseworkers visited in order to verify whether
the family was still eligible for welfare. The perception of the caseworker as a resource for problem
solving was rare.[47]

Distrust of the establishment is not the only
factor in low use of and reference to professional
caretakers. Several researchers suggest that much
of the problem is simply lack of information.[48]
Lack of familiarity and participation in organizations means little understanding of bureaucracies.
The poor often do not know that certain caretaking
agencies exist and they have no means of getting the
information that would lead them to these resources.

Despite this dim view of the effectiveness of
professional caretaking, a few studies take another

perspective. Freeman and Lambert emphasize that while
the public service agencies they studied did not have
high influence, they had more influence than voluntary
membership organizations.[49] Kurtz's study of clusters
of resource people in a Spanish-American community
isolated "public patrons" (social workers, teachers,
and other public employees) as one cluster and also
found a "super-cluster" of highly active resource-
handlers that included politicians, a mayor's assistant, and top welfare administrators. In that study,
the resource people, whether professional caretakers
or volunteers, primarily used informal channels to
those who came to them. Kurtz also suggests that
help given to the community was often inefficient--
for example, a real estate agent, tried to find medical help for a family while a doctor tried to find
housing. Further, the highly-involved core of sources
in the "super-cluster" handled an overload of help
requests that cut across multiple problem areas.[50]

Another recent study compared the perceptions of
professionals, indigenous workers, and clients in an
attempt to see what might be done to promote better
communication. Professional social workers were more
optimistic about the possibilities of changing the
social order but much less optimistic about the current state of affairs. The professionals saw more
inequality working against the poor in both job opportunities and treatment of children in school.
Both professional and indigenous workers were also
measured on their ability to predict the views of
their clients. Only 26 percent of the professionals
got high scores compared with 52 percent of the indigenous workers.[51]

Education, Employment, and Consumer Behavior

Considerable research on low-income respondents
has focused on these three behavioral areas. Sum-
maries of this research provide further examples of
the complex interrelationship between life style,
social relations, and inability to cope in the very
areas where achievement would be most likely to
break the poverty cycle.

Research in all three areas suggests that ghetto
values and styles are antagonistic to improvement.
In particular, education and employment emphasize
individual achievement but the ghetto dweller defends

himself against an alien world by emphasizing group
life and support.

Education

    "Low-education" is frequently used as a synonym
for "poverty." To be poor is to be less educated and
to have less opportunity for further education. To be
poor probably means that your children are attending
a public school with marginal resources and small
staff where custodial requirements predominate over
academic requirements.[52] There are, however, a number of contradictions in low-income educational values,
aspirations, expectations, and involvement.

    The literature suggests that for both the low-
income and the working-class person, "anti-intellectualism" is a value. The professor, the teacher, and
the writer are among the persons least admired by the
low-income community.[53] Intellectual concerns are
associated with the feared and hated establishment.
Abstract educational goals, achievement, and "educa-
tion-for-education's-sake" are middle-class values
rejected by the poor. The middle-class person will
rank education at the top of a list of values; the
low-income person ranks it below such concerns as
better housing, being clean, and having insurance.[54]

    Despite this surface rejection of education,
the literature strongly supports the premise that
education is valued by the low-income community.[55]
However, low-income people value education for different reasons than the middle class. Low-income
and working-class persons value education because it
can help them get a better job and earn more money.
Education often is seen as a necessary evil, a means
to an end. Education is desired but the discrepancy
between aspiration and expectation is large. Life
in the ghetto is such that the poor do not expect to
obtain for themselves or their children the education
they would wish. In practice, education must take
a secondary place to basic survival needs.

    Other studies have tapped various dimensions
of parental involvement in and perceptions of their
children's schools. One study showed that New York
City parents who were involved in school activities
were more favorable toward education in general but
less favorable toward the actual practices of the
school and teachers they personally knew.[56] Several
other studies suggest that education and its

accompanying improvement in occupational status neu-
tralize differences between ethnic and racial groups.
Given controls for education, attitudes and behaviors
of blacks and whites are often more alike than are
attitudes and behaviors of high- and low-educated respondents of the same race.[57]

Employment

Lack of employment and job skills are another
aspect of the poverty cycle. Because the low-income
person is unable to make individual gains, he de-empha-
sizes individual achievement. This attitude involves
him in a life style where getting, keeping, and doing
well in jobs receives low priority.[58] He is unprepared
for working in the primarily middle-class-oriented
work world. And his life conditions often lead him
to take high-paying, unstable, seasonal work instead
of lower-paying, regular jobs where he might learn
and advance.

Consumer Behavior

Considerable research documents the consumption
behavior of the poor.[59] "Compensatory consumption"
is the term applied by several researchers to low-
income behavior: the low-income person, frustrated
early in efforts to achieve through employment and
education, compensates for his lack of achievement
by consumption. Dealers selling high-priced, low-
quality goods under exorbitant credit terms make it
possible for the low-income person to consume despite
limited resources. The dealers also use the inter-
personal style of the ghetto to advantage, emphasizing
highly personal selling techniques, door-to-door
peddling, and friendship references.

Caplovitz provides the most extensive evidence
in his book The Poor Pay More. His study of residents
of New York City public housing showed that:

1. ownership levels of major durables (such as
phonographs, TV's, and washing machines) were as high
for his respondents as for the general population;
2. his respondents were highly dependent on
neighborhood sources for their goods and services;
3. they used department, discount, and chain
stores much less than did the general population;
4. one-half of his respondents bought from
peddlers and many considered peddlers friendlier
than store salesmen;

    5. the price paid for the advantage of imme-
diate consumption was high--high mark-ups and substantial credit costs often made prices exorbitant;
    6. most of the respondents used credit;
    7. most reported incidents when they or others
were cheated by shady sales practices; and
    8. most had no idea what professional sources
they might call on for legal help in dealing with
merchants.[60]

MASS COMMUNICATION BEHAVIOR

Media Usage

Usage studies of the poor concentrate on television consumption, give less attention to radio,
newspapers, and magazines, and almost entirely ne-
glect such media as movies and phonograph listening.
Common controls in such studies are income, age, sex,
and race, with occasional attention to more abstract
characteristics such as civil rights activity, alienation, and socialization.

In examining available research, it is obvious
that the poor are by no means deprived of the hard-
ware of media contact nor do they fail to make use
of them. The urban poor own radios and televisions
to virtually the same extent as the balance of the
population.[61] Allen found that television sets in a
Pittsburgh black ghetto were watched for an average
of 8 hours on weekdays and only slightly less on the
weekends. A Lansing, Michigan, study showed that the
poor watched television for an average of 5.2 hours
on weekdays compared with 2.0 hours for the general
population.[62] Low-income black teen-agers in Philadelphia watched television for 6.3 hours on a Sunday
compared with 4.6 hours by their white low-income
counterparts. On the other hand, white middle-class
teens spent an average of only 3.7 hours with television.[63] Similar differences were evident when total
time spent using television, radio, and the phonograph
are considered. The lower-class individual spent an
average of 7.3 hours per day with these media compared
to 4.0 hours for the middle-class person. Within the
lower class, blacks spent more time viewing than did
whites. Children also reflect class differences;
Friedman's study of sixth graders showed that lower-
class children watched television an average of 29

hours each week whereas the high-status child spent
only 15 hours per week.[64]

Although lower-class viewing is greater at any
one time, it is particularly heavier than middle-class
viewing during the late morning and most afternoon
hours of a given weekday. Low-income families start
viewing earlier in the day and cease later at night
than families in the general population.[65] The peak
viewing times for children have been shown to vary
somewhat by status; low-status children view most
during the dinner hours of 5 to 7 p.m. whereas other
children viewed maximally between 7 and 9 p.m.[66]

Despite the omnipresence of radio, there is considerably less information on its usage. In Allen's
sample of Pittsburgh ghetto blacks (predominantly
female), radio use was extensive and averaged 5.5
hours on weekdays.[67] Lyle found radio listening
"high" among Los Angeles Negroes of predominantly low
income.[68] However, Greenberg and Dervin found that
low-income families spent somewhat less time with
radio than does the general population.[69] On Sundays,
low-income blacks made less use of radio than either
low-income or middle-class whites.[70] Adult females
make heaviest use of the radio, particularly in the
morning hours when 100 percent of Pittsburgh black
ghetto households reported female radio use.[71]

Differences in newspaper reading seem to follow
class and income lines more than racial ones. Greenberg and Dervin reported that general population
respondents read the paper more often (77 percent
daily readers) and more extensively (39 percent reading the entire paper) than did low-income subjects
(65 percent daily readers, 17 percent readers of the
entire paper).[72]

In terms of black press readership, over 70 percent of Los Angeles blacks sampled read the major
Negro weekly.[73] Some 16 percent of a sample of
participants in the Detroit riots indicated regular
reading of the Michigan Chronicle, a black weekly
newspaper, but 47 percent regularly read the most
popular Detroit mass circulation daily.[74]

Generally, low-income adults read fewer magazines, although some magazines are regularly read.[75]
Only 10 percent of Lyle's black Los Angeles sample
indicated no regular reading of magazines[76] and Ingram
estimated that poor blacks consume about one magazine

per week.[77] In Lyle's sample, the median number of
magazines regularly read was three, these being a
combination of general magazines such as Life and
Look and Negro-oriented publications. Pulp and confession magazines also enjoyed a good following among
both low-income blacks and whites. Gerbner indicated
that pulp magazines were favored among young, low-
income females with children. In Allen's study, 83
percent of homes reported female readers compared to
only 12 percent adult male and 5 percent teen-age
readers.[78]

Little information is available on movie attendance and use of the phonograph. Some studies report
infrequent movie attendance among both middle- and
lower-class respondents, regardless of race. However,
use of the phonograph was much greater in the lower
class, particularly among blacks, both adults and
teen-agers.

One intriguing sidelight on usage deals with
parental control of children's media consumption.
Parental control of TV viewing is largely a myth.
In his study of three socio-economic groups, Friedman
reported that very few parents at any class level
prohibited specific programs. Viewing during the
dinner hour was equally common for all. Few children
watched programs recommended by the National Association for Better Radio and Television or Junior Scholastic.[79]

In contrast, Blood examined four social class
groupings of white mothers regarding the viewing behavior of children aged 2 to 18. He reported that
the lower-class mothers cited less control, fewer
bedtime rules, and more use of TV as a reward for
good behavior. He found that the father usually resolved conflict situations in lower-class homes,
generally in an authoritarian manner with fewer
reasons given for his particular program choices.[80]

Greenberg and Dominick examined the responses of
the young viewers themselves--groups of teen-age
middle-class whites, lower-class whites, and lower-
class blacks. Less than half of any of these groups
reported any household rules with respect to TV watching. Less than a fourth reported ever being punished
by denial of TV privileges. The only rule of any
prevalence was that of how late one could stay up:
one-half the whites indicated such a rule, as did one-
third of the blacks.[81] Thus, although middle-class

mothers indicate the existence of more rules than do
lower-class mothers, studies of the youngsters themselves provide little support for these contentions.

Media Content Preferences

On the surface, the urban poor appear to lack
strong content preferences, particularly with regard
to the broadcast media. In Allen's study of ghetto
blacks, the most common TV program preference was
"anything," except during the afternoon soap-opera
period and the 6 p.m. news hour. Most respondents
just switched on the set and rarely selected channels
in a planned fashion.[82]

However, more systematic evidence indicates that
low-income viewing is not entirely haphazard or an
imitation of middle-class preferences. Runciman contrasted program preferences of those with high and
low educations and found that suspense, western, and
soap-opera programs increased in popularity as education decreased. Among the highly-educated, there was
a stronger preference for public service programs.
Variety shows and situation commedies were about
equally appealing regardless of educational level.[83]
Greenberg and Dervin found that low-income individuals
tend to watch more "top-rated" shows than did a general population sample. Further, there was little
similarity in the popularity ratings of shows watched
by the two groups.[84]

Some attention has been given to racial differences in program preferences. Greenberg and Dominick
found relatively high agreement (correlation = .72)
between lower-class black and white teen-agers on the
relative popularity of various programs. However,
black teen-agers showed a preference for family-cen-
tered shows and a relative dislike of comedy and
variety programs.[85]

Carey's research indicates more extensive and
contradictory differences. Correlation of black/white
popularity rankings was noticeably lower (.50). Carey
claims that blacks do not favor family shows but prefer individual oriented programs with themes of conflict and loneliness as well as aggressive comedies.
Blacks and whites in this study did agree on which
shows were the worst--country and Western programs

and lower middle-class romantic music.[86] However,
Carey did not control for income in his study. Thus
the differences between his study and that of Greenberg and Dominick may be more due to income or class
than to race.

Singer found that a group of predominantly low-
income Detroit blacks preferred spy-detective-mystery
programs. Comparison is again difficult, since Singer
studied a specialized sample of riot-participants.[87]

Thus, data on racial differences in program
preferences is somewhat inconsistent and difficult
to compare across studies, although blacks and whites
seem to agree on most-favored and least-favored programs. It is interesting to note, however, that the
principal preference differences seem to be based more
on socio-economic than racial lines.

Few of the studies reviewed indicate radio program preferences by race or income criteria, probably
because of the relative homogeneity of radio programming from station to station and across various time
periods. Allen found that his ghetto sample preferred
"anything" on the radio, indicating little effort to
define program preferences. Some preference was found
among adult females and children for popular or gospel
music and among men for sports.[88] Little is known
about the growing number of "ethnic" radio stations.
A study by Larson indicates that ethnic-appeal stations can outdraw mass-appeal stations among the target minority.[89]

Ethnic preferences are more clearly manifest in
the print media, where numerous ethnically-oriented
publications may be found. According to Lyle, consumption of black newspapers is greatest where conditions of ghetto segregation are strongest. Readers
use the black press mostly for news of civic affairs
and entertainment; they use the white mass press for
national and international news and sports.[90]

Ethnic magazines also have strong appeal. In
Singer's Detroit sample, 58 percent were regular
readers of black periodicals.[91] Ebony was the most
preferred magazine among Allen's Pittsburgh blacks.[92]
In Los Angeles, Negro magazines and general magazines
(such as Life and Look) were regularly read by 60
percent of the respondents; 50 percent said they
read Ebony; 30 percent said they read Jet.[93]

Whites and blacks of the same income level showed many similarities in what they preferred to read in mass circulation newspapers.[94] Low-income whites and blacks gave very similar preference rankings to newspaper sections (correlation = .74). Differences on this measure were relatively major between the low-income and general population samples (correlation = .23). General population subjects preferred regular reading of the front page, comics, and sports, whereas low-income persons were most interested in scanning the headlines and reading the want-ads.

Attitudes Toward the Media

Media attitudes are commonly assessed in terms of the relative credibility of several media, usually in reference to their news content. Television is overwhelmingly the most preferred and most believed medium among the poor.[95] In Allen's ghetto sample, 77 percent felt TV was the most reliable and factual medium, followed by radio (12 percent), and newspapers (6 percent). Greenberg and Dervin found low-income respondents consistently more favorable than the general population toward television for world news.[96] However, the poor preferred local news from the radio; other adults preferred the newspaper, followed by the radio.

Some racial differences were evident.[97] While low-income whites indicated nearly equal preference among TV, radio, and newspapers for local news, blacks gave most preference to radio and very little to newspapers. Perhaps of greatest interest was that 22 percent of the blacks cited "people" as the most preferred source of local news compared to only 7 percent among the low-income whites. Such relatively high preference for inter-personal news sources was also evident among the rural poor where other people constituted the most preferred means of acquiring local news.[98] Perhaps the social isolation of urban blacks and the physical isolation of rural poor increase dependence upon personal sources of news.

Teen-agers generally paralleled adults in their view of TV as the most preferred and believable medium. Some 65 percent of low-income white and black teen-agers preferred TV news accounts if conflicting stories on the same subject were presented by radio and newspapers.[99] Half of middle-class teen-agers preferred television under the same circumstances.

Radio and newspapers were most trusted by about
15-20 percent of the low-income whites and blacks;
35 percent of the middle-class white teen-agers
showed more faith in the newspaper. When asked to
choose only one of the three major media, 66 to 75
percent of all groups selected television. Newspapers
were hardly mentioned. When asked which reporter
performed his job best, low-income whites and blacks
chose the TV newsman. Middle-class teen-agers preferred TV and newspaper reporters equally.

Though the data summarized above speak little
of racial differences in media attitudes, strong
feelings emerge when blacks assess the treatment of
blacks in the mass circulation press. Eighty-three
percent of Lyle's sample of Los Angeles blacks considered coverage of black-oriented news in the mass
press to be inadequate. Half of this sample felt
the majority press was consistently unfair to blacks;
only 13 percent believed both sides were regularly
reported in racial disputes.[100] Detroit blacks were
offended when the large dailies made light of Negro
claims or used racial designations in reporting crime
stories.[101] A CBS network report indicated wide disagreement between blacks and whites regarding the
general fairness of race coverage in the media. Although 64 percent of whites polled believed blacks
received too much attention in the media, only 10 percent of the blacks agreed. On the other hand, 46 percent of the blacks believed they received too little
attention--only 8 percent of whites agreed. Only 25
percent of the sample of either race believed coverage
to be adequate. Half of the whites believed the black
cause was fairly presented--only a fourth of the
blacks agreed. Some 52 percent of blacks believed
that their civil rights cause had been unfairly presented in the media--39 percent of the whites agreed.
Each race saw itself in a more righteous position
than the other.[102]

Gieber's interviews with civil rights leaders
and reporters revealed much the same disagreement:
black civil rights people were suspicious of the
press and reporters were resentful of being told
how to do their job by these individuals.[103]

Blacks are also critical of the black press,
although they feel that it is relatively accurate
and complete. The more educated blacks object to
frequent sensationalism and the less educated regret
the omission of local people from the news. Readers

are also skeptical about the papers' freedom from
advertiser pressure and censorship. In fact, 36
percent of sampled blacks preferred the trustworthiness of the mass circulation dailies and only 25 percent preferred the black weekly paper.[104]

Poor blacks seem to prefer that their racial
achievements be glamorously, perhaps even sensation-
ally, presented. They also like to see local people--
those most like themselves--in the news. Finally,
blacks want ethnic media that reinforce their culture,
give them racial and self pride, and air their griev-
ances.

Media Characterizations

As documented above, the poor consistently judge
television to be the most credible of the mass media.
We shall now consider to what extent media presentations, particularly television, correspond to reality,
either to the viewers or by more objective indexes.

In their study of teen-agers' use of and attitudes toward television, Greenberg and Dominick asked
the respondents to comment on a series of statements
about the perceived reality of TV programs, such as:
"The programs I see on TV tell about life the way it
really is." White middle-class teen-agers disagreed
most with such items, black lower-income respondents
agreed significantly more, and white lower-income
respondents were at an intermediate level of agreement. The poor, particularly the blacks, perceived
television as "showing it like it is."[105] In her
studies of slum children, Keller reports that the
majority society reaches these children (first and
fifth graders) through entertainment and escapist
stories on television.[106]

Relevant analyses of television and magazine
content have focused largely on the media presentation of occupational groups. They give evidence of
the discrepancy between media presentations and real-
life job distribution. In an analysis of 122 characters on 26 network programs, Gentile and Miller found
only 7 working-class characters. All were males, all
used improper English and the presentations were
seldom favorable.[107]

In a more systematic study, DeFleur analyzed
occupational roles in 250 randomly selected half-hour

segments, 436 job portrayals in all. Nearly one-
third of the jobs were law-connected. In terms of
the actual labor force distribution, upper-status
occupations were greatly over-represented and lower-
prestige jobs equally under-represented. Female
workers were more numerous than they actually are.
DeFleur also found portrayal of higher-status persons
more favorable, although stereotyped. Moreover, the
most favorably portrayed jobs were jobs that young
workers--or indeed most workers in any realistic
sense--were least likely to attain.[108]

Several studies of magazines yield related findings. Shuey analyzed 292 issues of six general circulation magazines. Using each picture containing a
Negro and the first succeeding picture containing a
white, he coded the occupation of the pictured persons as a less-than-skilled position, a skilled-labor
position, or a higher-than-skilled position. Of the
pictures in advertisements, 5 percent showed blacks
in higher-than-skilled positions compared with 86
percent of the whites so portrayed. Thirty-eight percent of the blacks in the pictures in the editorial
sections of the magazines were cast in higher-than-
skilled positions compared with 81 percent of the
whites. Census data for that time period indicated
that only 20 percent of the white labor force held
such jobs.[109]

Boyenton looked at Negroes in newspaper ads in
four cities that contained 14 percent of the total
black population of the United States. He found virtually none; in some 20,000 New York Times ads, there
were nine Negroes. Other newspapers and magazines
analyzed showed even fewer Negroes.[110] Yet in the
CBS study, 64 percent of the white respondents (compared to 10 percent of the blacks) said that blacks
were getting too much attention in the media.[111]

Similar analyses have included comparison with
some Negro media. Barcus and Levin examined 34
stories with Negro and non-Negro characters from
four white and four black general circulation magazines. They analyzed the closeness of the role-relationships between paired characters. They found
that intra-group role-relationships were consistently
closer than inter-group ones and that Negroes were
closer to non-Negro minorities than they were to
whites. Only 15 percent of the white magazine stories
had racial differences as a central plot compared to
73 percent of the stories in the Negro magazines.[112]

Berkman analyzed the advertising content of four issues of Ebony and Life. In Ebony, 20 percent of the ads were for alcoholic beverages; 5 percent of the Life ads were for such products. Other significant points of comparison were: automotive ads, 1 percent in Ebony and 17 percent in Life; patent medicine ads, 57 in Ebony and 22 in Life; and money-making opportunities, 51 in Ebony and 0 in Life.[113]

Lyle did the most comprehensive empirical study of the Negro media. He found that the perceived need for a Negro newspaper was highest in the central ghetto areas and lowest in the geographic areas farthest from the core city. Paradoxically, the blacks most publicized in these newspapers are the better-educated and highest-income blacks--those least likely to be living in the central ghetto. Lyle perceived that lower-income blacks may be resentful or jealous of the attention given those who have means to escape the ghetto.[114] Ingram maintained that poor blacks enjoy reading glamorous presentations of black accomplishments as, for example, in Ebony.[115]

Frazier, in his classic indictment of the Negro press, said that there was severe exaggeration of Negro achievements in the Negro press. He contended that this exaggeration was done to compensate for inferiority feelings and to serve as superficial gratification for the black bourgeoisie.[116] Since then, Rosen has found considerable changes in Ebony's editorial content. The changes made between 1948 and 1960 included more mention of discrimination and more intensity in discussions of discrimination, less mention of whites, more militant black ideology, and more emphasis on Negroes as agents responsible for integration attempts.[117]

Sargent et al. compared the coverage of integration in pictures in Life and Ebony for 1962-63. Ebony had far less violence in its photographic content and 10 times as many pictures of blacks and whites together.

The world as presented in the majority media is virtually devoid of the lower class, in both fiction and advertisements. Further, the correspondence between mass media fiction and real life is negligible by certain objective criteria but substantial in the view of the low-income audience.[118]

Motivational Concomitants
of Media Behavior

Alienation, social isolation, and anxiety--feel-
ings typical of many poor people--have been thought
to affect media usage, particularly television. The
basic hypothesis is that those who are isolated and
alienated compensate for their loneliness by high
media use, with an emphasis on fantasy-type programs
that depict isolation and alienation.

McLeod et al. found that highly alienated people
did not have higher television consumption or more
extensive viewing of programs that reinforced an image
of a hostile unpredictable world.[119] In terms of
newspaper reading, general radio listening, and specific consumption of radio news, Sargent and Stempel III
found no significant differences between those with
high and low alienation. They suggested instead that
the critical variable is poverty. However, the highly
alienated among relief cases viewed less television.
The authors argue that TV viewing and alienation may
both be methods of anxiety-reduction, although somewhat incompatible. The alienated person may find
television an unacceptable reminder of the society he
wishes to evade. In contrast, another person may find
the fantasy content of television a more acceptable
anxiety-reduction device.[120] Anxiety-reduction through
TV fantasy was supported by Hazard, who found that
highly anxious people showed less civic participation
as well as extensive viewing of high fantasy content
TV programs. Low social position was also related to
high use of fantasy content. This syndrome is prevalent, it was reasoned, in the lower class where
social and economic uncertainties breed anxiety.[121]

Others have studied television as an instrument
of social involvement. McCombs compared 1952 voting
survey data to similar information for 1964 and inter-
vening time periods and found that blacks made increased use of television particularly and newspapers
secondarily for political information. Similar increases were not evident in the white population,
whose usage remained constant or, in the case of TV,
declined. Although low media users among whites rose
from 29 to 41 percent over this 12-year period, low
media users among blacks dropped from 63 to 41 percent. Although part of the increase among blacks
could have been due to the increasing availability
of TV sets, McCombs contends that most was due to

increasing black civil rights activity and consequent
information-seeking behavior.[122]

Gerson found racial differences in adolescents'
use of television to obtain dating information. They
looked at television to reinforce dating ideas they
already had as well as to get new ideas. Basically,
lower classes, particularly blacks, used mass media
more heavily for socialization information. Blacks
who were poorly integrated into their own peer culture made more use of the media than those who were
more successfully integrated. Gerson suspected that
the blacks felt a need for information on how to
succeed in the white society.[123]

Greenberg and Dominick supported Gerson's suspicions, finding that low-income blacks made greater
use of TV as a "school-of-life" device than did
middle- and low-class whites.[124] The black teen-age
respondents indicated that they used TV more for
learning how to solve problems, things they couldn't
learn in school, and about people in all walks of
life. In sum, income differences among respondents
were associated with divergent motivations for watching television. Being both black and poor accentuated
the differences.

CONCLUSIONS

The poverty syndrome is a vicious circle with
far-reaching effects on life styles and communication
behavior. From a research standpoint, determination
of cause-and-effect relationships is frequently impossible. Typically, problems of the poor in one
aspect of living interact with those in another,
feeding the poverty cycle and progressively degrading
the quality of life. Consequently, the isolated
effect of one factor on the life of a poor person
is in most cases impossible to determine. Although
understandably imprecise, these studies effectively
catalog and explain conditions affecting the poor.
In a few instances, they also do an adequate job of
measuring the consequences of these conditions.

In terms of inter-personal contacts, family and
friends form a closely-knit network beyond which few
of the disadvantaged venture. While the middle-class
person concentrates on individual activities and
betterment, the lower-class person leans heavily on

kin and friends for aid and emotional support. The
poor lack the middle-class notion that the receiving
of aid obligates one to repay the favor. In low-income groups, help is usually received if others are
able to give it. Help from outsiders, such as social
service agencies, is suspect. Social workers raised
in the ghetto are generally better received.

Gossip is the prime activity of the low-income
communication network. Typically, conversation is
less verbal than in the middle class. Participation
in formal organizations other than church and fraternal organizations that parallel family and peer
group ties is infrequent. However, there is some
recent evidence of increased organizational activity
among low-income blacks.

The poor are heavy consumers of the mass media,
particularly television. Both television and radio
are as ubiquitous among the poor as in the rest of
the population. Low-income people view much more
television than the rest of society, starting earlier
in the morning and continuing later at night. Magazines and newspapers receive relatively little attention from the poor in comparison to the middle class.
Blacks in particular distrust general circulation
newspapers and frequently accuse them of being bigoted
or white-oriented. Although black-controlled newspapers receive a more favorable evaluation, they are
accused of ignoring the ordinary black man and presenting a sensational view of the world despite their
evident value in reinforcing black pride. Ethnic
radio stations have a similar value, as evidenced by
the fact that these stations frequently have greater
drawing power among the target minority than the
general audience stations.

More important are the findings that poor blacks
especially use television as a source of social information or thrills and excitement. Inconclusive
research also indicates that television may serve to
reduce anxiety by allowing easy escape into a fantasy
world. Content analysis of telelvision programming
has demonstrated that the TV world is exaggerated
and emphasizes the values and means of white upper-
middle-class society. Frequently, blacks have been
shown in inferior roles and occupations. Until recently, they have been entirely missing from advertisements. Thus, TV--the principal communication
link between the majority society and the ghetto
black and the poor--gives at best a distorted view.

There is some evidence that television recently has
encouraged political participation among blacks.
However, the general conclusion is that media content does little to break down and may in fact encourage the isolation of the poor and ghetto black
from the majority society.

NOTES

1.   Arthur Besner, "Economic Deprivation and
Family Patterns," Welfare in Review III, 9 (September, 1965), 20-28.

2.   Catherine S. Chilman, Growing Up Poor, U.S.
Dept. of Health, Education and Welfare, Welfare Ad-
ministration Publication No. 13 (Washington, D. C.:
Government Printing Office, May, 1966).

3.   Elizabeth Herzog, "Some Assumptions About
the Poor," Social Service Review XXXVIII, 4 (December,
1963), 389-402.

4.   Besner, op. cit.; Herbert J. Gans, The
Urban Villagers: Group and Class in the Life of
Italian Americans (Glencoe, Ill.: The Free Press,
1962); Elliot Liebow, Tally's Corner: A Study of
Negro Streetcorner Men (Boston: Little, Brown, and
Co., 1967); Lee Rainwater, Richard P. Coleman, and
Gerald Handel, Workingman's Wife (New York: Oceana
Publications, 1959).

5.   Liebow, op. cit.

6.   Besner, op. cit.

7.   Liebow, op. cit.

8.   Rainwater et al., op. cit.

9.   Chilman, op. cit.

10.   Chilman, op. cit.; National Advisory Com-
mission on Civil Disorders, Report of the National
Advisory Commission on Civil Disorders (New York:
Bantam Books, March, 1968).

11.   Chilman, op. cit.; Lenore A. Epstein, "Some Effects of Low Income on Children and Their Families," Social Security Bulletin XXIV, 2 (February, 1961) 12-17; Liebow, op. cit.

12.   Epstein, op. cit.

13.   Alice R. McCabe, "Re: Forty Forgotten Families," The Journal of the American Public Welfare Association, Public Welfare XXIV, 2 (April, 1966), 159-171.

14.   Besner, op. cit.; Catherine S. Chilman, "Child Rearing and Family Relationship Patterns of the Very Poor," Welfare in Review III, 1 (January, 1965), 9-19; Liebow, op. cit.; U.S. Government, Recent Trends in Social and Economic Conditions of Negroes in the United States, Current Population Reports, Series P-23, No. 26, BLS Report No. 347 (Washington, D. C.: Government Printing Office, July, 1968).

15.   Salvador Minuchin, Braulio Montalvo, Bernard Guerney Jr., Bernice Rosman, and Florence Schumer, Families of the Slums: An Exploration of Their Structure and Treatment (New York: Basic Books, 1967).

16.   Herzog, op. cit.

17.   Liebow, op. cit.

18.   Minuchin et al., op. cit.

19.   Ibid.

20.   Phyllis Levenstein and Robert Sunley, "Stimulation of Verbal Interaction Between Disadvantaged Mothers and Children," American Journal of Orthopsychiatry XXXVIII, 7 (January, 1968), 116-121.

21.   Gans, op. cit.

22.   Melvin L. Kohn, "Social Class and Parental Values," The American Journal of Sociology LXIV, 4 (January, 1959), 337-351; Robert R. Bell, "Lower Class Mothers' Aspirations for Their Children," Social Forces XLIII, 4 (May, 1965), 493-500; Besner, op. cit.; Chilman, op. cit.; Gans, op. cit.

23.   Bell, op. cit.

24. Gans, op. cit.; Chilman, op. cit.; McCabe,
op. cit.; Levenstein and Sunley, op. cit.; Minuchin
et al., op. cit.; Oliver C. Moles, "Child Training
Practices Among Low Income Families--An Empirical
Study," Welfare In Review III, 12 (December, 1965),
1-19.

25. James Walters, Ruth Conner, and Michael
Zunich, "Interaction of Mothers and Children in Lower
Class Families," Child Development XXXV, 2 (June,
1964), 433-440.

26. McCabe, op. cit.

27. David Caplovitz, The Poor Pay More (New
York: The Free Press, 1963); Chilman, op. cit.;
Kenneth B. Clark, Dark Ghetto: Dilemmas of Social
Power (New York: Harper, 1967); Paul Friedman and
Gerald M. Phillips, "Toward a Rhetoric for the Poverty
Class," Journal of Communication XVII, 3 (September,
1967), 234-249; David Gottlieb, "Goal Aspirations
and Goal Fulfillments: Differences Between Deprived
and Affluent American Adolescents," American Journal
of Orthopsychiatry XXXIV, 5 (1964), 934-941; Jules
Henry, "White People's Time, Colored People's Time,"
Trans-Action II, 3 (March-April, 1965) 31-34; Lola
M. Irelan, and Arthur Besner, "Low Income Outlook on
Life," Welfare in Review III, 9 (September, 1965),
13-19; Oscar Lewis, "The Culture of Poverty," Scientific American CCXV, 4 (October, 1966), 19-25; Liebow,
op. cit.; Jack L. Roach and Orville R. Gursslin, "The
Lower Class, Status Frustration, and Social Disorgani-
zation," Social Forces XLIII, 4 (1965), 501-510; U.S.
Gov't. (1968), op. cit.

28. Endell Bell, "Anomie, Social Isolation,
and the Class Structure," Sociometry XX (June, 1957),
105-116; Leonard Broom and Norval D. Glenn, "Negro-
White Differences in Reported Attitudes and Behavior,"
Sociology and Social Research L, 2 (January, 1966),
187-200; Chilman, op. cit.; Clark, op. cit.; Albert
K. Cohen and Harold M. Hodge Jr., "Characteristics
of the Lower Blue-Collar Class," Journal of Social
Problems X, 4 (Spring, 1963), 103-134; Leon F. Fannin
and Marshall B. Clinard, "Differences in the Concep-
tion of Self as a Male Among Lower and Middle Class
Delinquents," Social Problems XIII, 2 (1965), 205-214;
Franklin E. Frazier, Black Bourgeoisie (New York:
Collier, 1965, original ed. in French publication,
1955); Henry, op. cit.; Irelan and Besner, op. cit.;
Lewis, op. cit.; Liebow, op. cit.; Russell Middleton,

"Alienation, Race, and Education," The American Sociological Review XXVIII (December, 1963), pp 973-977.;
Roach and Gursslin, op. cit.; U.S. Gov't. (1968),
op. cit.

29. Caplovitz, op. cit.; Chilman, op. cit.;
Cohen and Hodge Jr., op. cit.; Gans, op. cit.; David
Gottlieb, "The Neighborhood Tavern and the Cocktail
Lounge: A Study of Class Differences," American
Journal of Sociology CXII, 6 (May, 1967), 559-562;
Henry, op. cit.; Irelan and Besner, op. cit.; Lewis,
op. cit.; Liebow, op. cit.; Conal E. Muir and E. A.
Weinstein, "The Social Debt: An Investigation of
Lower Class and Middle Class Norms of Social Obliga-
tion," American Sociological Review XXVII, 4 (1962),
532-539; Rainwater et al., op. cit.; Frank Riesman,
"Low Income Culture: The Strengths of the Poor,"
Journal of Marriage and Family XXVI, 4 (November,
1964), 417-421.

30. Clark, op. cit.; Henry, op. cit.; Liebow,
op. cit.

31. Caplovitz, op. cit.

32. Friedman and Phillips, op. cit.; Gans, op.
cit.; Henry, op. cit.; Liebow, op. cit.

33. Friedman and Phillips, op. cit.; Irelan
and Besner, op. cit.; Hugh McIssac and Harold Wilkin-
son, "Clients Talk About Their Caseworkers," Public
Welfare XXIII, 3 (July, 1965), 147-154; Roach and
Gursslin op. cit.; Leonard Schatzman and Anselm
Strauss, "Social Class and Modes of Communication,"
The American Journal of Sociology LX, 4 (January,
1955), 329-338.

34. McIssac and Wilkinson, op. cit.

35. Cohen and Hodge Jr., op. cit.; Gans, op.
cit.; Irelan and Besner, op. cit.; Lewis, op. cit.;
Rainwater, op. cit.

36. Clark, op. cit.; Frazier, op. cit.

37. Norman R. Kurtz, "Gatekeepers: Agents in
Acculturation," Rural Sociology XXXIII, 1 (March,
1968), 63-70.

38.   Robert M. O'Shea and Shirlene B. Gray, "Income and Community Participation," Welfare in Review IV, 4 (April, 1966), 10-13.

39.   Frazier, op. cit.; Gans, op. cit.; Kurtz, op. cit.

40.   Kurtz, op. cit.

41.   Gans, op. cit.

42.   Frazier, op. cit.

43.   Gans, op. cit.

44.   Caplovitz, op. cit.; Lewis Donohew, "Poverty 'Types' and Their Sources of Information About New Practices" (Paper presented at the International Communication Division, Association for Education in Journalism, Boulder, Colo., August 27-31, 1967); Lewis Donohew and B. K. Singh, "Modernization of Life Styles An Appraisal of the 'War on Poverty' in a Rural Setting of Southeastern Kentucky." (Lexington, Kentucky: University of Kentucky, August, 1968); Gans, op. cit.

45.   Clark, op. cit.

46.   Gans, op. cit.; Lewis, op. cit.; McIssac and Wilkinson, op. cit.; U.S. Gov't. (1968), op. cit.

47.   McIssac and Wilkinson, op. cit.

48.   Cohen and Hodge, Jr., op. cit.; Irelan and Besner, op. cit.

49.   H. E. Freeman and Camille Lambert Jr. "The Influence of Community Groups on Health Matters," Human Organization XXIV, 4 (Winter, 1965), 353-357.

50.   Kurtz, op. cit.

51.   Charles F. Grosser, "Local Residents as Mediators Between Middle Class Professional Workers and Lower Class Clients," Social Service Review XL, 1 (March, 1966), 56-63.

52.   Chilman, op. cit.; Clark, op. cit.; Gottlieb, op. cit.

53.   Chilman, op. cit.; Cohen and Hodge Jr., op. cit.; Rainwater, et al., op. cit.

54.   Richard B. Larson and Sara Sutker, "Value Differences and Value Concensus by Socio-Economic Status," Social Forces XLIV, 4 (1966), 563-569.

55.   Gans, op. cit.; Gottlieb, op. cit.; Irelan and Besner, op. cit.

56.   Richard A. Cloward and J. A. Jones, "Social Class: Educational Attitudes and Participation," in Education in Depressed Areas, edited by A. H. Passow (New York: Teachers College Press, Columbia University, 1963), pp. 190-216.

57.   Broom and Glenn, op. cit.; Caplovitz, op. cit.; also, see chapter 1.

58.   Friedman and Phillips, op. cit.; Lewis, op. cit.; Liebow, op. cit.

59.   Caplovitz, op. cit.; Laurence P. Feldman and Alvin D. Star, "Racial Factors in Shopping Behavior," in A New Measure of Responsibility for Marketing, edited by Keith Cox and Ben Enis, Conference Proceedings, Series No. 27 (Philadelphia: American Marketing Association June 17-19, 1968), 216-226; Frazier, op. cit.; Lewis, op. cit.; Rainwater, et al., op. cit.; U.S. Gov't. (1968), op. cit.

60.   Caplovitz, op. cit.

61.   T. H. Allen, "Mass Media Use Patterns and Functions in a Negro Ghetto," (Master's thesis, University of West Virginia, 1967).

62.   See chapter 1.

63.   See chapter 2.

64.   M. Friedman, Television Program Preference and Televiewing Habits of Children as Related to Their Socio-Economic Status (PhD dissertation, Yeshiva University, 1957).

65.   See chapter 1.

66.   Friedman, op. cit.

67.   Allen, op. cit.

68.   Jack Lyle, "The Negro and the News Media," in Jack Lyle, The News in Megalopolis. (San

Francisco: Chandler Publishing Co., 1967), Chapter
9, pp. 163-182.

69. See chapter 1.

70. See chapter 2.

71. Allen, op. cit.

72. See chapter 1.

73. Lyle, op. cit.

74. B. D. Singer, Television and the Riots,
mimeographed (London, Ontario: Department of Sociology, University of Western Ontario, June 7, 1968).

75. See chapter 1.

76. Lyle, op. cit.

77. Jim Ingram, "What Blacks Read--and Who They
Believe," Detroit Scope Magazine I, 39 (January 4,
1969), 6-8.

78. George Gerbner, "The Social Role of the
Confession Magazine," Social Problems VI, 1 (1958),
29-41; Allen, op. cit.

79. Friedman, op. cit.

80. Robert O. Blood Jr., "Social Class and
Family Control of Television Viewing," Merrill-Palmer
Quarterly VII, 3 (July, 1961), 205-222.

81. See chapter 2.

82. Allen, op. cit.

83. Alexander P. Runciman, "A Stratification
Study of Television Programs," Sociology and Social
Research XLIV, 4 (March-April, 1960), 257-261.

84. See chapter 1.

85. See chapter 2.

86. James W. Carey, "Variations in Negro-White
Television Preference," Journal of Broadcasting X, 3
(1966), 199-212.

87. B. D. Singer, The Detroit Riot of July 1967: A Psychological, Social, and Economic Profile of 500 Arrestees, a report prepared for the U.S. Department of Labor, Manpower Administration, Research Contract No. 81-24-68-03 (London, Ontario: Department of Sociology, University of Western Ontario, n.d.).

88. Allen, op. cit.

89. Carl M. Larson, "Racial Brand Usage and Media Exposure Differentials," in Cox and Enis, eds., op. cit., 208-215.

90. Lyle, op. cit.

91. Singer (1967), op. cit.

92. Allen, op. cit.

93. Lyle, op. cit.

94. See chapter 1.

95. Allen, op. cit.; see chapters 1 and 2.

96. See chapter 1.

97. See chapter 1.

98. Donohew and Singh, op. cit.

99. See chapter 2.

100. Lyle, op. cit.

101. Ingram, op. cit.

102. Columbia Broadcasting System, White and Negro Attitudes Towards Race Related Issues and Activities (Princeton, N.J.: Public Opinion Research Corp., July 9, 1968).

103. Walter Gieber, "How the 'Gatekeepers' View Local Civil Liberties News," Journalism Quarterly XXXVII, 2 (Spring, 1960), 199-205.

104. Lyle, op. cit.

105. See chapter 2.

106. Susanne Keller, "The Social World of the Urban Slum Child: Some Early Findings," American Journal of Orthopsychiatry XXXIII, 5 (1963), 823-831.

107. Frank Gentile and S. M. Miller, "TV and Social Class," Sociology and Social Research XLV, 3 (April, 1961), 259-264.

108. M. L. DeFleur, "Occupational Roles as Portrayed on Television," Public Opinion Quarterly XXXVII, 1 (Spring, 1964), 57-64.

109. Audrey Shuey, Nancy King, and Barbara Griffith, "Stereotyping of Negroes and Whites: An Analysis of Pictures in Magazines," Public Opinion Quarterly XVII (1953), 281-287.

110. William H. Boyenton, "The Negro Turns to Advertising," Journalism Quarterly XLII, 2 (Spring, 1965), 227-235.

111. Columbia Broadcasting System, op. cit.

112. F. Earle Barcus and Jack Levin, "Role Distance in Negro and Majority Fiction," Journalism Quarterly XLIII, 4 (Winter, 1966), 709-714.

113. David Berkman, "Advertising in Ebony and Life: Negro Aspirations vs. Reality," Journalism Quarterly XL, 1 (Winter, 1963), pp. 53-64.

114. Lyle, op. cit.

115. Ingram, op. cit.

116. Frazier, op. cit.

117. Bernard Rosen, "Attitude Change within the Negro Press Toward Segregation and Discrimination," Journal of Social Psychology LXII, 1 (1964), 77-83.

118. Leslie W. Sargent, Wiley Carr, and Elizabeth McDonald, "Significant Coverage of Integration by Minority Group Magazines," Journal of Human Relations XIII, 4 (1965), 484-491.

119. Jack McLeod, Scott Ward, and Karen Tancill, "Alienation and Uses of Mass Media," Public Opinion Quarterly XXIX, (Winter, 1965-66), 583-594.

120.   Leslie W. Sargent and Guido H. Stempel III. "Poverty, Alienation, and Mass Media Use," Journalism Quarterly XLV, 2 (Summer, 1968), 324-326.

121.   William R. Hazard, "Anxiety and Preference for Television Fantasy," Journalism Quarterly XLIV, 3 (Autumn, 1967), 461-469.

122.   Maxwell E. McCombs, "Negro Use of Television and Newspapers for Political Information, 1952-64," Journal of Broadcasting XIII, 3 (Summer, 1968), 261-266.

123.   Walter Gerson, "Mass Media Socialization Behavior: Negro-White Differences," Social Forces XLV, 1 (September, 1966), 40-50.

124.   See chapter 2.

CHAPTER **6** ANNOTATED
BIBLIOGRAPHY
ON COMMUNICATION
AND THE POOR

Brenda Dervin,
John Bowes, and
Bradley S. Greenberg

INTRODUCTION

When we first undertook our research projects
on the communication behavior of the urban poor, we
attempted to do the usual background search of existing literature. This search was found to be no
straightforward task. Although there is a huge
volume of literature available on the poor and a
considerable volume available on communication, the
overlap between the two is minimal. Extensive library searches were necessary in order to find even
a few jointly-relevant listings. The compilation in
this chapter is the product of a search of more than
3,000 listings.

Our overall purpose was to compile comprehensive
abstracts of empirical research on the communication
behavior of the urban poor. Specifically, we wished
to include:

1. As complete as possible a selection of
studies dealing with the mass and inter-personal communication behavior of the poor.
2. A selective sampling of classic and often-
cited studies on poverty life styles.
3. A selection of recent work on disturbances
in urban ghettos.

The publications included deal with one of the
areas specified above, describing low-income urban
respondents or comparing low-income respondents to

general population respondents. Because of the close
link between race and poverty, a number of studies
comparing blacks and whites have also been included.

Our search emphasized empirical works: We have
included only field surveys, laboratory studies, and
review and commentary articles based on empirical
work. We also required a post-1960 date except for
a few classic articles with data unavailable in more
recent work.

These criteria eliminated many possibilities:
for example, only two studies on the rural poor are
included. The myriad commentary and opinion pieces
on poverty are excluded as well as many small-scale
projects testing the results of specific poverty action programs. Studies dealing with the language
behavior of the poor were also eliminated because a
number of bibliographic collections on this single
topic are available elsewhere.

Our search did not exhaust the large volume of
literature available. Specifically, the search parameters included: (1) a review of Journalism Quarterly
and Public Opinion Quarterly, 1959-68; (2) a review
of Psychological Abstracts and Sociological Abstracts;
(3) a review of all listings in Poverty and Human
Resources Abstracts since its first publication in
January, 1966; and (4) a review of all listings in
five bibliographic and review publications:

Wayne A. Danielson and G. C. Wilhoit Jr.,
A Computerized Bibliography of Mass Com-
munication Research 1944-1964 (New York:
Magazine Publishing Association, 1967).

Freda L. Paltiel, Poverty: An Annotated
Bibliography and References (Ottawa, Canada: The Canadian Welfare Council, 1966).

Percy H. Tannenbaum and Bradley S. Greenberg, "Mass Communication," Annual Review
of Psychology XIX (1968), 351-386.

Verling C. Troldahl, George B. Robeck,
and Daniel E. Costello, Bibliography of
Mass Communication Research, mimeographed
(Department of Communication, Michigan
State University, April, 1965).

Agnes Woodward, <u>Poverty/Pauvrete:</u> Sup-
<u>plement 1</u> (Ottawa, Canada: The Canadian
Welfare Council, March, 1967).

Some relevant research undoubtedly has been
overlooked. We feel most confident about the completeness of our search for articles dealing specifically with the mass and inter-personal communication
behavior of the poor. However, the volume of literature dealing with poverty life styles is so large we
feel less confident about the completeness of our
coverage in that area. Since much work on ghetto
disturbances is both recent and unpublished, we know
we have missed some relevant material. Some researchers may also find our abstracts of their own
work wanting; for example, we omitted their self-
criticisms. We hope such shortcomings are overcome
by having made available in a single volume a comprehensive compilation of abstracts focusing on the communication behavior of the urban poor.

ANNOTATED BIBLIOGRAPHY

Allen, T. H. "Mass Media Use Patterns and Functions in a Negro
Ghetto." Master's thesis, University of West Virginia, 1967.

Purpose: To investigate the mass media use patterns of and their
effects on residents of a Negro ghetto.

Method: A field survey was conducted June 5-13, 1967. These dates
were chosen because they occurred prior to the start of school vacation
and summer TV reruns. The sample was comprised of 100 adult Negroes
living in the Hill area of Pittsburgh, Pennsylvania. The sample represented 1% of the 10,000 residents in this ghetto, where 87% of all Pittsburgh Negroes live. The median income is $3,000 compared with $5-
6,000 for other census tracts in Pittsburgh; median education is 8.2
years; and the unemployment rate is 19% among men and 7% among women. An adult occupant of each house or apartment located on the corner
of each major street in the three census tracts that make up the Hill
area was interviewed. Approximately 75% of the respondents were female. Respondents were asked to report not only their own media behaviors but also those of all members of their households. Therefore,
the data below represent multiple members of a household as reported
by a single member of the household. (Tabled data did not report Ns
used in computing percentages.) The paper reports only the frequency
marginals for the following variables, making no correlations: (1) inventory of media availability; (2) radio use; (3) newspaper use; (4) TV
use; (5) magazine use; (6) sources of news on public affairs; (7) perceptions of reliability of the media; and (8) knowledge on specific news.

Results
    Media inventory
    1.   100% of the respondents reported at least one radio in their
home; 64% reported two or more.
    2.   95% had at least one TV; 47% had two or more.
    3.   58% said they never received magazines; 42% received one
magazine.
    4.   86% did not receive a daily newspaper; 87% did not receive a
weekly; and 40% did not receive a Sunday newspaper. Those who did
receive newspapers received only one daily and/or one weekly.

    Radio use
    1.   70% indicated they had the radio on in their homes sometime
Saturday and 58%, sometime Sunday. On weekdays, radio use in households varied from a high of 63% to a low of 21%, depending on the time
of day. Peak usage times were between 8 a.m. and 1 p.m.; low usage
times were from 5 p.m. to midnight.
    2.   Respondents indicated that the females in their households
were the high radio users: 100% of the respondents noted female use of
radio on weekdays between 8 a.m. and 12 noon. Children were reported
to use the radio between 5 p.m. and midnight in 39% of the households.

3.   When asked what they liked best on radio, the answer was music
for the children (97% of the households); music and gospel singing for
the women (83% of the households); and baseball games for men (71% of
the households).

4.   The radio was on for an average of 5.5 hours Monday through
Friday, 4.0 hours Saturday, and 3.5 hours Sunday.

Newspaper use

1.   The adult woman was the biggest reader of the newspaper--in
75% of households, she read the paper at least sometimes. In 51% of
households, men read at least sometimes; in 28%, children read sometimes.

2.   Generally, newspaper readers read only one section of the
newspaper (73% of the households); 5% said all of the newspaper was
read.

3.   Newspaper sections liked best were sales and display ads (32%
of households); styles and fashions (24%); general news (18%); classified
ads (12%); local news (10%).

TV use

1.   On weekdays, at any given time of the day at least 14% of the
households had their TVs on: 24% from 7-9 a.m.; 14% from 9-12 noon;
17% from 12 noon to 1 p.m.; 89% from 1-5 p.m.; 100% from 5-7 p.m.;
and 96% from 7 p.m. to midnight.

2.   Nighttime viewing was primarily a family affair--95% reported
that everyone watched from 7 p.m. to 12 midnight. The weekday day-
time hours were popular viewing times for females, although the early
morning hours were used primarily by children (66% of the households
reported children watching from 7-9 a.m.).

3.   Weekend viewing was also a family affair except for the Saturday morning hours when in 67% of the households the audience was mostly
children.

4.   When asked what they watched on TV weekdays, respondents
most frequently said "anything." The exceptions were from 1-5 p.m.
when soap operas were on in 88% of the households and from 5-7 p.m.
when 100% of the respondents said the local news was on and 72% indicated that national news also was on.

5.   74% of the respondents reported that in their households the
TV set was just turned on and channels were not switched systematically.

6.   The TV set was on an average of 8-9 hours weekdays, 8 hours
Saturday, and 6-1/2 hours Sunday.

Magazine use

1.   The magazine with the greatest number of subscribers was
Ebony (38%), followed by True Detective (19%), True Story (15%),
Modern Romance (12%), and Secret (10%).

2.   The magazine readers were primarily women according to 83%
of the reports. Only 12% reported men reading magazines and only 5%
reported teen-age readers.

3.   When asked what interested them most in the magazines, respondents most frequently said "personalities" (72%). No other response
was made by more than 10% of the respondents.

Media attitudes
1.   In terms of media preferred for information on a public issue;
52% of the respondents preferred TV; 20% radio; 24% neighbors; 3%
newspapers.
2.   In terms of media most used as a source of information; 75%
said TV; 16%, radio; 6%, other people; and 3%, newspapers.
3.   In terms of media considered most reliable and factual; 77%
said TV; 12%, radio; 6%, newspapers; and 5%, no preference.

Barban, Arnold M. "Negro and White Reactions to 'Integrated' Adver-
tising: Some Preliminary Findings." Paper presented to Division of
Advertising, Association for Education in Journalism, Boulder, Colorado,
August 27-31, 1967.

Purpose: To test Barban's hypothesis that the reason for the relative
lack of integrated advertisements is that advertisers cannot predict the
results such ads would have--in either the black or white markets.
This study deals with white and black evaluation of "integrated" versus
segregated ads.

Method: In the winter of 1966-67, Chicago residents were selected
randomly to compose a sample including nearly equal numbers from
both races possessing middle-class incomes. Middle income was defined differently for each race. For whites, median income in the
sampled census tracts was $6-$8,999. For blacks, median income was
$3,500-$5,999. Of the 364 families sampled, 121 white and 125 black
returns were usable. Only those Ss over 18 years of age were considered. Subjects were shown ten pictorial ads grouped as follows:
1.   All the ads pictured whites only. The first showed relatively
intimate drinking and conversation. The second was made up of panels
of individual photos, i.e., no physical contact among people in ad--they
were socially independent. The third was a scene with a young couple
smoking cigarets. The fourth showed a young couple drinking soda.
2.   The ads showed integrated scenes. The ads were identical to
the first two in Group 1 except that both blacks and whites appeared.
Thus, there was one integrated scene of social and physical intimacy
and one of social and physical separation. There were only two ads in
this group.
3.   Identical to the four ads in Group 1 except that the ads pictured
blacks only.
Each group of ads was presented to a different sample group. Each
sample group was composed of about 40 blacks and 40 whites. Subjects
rated each ad on semantic differential scales, including indicants of
Osgood's activity, potency, and evaluation (active-passive, pleasant-
unpleasant, masculine-feminine, beautiful-ugly, good-bad, heavy-
light, friendly-unfriendly, for me-not for me, strong-weak, fast-slow).

Results
1.   Factor analyses of the scales for the two races were similar.
For both races, two main factors resulted: the first, an evaluative

accounted for 43% of white variance and 44% of black variance; the second, primarily an activity factor, accounted for 25% of white variance
and 19% of black variance. The few differences in scale structure that
did appear showed blacks tending to respond to activity (fast-slow) and
potency (strong-weak) adjectives as they did to evaluative adjectives
(good-bad). For whites, on the other hand, activity and potency adjectives loaded either on the second factor or on a later factor. Both races
had a third and fourth factor but their structures were not easily interpreted and the author did not label them. On the basis of this analysis,
the author suggests that black-white comparisons probably should be
limited to the evaluative dimension and to those scales to which both
races responded similarly.

  2.   Black-white responses to the 10 advertising stimuli differed
somewhat. In general, all respondents were favorable, (i.e., their
mean responses were on the plus side of neutral) to all three types of
ads--those with black, integrated, and white models. However, for
all three types of ads, black responses were more intensely favorable.
When a comparison was made of the two ads that were tested with the
three different model types, results indicated that each race preferred
ads with integrated models or models of their own race. When ads with
only black or only white models were tested, this trend was supported
for white respondents, who preferred white models. Blacks, on the
other hand, showed no consistent pattern--they preferred the black or
the white model ads equally well.

Barban, Arnold M., and Grunbaum, Werner F. "A Factor Analytic
Study of Negro and White Responses to Advertising Stimuli." Journal
of Applied Psychology XLIX, 4 (1965), 274-279.

Purpose: To develop adequate techniques to measure group reactions
to advertising and mass media concepts, i.e., techniques with compar-
ability for different groups of respondents. In addition to the methodological focus, the authors compared Negro and white use of semantic
differential scales in judging concepts as well as differences in the
actual judgments made.

Method: Osgood's semantic differential technique was used as the
measuring instrument, although scales were not Osgood's originals.
Ss were 181 freshmen from English classes in two Texas universities--
93 white students and 88 black students. The Negro students attended
a Negro university. The study was conducted in the spring of 1963.
During administration 10 concepts were presented to the Ss, each to be
rated on 22 scales. The concepts were presented in slide form and included: (1) the word "advertising"; (2) a two-color cigaret ad with line
drawings of people; (3) a national magazine cover showing a Negro
singer; (4) a local Negro newspaper masthead; (5) a four-color cigaret
magazine ad with white models; (6) a four-color magazine ad with both
Negro and white models; (7) the call letters of a local radio station;
(8) a four-color magazine cigaret ad showing no people; (9) a national
Negro magazine cover; and (10) the same as (5) but with Negro models.

Results

1. Negro and white Ss uses of the 22 scales were highly similar.
A scale by scale factor analysis produced essentially two dimensions of
judgment for both samples. The first factor for both samples was an
evaluative type dimension with the following adjectival pairs showing
the highest loadings; ugly-beautiful, low class-high class, dull-sharp,
unfriendly-friendly, sad-happy, good-bad, for me-not for me, and
unpleasant-pleasant. Factor loadings for all these concepts were .60
or above, with loadings for Negroes versus whites highly similar. Variance accounted for on this factor was 74% for whites, 73% for Negroes.
The second factor, accounting for 8% of white variance and 9% of Negro
variance, produced the highest loading for the strong-weak adjectival
pair. No other adjectival pairs were loaded highest on this factor, but
pairs such as active-passive and heavy-light were second highest on
this factor. All adjectival pairs except strong-weak loaded highest on
factor 1.

2. Negro and white Ss actual judgments of the 10 concepts differed.
A concept by concept factor analysis produced essentially two factors.
For Negro Ss all 10 concepts loaded highest on factor 1--a general advertising, media factor. For white Ss, all but two concepts loaded highest on factor 1. The two concepts which loaded highest on factor 2 for
whites were Negro weekly newspaper and local Negro radio station. The
whites also showed higher loadings than Negroes on factor 2 for the
magazine cigaret ad showing both Negro and white models. Factor 2
seemed aligned with a "Negro" media dimension. Variances accounted
for were: on factor 1, 68% for whites, 81% for Negroes; on factor 2,
18% for whites, 8% for Negroes. These results suggest that although
Negroes do not differentiate Negro versus major society media in their
judgments, whites tend to do so. Interestingly, the presence of Negro
versus white models did not seem to be the important factor, for only
when a magazine ad was integrated did the whites tend to judge it with
the Negro media.

Barcus, F. Earle, and Levin, Jack. "Role Distance in Negro and
Majority Fiction." Journalism Quarterly XLIII, 4 (Winter, 1966)
709-714.

Purpose: (1) To formulate a scale by which the various characters in
a randomly selected group of short stories may be ranked in terms of
the degree of expected intimacy between them, i.e., their role distance
and (2) to use the resulting scale to determine whether role distance
between fictional characters is influenced by the ethnic groupings to
which these characters are assigned.

Method: A group of relevant short stories (containing both Negro and
non-Negro characters) was selected from majority-oriented and Negro-
oriented magazines published in 1964 and 1965. The majority magazines
were Saturday Evening Post, Ladies' Home Journal, Playboy, and True.
The Negro magazines were: Negro Digest, Bronze America, and Elegant.

All issues for each magazine published between April, 1964 and March, 1965 were included. The search produced 15 relevant stories in Negro magazines and 19 in majority magazines. A "character sheet" was coded for each identifiable character in the relevant short stories, list- ing such items as the character's sex, age, occupation, and nationality. This character analysis yielded 18 different role types, such as husband, fiance, uncle, teacher, employer, sheriff, and thief. A "relationship sheet" was made for all possible pairs of roles--153 in all. Then, each pair was assigned to a role distance scale. The scale had scores from 1 (close relationship, such as husband-wife) to 8 (distant relationship, such as thief-victim). Eight judges, all undergraduate students, assigned each of the possible pairs to these scales. A median score for their judgments on each relationship was computed. Then, these medians were applied to the actual character dyads found in the magazine fiction, and the character dyads were divided into different types of ethnic pairs.

Results
    1.   In general, intimate relationships between intra-group mem- bers were more prevalent than between inter-group members.
    2.   In both majority and Negro fiction, social relationships were determined by a generalized preference for intra-group relations.
    3.   Negroes in Negro-oriented stories were most likely to associ- ate with other Negroes.
    4.   In both majority and Negro fiction, Negroes had closer role relationships with non-Negro minorities than with the white majority.
    5.   When classified according to plot, only 3 of 19 majority fiction stories were interracial (i.e., racial differences were central to plot), in comparison with 11 of 15 Negro short stories.

Bell, Endell. "Anomie, Social Isolation, and the Class Structure." Sociometry XX (June, 1957), 105-116.

Purpose: (1) to gather new data for the hypothesis that economic status is an important determinant of anomie; (2) to isolate other variables relevant to anomie, particularly social isolation; and (3) to relate both unit and personal measures of economic status to anomie.

Method: The study included 701 interviews in four San Francisco cen- sus tracts selected according to their scores on the Sherky urban typology. The four areas include a low-rent rooming-house district (low in economic status and family organization), a low-rent single- home district (low in economic status and high in family organization), a high-rent apartment area (high in economic status and low in family organization), and a high-income single-family housing area (high in economic and family status). Sampling was done with probability sampling methods. Respondents were adult males over 21 years of age. The five-question Srole anomie scale was administered to each respondent. In this scale, increased alienation is indicated by (1) the conviction that community leaders are indifferent to the needs of people;

(2) the perception of chaos in the social order, producing the feeling
that one can do little to direct one's life; (3) the view that the respondent
and others like him are regressing from the goals they have reached;
(4) the feeling that internalized group norms, values, and goals are
losing meaning; and (5) the feeling that close personal relationships are
no longer predictable or supportive.

Results
    1.   Anomie is inversely related to economic status.
    2.   Anomie is positively related to the extent of the respondent's
social isolation. Isolated males particularly have higher anomie.
    3.   Respondents showed high variability in extent of "personal
demoralization." This variability was accounted for by differences in
the frequency of their formal and informal contacts, age, and position
in the social structure.
    4.   Respondents originally from rural areas had higher anomie
scores.

Bell, Robert R. "Lower Class Mothers' Aspirations for Their Children."
Social Forces XLIII, 4 (May, 1965), 493-500.

Purpose: To test the hypothesis that several status levels exist in the
Negro lower class and that these differences can be distinguished by
measurable characteristics. Since the mother is very often the center
of the lower-class family, her values and aspirations are important.
Thus, it would be useful if she could be placed in a status hierarchy
existing within the range of the Negro lower class, according to variations in her aspirations for her children.

Method: Interviews were conducted in 1963 with 202 Negro mothers,
each with two or more children, one of whom was in nursery school
or kindergarten. Respondents were selected from three Negro, lower-
class districts in Philadelphia. Negro females administered the 102-
item questionnaire. The focus of the questionnaire was the mothers'
views on marriage, their roles as mothers, child rearing, and their
expectations for their children.

Results: On the basis of the questionnaire, four levels of lower-class
Negroes were constructed:
    1.   Low-status mothers with low education, many children (no
more than 8 years of school, at least 7 children.)
    2.   Middle-status mothers with low education, few children (no
more than 8 years of school, no more than 6 children).
    3.   Middle-status mothers with high education, many children (9
or more years of school, at least 7 children).
    4.   High-status mothers with high education, few children (at least
9 years of school, no more than 6 children).

To maximize differences, only groups 1 and 4 were compared. Primary differences between the two groups with respect to aspirations for their children were as follows:

1. High-status mothers wanted education for their sons (65% versus 44%) and daughters (61% versus 39%) more than did low-status mothers.

2. Both high- and low-status mothers (47%)wanted professional jobs for their sons, and nearly the same percentage believed that a young man who worked hard could earn $10,000 a year (low-status=72%, high-status=74%). However, a far greater proportion of high-status mothers believed that hard work and ambition were necessary for success (low status=69%, high status=95%).

3. More higher-status Ss felt that their sons should not marry before their 24th birthday. A similar pattern was found where daughters were concerned.

4. Both low- and high-status mothers preferred that their sons and daughters have less than two children rather than four or more. This difference was greater for daughters and for low-status respondents.

5. When mothers were questioned on "American Dream" or abstract, aspiration values, there were few significant differences between low- and high-status mothers. The lack of differences is explained by low status Ss being more influenced by concrete realities (subsisting) than abstractions. This, it is suggested, points up Rodman's theory that lower-class people develop alternate values instead of just abandoning those of general society ("lower-class value stretch"). Thus, the lower class has a wider range of values and lower commitment to them--adjusting their values to a deprived condition.

6. Reservations on these findings are necessary because aspirations discussed were verbalized only; 30% of the sampled mothers couldn't be interviewed, underrepresenting working mothers; and the study considered the mothers' influence independently of others who also may be influential in determining the child's future, such as the father, school, and peers.

Berkman, David. "Advertising in Ebony and Life: Negro Aspirations vs. Reality." Journalism Quarterly XL, 1 (Winter, 1963), 53-64.

Purpose: To determine the distinctive characteristics of ads for blacks and explore whether the unique qualities of such ads are due mostly to the demands of the target groups or to assumptions by advertising agencies.

Method: Four issues of Ebony and Life were sampled for 1963--one issue for each quarter of the year. Since the page size, layout, typography, and content of the two publications are similar, the two magazines were well-suited for comparison. The four issues of Ebony contained 809 ads totaling 17,552 column inches. The four issues of Life contained 385 ads totaling 16,799 column inches.

Results: Below is a compilation of quantitative results from various
sections of the article.

	Number of different advertisers	
	EBONY	LIFE
Food, candies, soft drinks	26	33
Tobacco products	10	10
Alcoholic beverages	42	21
Patent medicines	57	22
Nonracial cosmetics	7	8
Motor vehicles	2	25
Furniture and home improvements	9	41
Appliances	14	26
Recreation	24	13
Travel and communication	13	7
Cleansing agents	2	6
Men's apparel	29	17
Women's apparel	15	11
Financial	8	12
Moneymaking opportunities	51	0
Negro cosmetics	50	0
Motor vehicle accessories	3	17
Miscellaneous	6	9

    The author based his quantitative analysis on the theory that the two
magazines would have both differences and similarities. He suggested
that the similarities would reflect middle-class America, to which the
black wants to gain entrance. The differences would reflect the lower
socio-economic status of the black. Within this context the author
emphasizes the following results:
    1.   The two magazines were very different in terms of ads for
motor vehicles and accessories. Ebony had 5 motor vehicle ads occupy-
ing less than 1% of total advertising column inches; Life had 40 ads in
17% of total advertising column inches. The author suggests that this
disparity contradicts the stereotype of the "Negro and his high-priced
car" and reflects the advertisers' belief that the Negroes' desire for
cars is not translated into sales. The author also noted that the few
car ads in Ebony were for lower-priced models, perhaps suggesting
that high-priced car advertisers do not want their prestige hurt by advertising in Negro magazines.
    2.   The number of ads for furniture, home improvements, and
appliances in the two magazines also seems to reflect the Negro's lower-
class status. Here, the author suggests, are classes of products requiring large expenditures that many Negroes cannot make.
    3.   The number of ads for alcoholic beverages reflects an opposite
trend, with 22% of Ebony's total advertising space devoted to this type
of ad (97 ads), compared to 5% of Life's advertising space (22 ads).

4.   The high proportion of patent medicine ads in Ebony is expected, the author says, because lower-class people work in more demanding jobs and generally suffer from more illnesses.

5.   The author suggests that the much larger number of ads dealing with moneymaking opportunities in Ebony is another reflection of the black's lower-class status.

6.   An analysis of the models used in Ebony's advertising revealed few dark models. Interestingly, children shown in Ebony's ads were likely to be darker. Of 34 ads showing children, 19 were dark, 10 were light, 5 in-between. Perhaps the advertiser feels that higher status accrues to a product displayed with lighter-complexioned adults; he also may sense that children's pictures must be realistically similar to the reader's own children.

Besner, Arthur. "Economic Deprivation and Family Patterns." Welfare in Review III, 9 (September, 1965), 20-28.

Purpose: The article summarizes research on the family patterns of the economically deprived. The effort is to isolate the particular differences of this group as compared with middle class family patterns. The summary is in the form of sociological narrative rather than citation of data.

Results
1.   Lower-class Ss are more influenced by residential proximity--"the girl next door"--in selection of a mate than are middle-class Ss. Courtships are short; there is also a relative absence of strong feelings about the marriage decision.

2.   Lower-class married couples retain kin ties and pre-marriage friendships rather than following the middle-class tendency to drop friends who are unacceptable to either spouse.

3.   Lower-class families are not generally close. Spouses are relatively isolated emotionally from one another.

4.   Husband and wife in lower-class homes have fewer overlapping responsibilities. Further, there is little joint social participation inside or outside the home; family members go their separate ways for diversion.

5.   Generally, in the lower-class family the male feels dominant and the wife downtrodden. This is because the husband places primary value on the physical satisfaction obtainable from his wife and the housework she performs. The wife suffers from a lack of openly expressed affection.

6.   The strongest relationships in the lower-class family may be between mother and child; children may compensate for the husband's inattention.

7.   The deficits of the lower-class family seem epitomized in the single-parent household that is characteristic of 25-40% of slum families. The middle-class marriage norms of economic support, love, and companionship are often absent since the lower-class mother

frequently has a succession of temporary companions during her fertile
years. Obviously, this situation is often detrimental to the social and
emotional development of children.

     8. Lower-class parents are more concerned with developing
"respectable" behavior in their children--obedience, neatness, discipline. Middle-class parents often take such behavior for granted, concentrating instead on developing the child's self-reliance and independence.

Blood, Robert O., Jr. "Social Class and Family Control of Television
Viewing." Merrill-Palmer Quarterly VII, 3 (July, 1961), 205-222.

Purpose: Recognizing that television may profoundly affect, perhaps
disturb, family activities and that parents frequently regulate their
children's viewings, the authors wanted to examine social-class differences in the norms held by parents, their means of transmitting and
enforcing norms and values, and their effectiveness in so doing.

Method: Some 102 interviews were held with white mothers with at least
two children from 2 to 18 years of age. The survey was held in 1957 in
two sections of Ann Arbor, Michigan, --one a working-class district and
the other, middle-class. Class distinctions were made on the basis of
the husband's job and education as follows: (1) lower-lower--unskilled
with only grade or some high school education; (2) upper-lower--skilled
job, high school completed; (3) lower-middle--supervisors or small
businessmen with high school or business school background; and (4)
upper-middle, professional people with a college education. The author
admits that the sample is not representative due to the unique class
make-up of Ann Arbor.

Results
     1. Level of viewing. Middle-class children, particularly those
in the upper-middle class, view fewer hours than those lower on the
scale.
     2. Control of viewing. Control was either amiss or missing in the
lower-lower class, which failed to see that TV could or did curtail other
activities of their children. Middle-class parents wanted their children
to engage in other activities, feeling that too much TV wasn't desirable;
these parents exercised control when they felt it consumed too much of
their children's time. Middle-class homes more frequently had a "bedtime" rule for the children, though the majority of mothers applied it
flexibly. Late viewing was allowed for special shows, particularly in
the upper-middle class. Lower-class homes used extended TV privilege
more as a reward.
     3. Resolution of viewing conflicts. Since there were five chan-
nels received in Ann Arbor, viewing conflicts were frequent. In lower-
class homes, the father would dictate the program choice of the hours,
while in middle-class homes, the wife or children usually won out. In
the middle-class home methods of resolving conflicts were more

democratic; in the lower-class situation the father's decision was final.
In the upper-class home more suggestions and objections were given
regarding program choices. In the lower-lower class, when no order
was forthcoming, no other controls were operative.

Boyenton, William H. "The Negro Turns to Advertising." Journalism
Quarterly XLII, 2 (Spring, 1965), 227-235.

Purpose: To quantitatively measure the number of Negroes appearing
in American newspaper and magazine advertising. Critical comments
and historical citations supplement the content analysis.

Method: Four major U.S. cities were selected for the newspaper study
because their combined population figures indicated they included 14%
of all U.S. Negroes. The papers studied were the New York Times,
Los Angeles Times, Chicago Tribune, and Philadelphia Inquirer. The
following magazines were also studied: New York Times Magazine,
Life, Atlantic, and Good Housekeeping. Issues of newspapers and
magazines were randomly selected for the time periods indicated below.
An ad was classified as Negro if it contained a "dark face." Negroes
who were obviously non-American were excluded.

Results: In general, the results indicated an extremely low level of
ads with Negro models, e.g., 9 ads in 43 issues of the New York Times,
2 in 5 issues of Chicago Tribune, and no other publication with higher
frequencies. The author noted that even the one publication that gave
considerable attention to Negroes in its editorial content, New York
Times Magazine gave almost none in its ads. Despite considerable
pressure prior to this study from Negro groups on advertisers, the
results indicate that Negroes have only token placement in ads. The
author suggests that integration is low and slow because: (1) social reform has not been part of advertising historically; (2) advertisers
prefer not to advertise in minority media because they want to influence
the general population; (3) more whites use the mass media than Negroes;
(4) Negroes are not in as favorable an economic position as whites; and
(5) no one actually knows how to appeal to the Negro consumer. The
authors added that some evidence suggests that the use of Negro models
may be detrimental in appealing to Negroes.

Broom, Leonard and Norval D. Glenn. "Negro-White Differences in
Reported Attitudes and Behavior." Sociology and Social Research L, 2
(January, 1966), 187-200.

Purpose: To discover Negro-white attitude differences and determine
whether these differences can be accounted for by region, age, and
education. Analysis was completed on available data.

Method: Data were gleaned from 32 basic types of questions asked on national public opinion surveys between 1950 and 1961 (obtained from Rober Public Opinion Research Center, Gallup, and National Opinion Research Center). Sample sizes averaged 1,437 for whites and 194 for non-whites. In addition to race, three other independent variables were considered: (1) education level--a year or more of college, at least one year of high school but no college, and no more than an eighth grade education; (2) regional difference--southern whites compared to non-southern whites (the Negroes were primarily southern); and (3) age--under 40 and over 40. Because Negroes are primarily southern in origin and of lower education, it was hypothesized that their responses would be similar to those of southern whites and low-educated whites. The dependent variable for all attitudes and behaviors was computed as an "index of dissimilarity." This index was the percentage of respondents in either race whose responses would have to be different in order for the percentage response distributions of the two races to be equal. The higher this score, the greater the difference between the groups being compared. Dependent variables included attitudes and behaviors on the following topics: religion, authoritarianism, morality, international affairs, domestic political-economic issues, child rearing and discipline, work, and religious and ethnic minorities.

Results
1.   The table below shows the dissimilarity indexes obtained.

Topic	Average Index of Dissimilarity		
	Negro versus White	Southern versus Non-Southern White	High- versus Low-Educated White
Religion	13.6	15.7	10.2
Authoritarianism	7.2	13.8	23.6
Personal morality	7.1	25.3	18.9
International Affairs	14.1	9.5	17.1
Domestic political-economic	19.6	5.6	11.1
Work	11.6	12.1	15.8
Religious and ethnic minorities	9.7	26.6	16.8

2.   In general, differences between blacks and whites were smaller than differences between southern and non-southern whites or between high- and low-educated whites. Controlling for age, Negro-white differences showed no distinct trend, indicating that they had not lessened among the young.
3.   The greatest black-white differences were found on attitudes toward domestic political-economic issues, international affairs, religion, and work. The smallest black-white differences were found on authoritarianism and personal morality.

4. An analysis of actual responses of Negroes in comparison with southern whites and low-educated whites indicated that these two control variables did not account for Negro-white differences on 14 items, but did on 18 items. For example, Negroes were more likely to believe in the devil, more likely to disapprove of pre-marital sex relations, more likely to say a person can't be Christian if he doesn't go to church, and more likely to believe that the world can't get out of the "mess" it's in. In comparison with college-educated and non-southern whites, southern whites and grade-school whites responded as did Negroes. However, Negro responses varied from responses of southern whites and low-educated whites for 14 items. For example, Negro attitudes toward a Catholic or Jewish president were more favorable as were responses of college and non-southern whites. A larger percentage of Negroes than any white category said they thought churches should express their views on day-to-day social and political questions. More highly-educated persons said that both good and bad nations should be allowed to join the United Nations; this response was also more characteristic of Negroes. Therefore, according to the authors, important black-white differences cannot be accounted for by education and residential differences.

Burma, John W. "An Analysis of the Present Negro Press." Social Forces XXVI (1947), 172-180.

Purpose: This 1947 article, based primarily on secondary sources, examines the communication role played by the Negro press. The author notes that the Negro press and the church are considered the two most important and influential agencies for social control and molding of public opinion within the black community.

Method: A poll of secondary sources on the subject was compiled as well as an analysis of examples of Negro journalism derived mainly from the Chicago Defender.

Results
1. Size of black papers. Although the number of black newspapers was decreasing, circulation and advertising inches were increasing. The author notes that in 1943 there were 155 Negro newspapers and that this number decreased 15% in two years. Effective circulation of these papers was considerably greater than actual circulation. One-third of urban Negro families subscribed to a Negro paper, but actual circulation was estimated at three to six million. Newspapers are likely to be passed from family to family and are commonly found in barbershops, shoeshine stands, lodge halls, and poolrooms. In addition, their contents often are passed by word of mouth.
2. History and growth. Growth of the black press parallels the rise of black protest and literacy. The several wars of the twentieth century increased the popularity of the black press because the black community wanted to know what was happening to black soldiers overseas.

3. Major functions. The Negro press is first an organ of protest
and militancy and, secondly, a purveyor of Negro news. It is a fighting
press and a safety valve in which certain stereotyped modes of compensatory behavior are regularly exhibited. It thrives on racial interpre-
tations of the news, creates black heroes, and stresses opportunity for
individual and racial advancement. A Chicago Defender poll showed
that the black press was influential in forming opinions within the Negro
community.

4. Important characteristics. The level of protest in black papers
is probably greater in terms of intensity than actual space. The black
paper is supplementary in that it does not attempt to compete with the
white press on such subjects as foreign affairs or finances. The papers
rely heavily on sensationalism (44% use sensational methods) to make
their points. Sensationalism would be a logical policy because of the
lower-class status of many readers. Editorial policy is mainly protest
about inequalities. For example, a study of editorials in the largest
Negro paper over a period of 12 years showed chief emphasis on social
conditions, politics, and economics. The society columns are imitations
of those in the white press, tending to exaggerate social affair. This,
of course, is indicative of the middle-class black's struggle for status.
Comics are not emphasized as they are in white papers. The three types
of comic characters that do appear -- humorous, propagandistic, and
some combination of both -- never poke fun of blacks. One striking
characteristic of the black press is the amount and character of its
advertising. The average white daily gets two-thirds of its income from
ads and one-third from circulation; these proportions are reversed for
the Negro press. Furthermore, only the largest black papers receive
national ads. Most ads are placed by Negro firms that minister to
"racial" needs.

5. Social control of the black press. Although the black press is
primarily an instrument of the black middle class, it is not free of control from the lower-class blacks who form the majority of its readership.

Caplan, Nathan S., and Paige, Jeffrey M. "A Study of Ghetto Rioters."
Scientific American CCXIX, 2 (August, 1968), 15-21.

Purpose: The authors hoped to test some traditional hypotheses on the
cause of riots by examining the 1967 riots in Newark and Detroit.

Method: The researchers interviewed rioters in both cities in an attempt
to determine their characteristics and attitudes. A probability sample
of blocks (weighted by number of dwelling units) was selected in each
city in census tracts where violence had taken place. Trained black interviewers were assigned to selected dwelling units. In Detroit interviewers enumerated every person in assigned units over 15 years of age
and interviewed every other person. In Newark Negro males 15 to 35
years old were listed and all were interviewed. Completion rate was
67% of eligible respondents in Detroit and 66% in Newark. Only 3%

refused interviews; the rest could not be located. In Detroit 11% of the total 437 respondents identified themselves as rioters. In Newark 45% of the 236 persons interviewed admitted rioting.

Results: Basically three traditional theories about riots were examined for their merit.

1. Riffraff theory. This theory holds that people riot because they are lower-class, emotionally disturbed, unassimilated migrants. This theory was not verified. Income differences between rioters and non-rioters were slight. Rioters' incomes were definitely not as low as the very poorest group of citizens. Furthermore, the rioters were not the least-educated individuals in their areas. They were not recent immigrants to the North but long-time residents. Finally, the rioters were not particularly deviant individuals, nor did they have more acute personality problems than non-rioters. They did not indicate any radically different societal values.

2. Relative deprivation theory. This theory blames riots on the supposed fact that blacks are far lower on the social-economic ladder than are whites. Rioters and non-rioters responded similarly when asked whether this social-economic gap was increasing: 36% of the rioters said it was increasing, as did 38% of the non-rioters. However, there was a significant difference when both groups were asked if the gap between better-off and poor Negroes was increasing: 39% of the rioters felt the gap was increasing, compared to 27% of the non-rioters.

3. Blocked-opportunity theory. This theory states that blacks riot because whites have constantly blocked their upward mobility. Generally, this hypothesis was verified: blacks were sensitive to discrimination and said that bias was imposed on them in jobs and education. In Newark 69% of the rioters and only 50% of the non-rioters, felt racial discrimination constituted the major obstacle to better employment. Furthermore, more than half of the rioters felt discriminated against in school, compared with less than a third of the non-rioters. Responses from both Newark and Detroit indicated that blacks had a strong sense of racial pride and were bitter over the inferior status accorded them by the white power structure. Rioters in both cities indicated a much higher level of racial pride than did non-rioters. They were also more likely to blame their status on discrimination than on lack of training. The rioters' anger was best expressed by their answers to the question "If the United States got into a big war today, would you personally feel this country is worth fighting for?" In Detroit 99% of the rioters, but only 15% of the non-rioters, felt the country was not worth fighting for. In Newark 53% of the rioters and only 28% of non-rioters felt the country was not worth fighting for. Finally, it was clear that the blacks interviewed were as resentful of higher-status blacks as they were of whites; rioters were significantly more antagonistic to affluent blacks.

Caplovitz, David. The Poor Pay More. New York: The Free Press, 1963.

Chapter 1--Introduction. This book reports a field survey of 464 low-income families in four public housing projects in Harlem. The

study was conducted by the Columbia University Bureau of Applied Social
Research. The four housing projects were not drawn randomly, but
were selected because they were near the three settlement house spon-
soring agencies. The purpose of the study was to describe the consumer
practices of the poor and to estimate the proportion and type of families
that have major consumer problems. Data are presented in cross-
tabulational form.

Families were drawn into the sample with a stratification technique
designed to make the sample representative of all families living in the
four housing projects. The sample had roughly 25% Negroes, 25%
whites, and 50% Puerto Ricans. Incomes ranged from under $2,000 to
more than $5,000. Less than half of the household heads were born in
the United States, and 21% were born in the South. About half of the
household heads had some high school education and 17% had at least
completed high school. Some 71% of the families included both parents
and children; 19% included only a mother and children.

Chapter 2--The Merchant and the Low Income Consumer. This
chapter sets the stage for the rest of the book by portraying the economic
community in which the poorer consumer lives and buys. It describes
in detail how merchants, selling high-cost but shoddy goods, are able
to operate in low-income areas. The basic function of the low-income
marketing system, Caplovitz says, is "to provide consumer goods to
people who fail to meet the requirements of the more legitimate, bureaucratic market, or who choose to exclude themselves from the larger
market because they do not feel comfortable in it . . . . The system is
extraordinarily flexible. Almost no one--however great a risk--is
turned away . . . . Even a family on welfare is permitted to maintain
its self-respect by consuming in much the same way as do its social
peers who happen not to be on welfare."

Chapter 2 also covers the following topics:

1. Compensatory consumption (the tendency of persons whose
status aspirations are cut short to shift their aspirations to the realm
of consumption).

2. Merchandising in the low-income area. The major point is
that the exploitative merchant continues to operate because he serves
a function.

3. Specific merchandising practices. From interviews with 14
merchants in the Harlem area, Caplovitz develops a lengthy description
of these practices. They include the absence of price tags on products; markups that range from 100% to whatever the traffic will bear;
use of personalized techniques such as first names or calling the
assistant manager to give the customer a "special deal."; use of the
community social network for sales purposes, (telling customers they'll
get a discount if 10 friends buy, passing peddlers from mother to
daughter); cooperation among merchants and "kickbacks" to merchants
who send low credit risks to merchants who will accept them; and finally, prevalence of low quality merchandise.

4. Eschewing the more formal techniques of collecting payments.
Repossession, garnishment, and turning contracts over to high-pressure
credit agencies are frowned upon because they alienate customers. More
often, personal ties are used.

5.   Unethical and illegal practices. In general, typical exploita-
tions include: selling old merchandise as new; using bait advertising to
lure customers; running fake contests; giving away free gifts and then
charging for them, and never actually stating the price before sending
payment book to the customer.

Chapter 3--Buying Patterns: Purchases of Major Durables.
Caplovitz answers the question "do low-income families buy major
durables?" with a resounding affirmative. Comparison with evidence
from a study of the general population in New York City shows that
these low-income families have a level of ownership comparable with
the higher-income general population. A far greater proportion of
these families than the general population own relatively new televisions
and washing machines. Moreover, these families tend to own the more
expensive models (such as console televisions and phonographs) and
75% planned a major purchase for the near future.

Chapter 4--Shopping Patterns I: Scope of Shopping. Scope of shopping was tapped by a number of items asking families where they prefer
to shop and where they have shopped. Findings show that 50% of the
sample was highly dependent on neighborhood sources. In comparison
with the general New York City population, these consumers are more
likely to use independent dealers and peddlers than department stores,
discount stores, and chain stores.

Chapter 5--Shopping Patterns II: The Peddler Economy. Caplovitz
distinguishes two kinds of peddlers (from the consumer's perspective)--
one offering traditional credit and the other offering bureaucratic credit.
The traditional peddler depends on personal contacts and does not use
installment contracts. The bureaucratic peddler is well-known for his
dotted line contract and high-pressure techniques.
   More than 50% of these consumers had bought from peddlers, although this data was not easy to obtain. Caplovitz notes that families
would deny they bought from door-to-door salesmen, but would report
that their clothes came from "Charlie," a trusted peddler.
   Caplovitz found that most families realized the peddler's prices
were higher, but they were generally satisfied with the products. Most
said the peddler was a "nicer person" to deal with than salesmen in
stores. Some 50% of the families had been dealing with the same peddler
for more than a year; 33% for more than two years. There was also
much unsystematic evidence that peddlers operated within social networks, passed from mother to daughter and friend to friend.

Chapter 6--Price Patterns: Costs of Major Durables. The prices
these consumers pay for appliances tend to be quite high--prices for
televisions, for example, ranged from $100 to more than $900 with 85%
paying more than $200, 40% more than $300, and 13% more than $400.

Chapter 7--Credit Patterns: Sources and Users of Credit. In the
survey, 59% said they thought credit was a bad idea, 26% said it de-
pended, and 15% said it was a good idea. A much higher proportion in
this sample (59%) thought credit was a bad idea than in a nation-wide

sample (33%). Despite their verbal answers to the attitudinal question, 66% of these families used credit.

Chapter 8--Family Finances: Debts and Assets. In this sample 35% of the families had no debts and 5% were more than $1,000 in debt. Caplovitz asserts that solvency would be a more meaningful measure of family financial stability than debts. To construct an index of insolvency, he obtained measures of family savings and insurance: 73% of his sample had no savings or less than $100 in savings; 13% had at least $100 in savings; and 13% had more than $100. However, 74% had some form of life insurance, including 25% who had 20-year endowment policies on their children.

Chapter 9--The Marginal Families: Consumption and Insolvency. Caplovitz presents an exhaustive analysis of marginal families (those with low solvency). The correlates of insolvency included: use of credit (families who consistently used credit were more likely to be insolvent); future buying aspirations (families who planned major durable purchases in the near future tended to be insolvent); age (younger families were more often insolvent); family size (larger families were often insolvent); income (lower income correlated with insolvency); and race (non-white families were more often insolvent).

Nonwhites are more active consumers and more likely to use credit, pay higher prices, buy from peddlers, and be insolvent. To explain these facts Caplovitz controls all variables that might account for the racial difference. He finds that age, family size, use of credit, shopping scope, income, and length of time in the city do not explain the racial difference.

He finds that when insolvency and race are controlled for occupational status, higher-status nonwhites are no more likely to be insolvent than higher-status whites. As status of nonwhites increases, insolvency decreases. For whites the relationship is reversed. No whites are insolvent at the lowest status level, but equal proportions of whites and nonwhites are insolvent at the middle- and higher-status levels.

Caplovitz finds that the marginal, more insolvent families are: more likely to expect trouble providing for their families; more likely to be considered "problem" families by housing project managers; less likely to be members of voluntary associations or other community organizations; and less likely to have voted in the most recent elections. Insolvent whites were likely to report knowing at least five neighbors. For Negroes the trend was similar. However, insolvent Puerto Rican families were more likely to be isolated.

Chapter 10--Consumer Problems I: Shady Sales Practices. In this chapter Caplovitz presents anecdotal material from the interviews, essentially case histories of exploitation. Some 40% of the families said they had been cheated, and 60% reported an actual incident. The families who had problems with merchants and payments were more likely to be nonwhite, and users of credit and peddlers.

Chapter 11--Consumer Problems II: Consequences of Missed Payments. This is another anecdotal chapter, with the emphasis on what happens to families who miss payments because of illness, job loss, or indignation when they realize they've been cheated. The major theme is that the poor are "too naive, too uninformed, too intimidated to know their rights or to exercise them when they do. As a result, the laws designed to protect them as well as the merchants often operate as an aid to the merchant's exploitation of them."

Chapter 12--Coping Patterns: Apathy, Ignorance, and Ineffectiveness. Several past studies have shown that working-class people take their problems to professionals less frequently than people in higher social strata. This study concurs; 50% of the families did nothing about their problems; 40% tried to deal (usually unsuccessfully) directly with merchants; 9% sought professional help but found little satisfaction.

The most usual response was apathy or a tendency to self-blame. The next most usual response was to try to get satisfaction from the merchant by stopping payments--such efforts often resulted in the families being charged court costs for suits. Those who did seek professional help usually could not be helped because they had lost the papers that would have proved their cases. In comparing knowledge of sources of help, Caplovitz again found that "traditionalism" was important. The newest migrants to the city--the Puerto Ricans--were not nearly as well-informed as Negroes and whites. Interestingly, Negroes were more informed than whites. Scope of shopping and formal education was another correlate of knowledge of aid sources included. The "learning from experience" notion was not strongly related to knowledge of sources. Those families that had had bad experiences were not more likely to know sources of aid.

Carey, James W. "Variations in Negro/White Television Preference." Journal of Broadcasting X, 3 (1966), 199-211.

Purpose: To verify the author's contention that television program preferences of Negroes and whites differ significantly. Author further argues that Negroes are more likely than whites to prefer some programs of higher quality (dramas) as well as programs that reflect Negro experience. Briefly stated, the author's hypotheses were: (1) there would be ethnic differences in TV program selection; (2) selection patterns would vary greatly in the case of individual programs and program categories; (3) these selection differences would be explainable in terms of historical ethnic factors.

Method: A nation-wide sample of more than 5,000 families (10% black) was surveyed during one week in October, 1963. Respondents were asked what programs they had watched "yesterday." The daily samples were each 1/7th of the total of 84 black and 641 white respondents. Program preferences of blacks were contrasted to those of whites by comparing the popularity rankings of some 80 programs compiled separately for each of the two racial groups. Rankings of program popularity were derived by converting the proportion of each sample group watching specific programs to ranks.

Results
       1.   Correlation between the two sets of ranks was .5 (rho), in-
dicating that agreement was far from perfect and that other factors
were at work. The author speculates that social and economic factors
may explain the differences. More likely, he reasons, differences are
due to discrepancies in background, personality, and life style. In
short, the black rejects white-oriented shows that typically emphasize
families, organizations, and other "foreign" life styles.
       2.   Blacks and whites seem to agree on what shows are liked
least and what constitutes a bad show.
       3.   Differences in preferential viewing times between the races
could have accounted for some differences. Blacks prefer weekends;
whites like early and midweek times.

Carter, Roy E., Jr. "Racial Identification Effects Upon the News
Story Writer." Journalism Quarterly XXXVI, 3 (Summer, 1959),
284-290.

Problem: To determine the effect of knowing the race of a crime suspect on how a reporter interprets and writes a story. Two hypotheses
were tested: (1) Negro suspects are likely to be judged less guilty than
white suspects by reporters or news writers; and (2) stereotyped content will be used more often in stories on Negro suspects.

Method: Students at two non-Southern and three Southern universities
(University of California, University of Wisconsin, University of Texas,
Florida State University, and University of North Carolina) were subjects, including 77 men and 65 women. Three weeks before the experiment, the students filled out a questionnaire whose purpose was to obtain
demographic data and to elicit their attitudes on race and the press.
Subsequently, the students were divided into two groups to write a news
story on a crime. One group was handed a "fact" sheet informing them
that the suspect was Negro. The other group was given identical information on the crime except that the suspect was not given as Negro.
Following this task, the students filled out questionnaires on problems
they encountered in writing the story and their perceptions of the news
event. Included in this questionnaire were items to ascertain views on
the guilt or innocence of the suspect, attitudes toward the descriptions
of the people used in the "fact" sheets, and opinions on the story's display value for a newspaper.

Results
       1.   The most significant finding was that the student journalists
perceived the Negro suspect as less guilty than the white suspect except
for the Texas subjects who treated both suspects equally.
       2.   Regionally, the Negro suspect faired better in the North than
in the South.
       3.   Little use was made of the 11 included stereotyped items in the
"fact" sheets, but on the whole Southerners used this material more
often.

4. Southerners writing the Negro suspect version of the story used more of the stereotyped items than Southerners writing the white suspect version. On the other hand, northerners used more of the stereotyped material with the white suspect. However, these findings only point to a trend and were not significant.

5. Both regions would have given the white suspect story better display in the newspaper. Northern students felt the story deserved more prominent display than Southern students irrespective of the suspect's race but this result also should be taken as inconclusive.

6. A content analysis showed no difference in fairness in writing about the event. No students convicted the suspect in the story or included potentially libelous statements.

Chilman, Catherine S. "Child Rearing and Family Relationship Patterns of the Very Poor." Welfare in Review III, 1 (January, 1965), 9-19.

Purpose: To summarize research on family patterns of the very poor (incomes of $3,000 and under) as contrasted with other low-income groups (i.e., the employed poor). The article also includes recommendations for future research and action programs.

Results
   Limitations of past research
   1. Past research has tended to use the term "culture of poverty." The author prefers the term "subculture of poverty" because research indicates that the poor subscribe at least partially to much middle-class culture, adapting it to their own disadvantaged situation.
   2. Past research has tended to ignore different subgroups of the poor, combining such groups as the unemployed poor, employed poor, and welfare poor, into one group. Past research has also ignored the differential behaviors of children and adults of different sexes.
   3. Past research has tended to lack methodological precision, paying too little attention to the nature of the sample, reliability of interview and observation techniques, use of standardized tests, and differences between people within poverty subgroups.
   4. Generalizations from research are cast in "middle-class" perspective because these are the "standard" behaviors against which other behaviors are measured. The author sees this as a limitation, but notes that middle-class standards determine advancement and success in our society.

   Summary of findings on child rearing and family relationship patterns. In reporting findings, the author compares behaviors of the very poor to "ideal" behaviors (i.e. behaviors which past research have found to be conducive to child growth and marital adjustment).
   1. Child rearing practices. The very poor tend to give their children limited freedom for exploration and little guided experience-- fewer years of parental control and abrupt rather than gradual termination of control. They tend to use harsh and inconsistent discipline

(physical or verbal) that is based on whether behavior annoys the parents. The poor also tend to judge misbehavior of children by pragmatic outcomes, using "staying out of trouble" as the criterion and ignoring reasons for misbehavior. In general, poor parents tend to be authoritatian. They engage in little discussion with their children.

2. Marital relationships. The very poor have high divorce and separation rates and are frequently one-parent families in which the male is seldom or never at home. Courtships for the very poor are short, and marriage often occurs because of pregnancy. Teen-age marriages are common. Verbal communication is low, and little affection is shown. The masculine and feminine worlds are quite separate even to maintenance of separate friends. The marriage relationship is generally exploitative, with regard to sex in particular. Moreover, attitudes toward sex are punitive and repressive.

3. General attitudes. The poor are fatalistic and apathetic. They have little belief in the long-range future, and tend not to defer gratifications. They are not interested in objective evidence and engage in magical and rigid thinking. They fear and distrust the unknown, and tend to rely on personal characteristics rather than expertise as a measure of success. They are nonintrospective and unaware of the subleties of interpersonal relationships. Their attitudes toward aggression are inconsistent, alternating between encouragement and restriction. They seem to have low self-esteem and demonstrate little skill in the middle-class norms of dress, manners, speech, and games.

4. Demographic characteristics. The very poor tend to have large families and high mobility. They frequently reside in multiple dwellings. Characteristically they have less than a high school education.

Chilman, Catherine S. Growing Up Poor. U.S. Dept. of Health, Education and Welfare, Welfare Administration Publication No. 13. Washington, D.C.: Government Printing Office, May, 1966.

Purpose: The emphasis is on family-life patterns and child-rearing practices of the urban poor to show how the child is enveloped by the poverty cycle. Much attention is given to contrasting the conditions of the slum child with analogous conditions that lead to optimum child development. Suggestions are made for future research.

Results
Emotional health. The fatherless home seems to be one of the main causes of emotional problems.

1. Child rearing. Child-raising patterns of the very poor are most likely to militate against good emotional adjustment. But "good adjustment" is a strongly middle-class standard and could well be maladaptive in the poverty milieu. Thus, environmental modification must be synchronous with changes in child-rearing patterns.

2. Anxiety. Generally, poor people's methods of coping with overwhelming anxiety such as that wrought by hopeless conditions in maladaptive, i.e., expulsive, violent, or expressive. Middle-class anxiety

is more optimistic, that is, it creates a competitive striving for goals
perceived as attainable.

    3.   Mental illness. Life experiences and poor physical health
make for more mental illness.

    Education. The life patterns of the very poor do not promote edu-
cation. Boys especially are affected by the detrimental environment,
largely created by their parents in the most immediate sense. Much
research indicates that the early years (0-6) are particularly crucial
for intellectual and emotional growth and that change will have to begin
in infancy if the cycle of poverty is to be broken. Other evidence indicates that there is more extreme intellectual variability in the very
young than at age 18; this variability seems accentuated in the very low
class. Thus, generalizing about intellectual development from middle-
class data is very hazardous when applied to the lower class. Enriched
educational experience for the very young is one method of breaking the
cycle. However, enrichment programs for adults are also indicated,
partly so that enrichment of the young is reinforced at home. Finally,
due to extreme inter-subject variability, a variety of strategies based
on individual diagnosis is needed. Group solutions based on middle-
class data are not the way to improve education among the poor.

    Social acceptance and conscience formation. The slum child has
little opportunity to learn social skills that are common in the middle
class. Lack of rewarding social contacts contributes to the depressed
life style. Low inter-personal trust is normative. However, whether
this depression exists in poverty backgrounds outside crowded urban
areas has yet to be demonstrated. Some advantages do accrue to this
life style, including casualness in relationships, quick humor and ex-
pressiveness, occasional compassion, and the capacity to enjoy plea-
sures of the moment. Unfortunately, whatever the advantages, lower-
class socialization runs counter to that of community services such as
health, welfare, and police. The hypothesis for poor conscience formation among the very poor is basically one of low self-esteem that inhibits
ego strength necessary for moral character. Again, poor conscience
is a middle-class judgment and the very poor may have a different moral
code rather than no code at all. The implication of this section is that
the poor must take on middle-class standards in order to advance.

    Family life styles. This chapter focuses on the maladaptive marriage
adjustment of the poor. Komarovsky found that compared to a skilled
labor group, the very poor males were less likely to value conversation
and companionship in marriage and more likely to view the woman's
world as entirely separate. More lower-class couples rated their relationships as unhappy. They found less emotional release in recreation
and social interaction; instead they employed violence and quarreling
alternated with repression and withdrawal. The higher employment
among black females often antagonizes black males who feel their masculinity threatened. A St. Louis study found that marital quarrels increased with unemployment and tapered off when the male was employed.
Family planning among the very poor was found to be inadequate, adding
the burden of many children to an already strained marriage.

Intervention strategies. Planned changes in cultural patterns are difficult to effect and some of the poor, particularly whites, might be highly resistant to change. It is necessary to fight the dysfunctional effects of anxiety--rigid, fatalistic, anti-intellectual behavior and chronic psychic depression--without imposing a new set of middle-class values and goals. Primary concern is given to enrichment of the very young in order to break the poverty cycle. Methods range from day care centers for the very young to vastly improved conditions in the slum school. It is also necessary to provide basic adult education. Supportive, non-frustrating instruction in small groups may be adequate to make up for earlier deficiencies. Family intervention approaches range from guidance in impulse control for parents to various community and family planning centers. Therapeutic services also might be established in low-income housing. Finally, adequate income support (relief) is recommended, with bonuses for desired behaviors such as improved child care.

Research implications
1. Methodological refinements. The author suggests that more care be taken in sampling to assure an adequate size; more reliability and validity be attained with instruments; better care be taken in analyzing results; and better attention be paid to questions asked, in particular the inclusion of questions that seek to discover the strengths as well as the weaknesses of the very poor. Attention to the variation within groups is also necessary, since variance of the poor may be greater than for the middle class along the same dimensions. More longitudinal research is also needed with more explicit definitions of the behavior under study. More multidimensional studies are needed, tapping learning styles, coping capacity, and vulnerability to stress. Biological factors (unspecified) also may be of importance.
2. Cognitive development questions. We need to find out to what extent the early years are crucial, whether there are "critical stages" of learning, and how best to enlarge learning potential after adulthood has been reached.
3. Family and "life style" research. Questions raised include the following: what family and life style variables of the very poor who stay married exist in contrast to those who don't. What is the extent of variation of key characteristics within the very poor subgroup, that is, what sort of individual differences are most critical at this level which may be distinct from those of more advantaged people? Finally, studies of the very poor child should not be isolated from studies of the very poor adult; families should be studied as units.
4. Experimental action research. Such research is needed to determine if various treatments and other remedial programs have their intended effects. Ideally, such effects should have specific behavioral outcomes that can be evaluated as objectively as possible.

Clark, Kenneth B. Dark Ghetto: Dilemmas of Social Power. New York:
Harper, 1967.

Purpose: To interpret data--official demographic statistics, statements
from interviews, and impressions of the author resulting from his two
years' work with Haryou (Harlem Youth Organization). Rather than
treating ghetto life in a detached manner, the author approaches the
reader on a personal level. Data used were obtained from existing
sources such as the city education department. Interviews were collected
principally by the Haryou Organization. In describing the plight of the
black ghetto by examining conditions in Harlem, the book stimulates
questions more than answers them.

Results
     Economic and social decay. Clark acknowledges that the economic
situation is poor. Most workers leave Harlem to work outside, leaving
the profits of their labor to other parts of the city. Businesses in the
ghetto are disproportionately service industries geared toward satiation
of personal needs. Banks, large stores and apartments -- mostly are
owned by outside, frequently absentee interests. Housing, of course,
is sub-standard by comparison in absolute and relative terms to the
balance of the city. According to projections, semiskilled as well as
unskilled jobs will become increasingly less over time. Since many
persons in the ghetto are unskilled and training efforts seek to make them
semiskilled, the occupational employment outlook is bleak. Despite
their touted liberalism, unions effectively bar blacks. Family life is
also depressing. Often the household is a matriarchy, on ADC, and
without the father present. Clark advances Haryou as a reasonable
effort to interdict the destructive cycle of ghetto existence, particularly
by sensitizing its participants to the values in organizing to achieve
social change. Upwardly mobile blacks, although they sometimes deny
their origins, often force whites to reconsider their stereotypes. These
blacks often force integration in formerly segregated suburbs.

     The psychology of the ghetto. Ghetto life is debasing. Fantasy is
a prime protective device for the black child who feels a sense of inferiority and shame because of his blackness. Teen-agers assume a
pretense of sophistication in illicit activities or sexual prowess. Whites,
including some social workers, may promote the status quo by attempting
to help clients adjust to their pathogenic environment. Stringently applied
middle-class values perpetuate rather than ameliorate problems. Clark
argues for abandoning "statistics" and "objectivity" as sole criteria for
ghetto study, explaining that this approach creates distortion rather than
"feeling."

     The pathology of the ghetto. According to Clark, the destructive
qualities of the ghetto are self-perpetuating. Emotional illness is high--
Harlem shows the highest mental ward admission rate in New York City.
Yet these figures fail to account for the many unreported and undiagnosed
problems. Nor do they take into consideration the tendency of agencies
to accept only patients who seem "reachable." Facilities for care of such
people are limited. Drug addiction, homicide, delinquency, and emotional

illness feed upon each other, furthering the physical and psychic erosion of ghetto residents. Haryou's prevention and rehabilitation program begins with children and teen-agers, organizing them into Cadet Corps and Academies that are somewhat militaristic with insignia and slogans to contribute to constructive ego development. However, adequate recreational facilities and part-time organizations cannot do the rehabilitation job alone. Many service organizations in the ghetto are controlled by policies formed elsewhere; according to the author, such policy control should be altered. Clark suggests that halfway houses be established to ease the transition of former prisoners and juvenile offenders back into the social system on an improved basis, hopefully by involving them constructively in the eradication of community problems. Narcotics control that offers easy access to medical and psychological rehabilitation is also necessary, says Clark. And finally, fundamental social change is needed. As a start, juvenile delinquency and narcotics must be controlled. Crime control will come by changing environmental and social conditions that induce violence rather than by concentrating on the reform of a given individual. There is much need for scientific study in this area. But, says Clark, lack of data is no excuse for continued social oppression.

Schools. When given better instruction, ghetto children usually respond quite well. However, ghetto schools are usually the dumping grounds for mediocre teachers and administrators who see their jobs in the ghetto as providing custodial control rather than education. In short, says Clark, the ghetto school needs money, talent, and innovation. Otherwise, ghetto children will continue to fall below the achievement levels of the balance of the city and there will be a consequent persistence of pathological conditions in the ghetto.

Ghetto power structure. Clark sees the black politician as a second-class citizen in the power hierarchy who have little or no success in getting control of large funds or bureaucracies. Jones and Powell are two exceptions to this rule, both having established a considerable political base.

The press. In order to be successful, the black newspaper must reflect the atmosphere of the ghetto as well as its aspirations and protest. Flamboyant headlines and make-up and articles on scandal and crime seem necessary to attract readership, but they also reinforce the white stereotype view of the black. Exaggeration of Negro successes and the nature of some products advertised help feed the fantasies of the ghetto resident. Militancy often makes rational assessment of civil rights strategies impossible, thereby promoting absolutism. The white power structure grows immune to Negro press sensationalism and repeated flamboyance dulls the urgency of response; thus, the paper dissipates its power. Middle-class Negroes judge the black press largely by the same criteria applied to the best of the white press; they therefore tend to reject it. Some of the white press, especially the New York Times, is making an effort to include blacks in news stories other than those about sex and violence. Every New York metropolitan daily has Negro reporters who are used in viable positions rather than as

show-pieces for liberal intentions. The author commends the efforts
of middle-class Negro publications such as Ebony, Jet, and Tan.
Although these publications also feed black fantasies, they encourage
blacks to achieve. Because of their comparatively restrained nature,
these publications may attain far greater power than their flamboyant
relatives, the newspapers.

Churches and social services. Those run by Negroes have little
real power and serve largely as temporary emotional palliatives. There
are a few exceptions: such leaders as Ralph Abernathy, Adam Clayton
Powell, and the late Dr. Martin Luther King, Jr., have been able to
couple religion to social action programs. Unfortunately, individuals
who are successful in directing their energies to larger problems and
are considered able contenders in the larger arena suffer a decline in
influence and usefulness within the ghetto. Such people may be regarded
as deserters for failing to meet a prime demand of the ghetto--restricted
vision. The basic rule is to present a single voice of protest and rebellion to the white world. A second rule is that no issue can take precedence over the question of racial oppression. Clark reports that
violating these rules tends to destroy an individual's effectiveness and
influence. Thus, the power of the black may depend upon a critical
mass who are somehow able to control the ambivalence they feel toward
themselves and consequently develop respect for those blacks who are
worthy of confidence. According to the author, the real tragedy is that
blacks have not taken themselves seriously because no one else has.

Change. Numerous strategies for breaking the destructive cycle
of the ghetto are listed. A caveat is posted for those who fall prey to
status quo forces that permit the power of those wanting social change
to be dissipated in the sham appearance of social action. Strategies
range from prayer (hope for divine intervention) to direct encounter
(such as sit-ins) to dramatize the injustices of the system.
Finally, the author sees hope in the emotional interdependence of
the black and the white. The black needs to be freed of his fear, and
the white, freed of his guilt. What is necessary is the destruction of
the black's fantasy acceptance of the status quo and extreme militancy.
The author sees both as fantasies that protect the black from the painful
necessity of relating to the white. On the other hand, the white liberal
needs to control his often visceral racism and ambivalence toward the
black. The author concludes that the eradication of each fantasy is
a necessary, however painful, process.

Cloward, Richard A., and Jones, J. A. "Social Class: Educational
Attitudes and Participation." In Education in Depressed Areas, edited
by A. H. Passow. New York: Teachers College Press, Columbia
University, 1963, pp. 190-216.

Purpose: (1) To determine the attitudes of low socio-economic families
toward the educational system and the amount of participation the parents

in these families have in the system; and (2) to help formulate a strategy for dealing with the problem of underachievement in the schools by students from low socio-economic families.

Method: A survey was made of residents living in the lower east side slums of Manhattan. Each interviewee was asked a series of questions concerning education, job, family income, attitudes toward the schools and education, and contact with the school via (PTA) or visits. The author constructed an "involvement index" ranging from those having no contact at all with the schools to past or present officers of the PTA.

The sample consisted of 1,250 households selected randomly from the slum area. In each household one person at least 20 years of age was chosen randomly to be interviewed; the total number of interviews was 988.

Results: Of the sample, 44% were categorized as lower class, 36% as working class, and 20% as lower-middle class. The lower-class person was employed as an unskilled or service worker, had less than an eighth grade education, and lived in a family whose income per person was less than the minimum wage. The lower-middle-class person was a professional or semi-professional, had some college education, and lived in a family whose income per person was above the national median. The working-class person fell between these two extremes.

Using the 260 families with children in the public schools, the following levels of involvement were found: 4% had been past or present officers of the PTA; 7% had attended most or all of the meetings; 15% belonged to the PTA but had attended few meetings; 45% were not in the PTA but visited the school; and 29% had no contact with the school.

1.   Education was found to be valued differently by the different social classes. The higher a respondent's social and economic level, the more he valued education. However, most respondents from all social classes believed one needs a good education to get ahead. Lower-class respondents did not value education for "education's sake" but as a means to a job. Education was also seen as part of the "good life" more by working-class people than by middle- or lower-class people.

2.   There was a popular belief that the school system and the community were not in agreement. Interestingly, middle-class respondents were more adverse to the school than lower-class respondents.

3.   The more years of schooling a respondent had, the more likely he was to disagree with the statement that teachers were really interested in their students.

4.   Respondents with children in school had different attitudes than those who did not have children in school.

5.   Parents who were more involved with the school, i.e., visited the school or were active in the PTA, valued education more than less involved parents.

6.   Parents who were more exposed to the school were less favorable to the school system than parents who were less exposed.

Cohen, Albert K., and Hodge, Harold M., Jr. "Characteristics of
the Lower Blue-Collar Class." Journal of Social Problems X, 4
(Spring, 1963), 103-134.

Purpose: After determining in a descriptive manner some characteristics of the blue-collar class, the authors hoped to interpret these
characteristics as working-class adaptation to conditions.

Method: The sample was composed of some 2,600 male heads of households residing in the San Francisco Bay region. Subjects completed at
least one of nine different schedules largely composed of forced-choice
items. Subjects were white, Mexican, and black and were thought to
comprise a representative blue-collar sample. Characteristics showing
a difference of $p < .05$ from other social strata were considered lower-
class.

Results: The results were interpreted ex post facto to represent
adaptation of the blue-collar class to its life conditions. The major
conclusions are listed below.
    1.   Simplification of the experience world.   The blue-collar person
is exposed to a narrow range of experience and is not subject to high
expectations. Workday rules are less complex than for other classes
and the individual is happy that he doesn't need to assume "public
service" roles.
    2.   Powerlessness.   The blue-collar person feels rather useless
and insecure, particularly since he is usually unskilled and expendable
at work. Since his bargaining power is weak, there is little he can do
if he is dissatisfied with his job.
    3.   Deprivation.   He is continually forced to curtail his aspirations,
lest they exceed his limited capacity to attain them.
    4.   Insecurity.   His ability to deal with unexpected expenses is
slight and persistent unemployment threats make for economic and
emotional instability. If unemployed, it is often difficult for the blue-
collar person to move knowledgeably and skillfully through the welfare
bureaucracy.

Discussion: A prime mode of adaptation to these conditions is to build
social networks that function largely as mutual insurance schemes.
Tight family relationships and strong ties to neighbors and relatives
provide emotional and economic support if needed. In short, the blue-
collar person must devise methods of reducing insecurity and enhancing
power that are not dependent upon achievement. The knowledge that
help is close and the self-esteem gained by helping others out of tight
situations satisfy these needs. Unfortunately, since spouses in the blue-
collar class characteristically do not relinquish mutually unacceptable
friendships made prior to marriage, an element of instability is often
present in the family.
    Other forms of ego protection are also evident. Participation in
voluntary organizations is lowest at this level, a characteristic indicative of the blue-collar unwillingness to go outside his tight circle of
extended family and neighbors. New people and situations are feared.
Anti-intellectualism is prevalent--college professors and writers are

among those least admired by the blue-collar class. Moreover, least
liked activities include fine arts--concerts and ballet as well as some
TV programs that are considered "too high-brow." Deviants, "un-
Americans," and athiests are rarely tolerated. Frequently, an attitude
of truculent toughness and extra-punitiveness is manifested in an attempt
to salvage a sense of worthwhile identity in a world where lives are
largely determined by external, often unknown, constraints and decisions.

Columbia Broadcasting System. White and Negro Attitudes Towards
Race Related Issues and Activities. Princeton, N.J.: Public Opinion
Research Corp., July 9, 1968.

Purpose: This survey was made in a year of racial crisis in order to
secure fresh information on how the black views himself, his needs,
his race, the white community, black violence, and the nation. A
similar questionnaire was administered to whites.

Method: A national probability sample composed of 587 whites and 478
blacks was selected and interviewed between May 22 and June 16, 1968.
To minimize bias, white interviewers interviewed white respondents
and blacks interviewed black respondents.

Results
      The Negro in the community. Nearly 45% of the blacks felt that
they had not made progress because of discrimination; 49% of the whites
thought that the Negroes hadn't worked hard enough. Most blacks (78%)
thought they were not making enough progress toward their goals. Only
28% of the whites agreed. Similarly, a majority of blacks (60%) thought
that their local government favored whites over blacks. Only 12% of
the whites agreed and 56% of the whites thought that their local government was fair to both races. Both whites and blacks singled out local
government and white religious leaders as those most interested in
helping the black.

      White racism. Some 43% of whites believed blacks were not as
civilized as themselves; 10% of the blacks agreed and 81% disagreed.
Whites also showed a greater tendency than blacks to attribute unfavorable statements to the other race. However, many of both races attributed unfavorable statements equally to whites and blacks. Common
white criticisms of blacks centered on high crime rates, depreciation
of neighborhoods, laziness, poor care of children, and detrimental
effects on the school system. Using the same list of statements, blacks
seemed more critical of themselves than of whites or attributed the
unfavorable statements equally to both races. They criticized whites
significantly more than themselves only on high crime rate. Using
questions that have face validity as racism indicators, some 34% of
whites interviewed displayed low racism; only 5% showed the highest
level. Regarding the President's report on racial disorders (which
blamed white racism for much of the Negro's plight), 74% of blacks

agreed and 9% disagreed; only 31% of whites agreed and 55% disagreed.
Some 42% of blacks laid the blame for racial strife mostly upon whites;
31% of the whites blamed the blacks. About half of each group said
both races were equally at fault. Blacks tended to think that whites
were not sympathetic to black problems and did not want equality. As
expected, whites saw themselves as somewhat more sympathetic and
desirous of equality though only 31% of whites thought that their race
really wanted equality. To a question advocating a separate country
for blacks as a solution to the race problem, a majority of whites
(56%) and blacks (84%) answered that it was not a good idea. However,
33% of whites and 5% of blacks approved.

Negroes and the media. Some 64% of whites felt that blacks were
given too much attention in the media; only 10% of blacks agreed. Some
46% of blacks thought that they were not given enough exposure; only
8% of the whites agreed. About a fourth of each group thought attention
given to blacks was adequate (28% of blacks, 21% of whites). About
half of the whites thought the media presented the Negro cause accurately
and fairly; only 29% of the blacks agreed. Some 52% of blacks thought
their case was not fairly or accurately considered; 34% of whites agreed.

Attitudes toward protest and violence. Both blacks and whites
agreed that potentially violent demonstrations were not good forms of
protest and favored peaceful meetings instead. However, racial disagreement occurred in terms of intermediate level protests. Whites
tended to disapprove of peaceful demonstrations, store boycotts, and
picketing businesses; blacks tended to approve of such methods. When
whites were asked to put themselves in the place of a Negro who saw
rioting as a way to get help for his problems and indicate whether under
these conditions they would join a riot, 76% said that they wouldn't, and
only 15% said they would. Whites believed riots were caused primarily
by youth looking for excitement (44%); overcrowding in black areas
(40%); a Negro rebellion against poor treatment (39%); or a nation-wide
Communist plot (35%). Blacks discounted the Communist plot theory
and to a lesser extent the youth-looking-for-excitement explanation;
they laid primary blame for riots on: a rebellion against bad treatment
(56%); overcrowding (45%); and desire for equality (31%). Blacks and
whites tended to agree that police arrest of looters, burners, and riot
instigators would be the best means of riot control. Few in either race
approved of a hands off-policy during riots (14% of blacks, 8% of whites).
Blacks tended to favor police methods short of using guns (79%), as, to
a lesser extent, did whites (54%). A majority of both races disapproved
of shooting several rioters as examples; 35% of the whites and 7% of the
blacks approved of such action. Whites believed the police should be
tougher in handling riots (70%) and that treatment of blacks by police
has been either soft (27%) or fair (58%). Blacks disagreed; 45% of blacks
felt police should be softer; 20% felt they were just right; and 59% felt
they were brutal.

Negro wants and needs. Generally, blacks were significantly more
dissatisfied than whites in four key areas: education, income, jobs, and
neighborhoods. Of the four areas, blacks were most satisfied with their

neighborhood (70%) and least satisfied with the quality of education
(42% satisfied). Predictably, blacks were more in favor of various
agencies and facilities to improve Negro living than were whites. There
was a decrease in white as well as black approval of relatively radical
proposals such as new communities especially built for Negroes (17%
blacks in favor, 21% whites in favor) and black control of black communities (22% blacks in favor, 26% whites in favor). Issues such as
provision of black housing in all white neighborhoods, busing of school-
children, and stronger enforcement of anti-discrimination laws, differentiated the two samples markedly. Issues such as improved schools
for Negroes, more efforts by blacks to help themselves, and more
attention by local government to Negro problems met with fairly high
approval by both races.

Some effects of age, education, and place of residence (whites
only). Predictably, southern whites with less than a high school education took a harder line toward blacks. They were more likely to be
in favor of a separate black nation and harsher control of blacks by
police. Age had less effect than residence and education, but those
more than 30 years of age tended to have a harsher attitude toward
blacks.

Darrow, Charlotte, and Lowinger, Paul. "The Detroit Uprising: A
Psychosocial Study." Paper presented at the Academy of Psychoanalysis
meeting in New York City, December, 1967.

Purpose: To study the committed young Negroes who were most active
in the Detroit riot of 1967. Their actions, attitudes, and thoughts concerning the riot and other racial issues were sought.

Method: Twelve interviewers were picked from the Negro community.
These included men and women between the ages of 20 and 30 who were
active in the disturbance and in a black power organization, staff members of a new activist Negro newspaper, and militant black students.
These interviewers were asked to interview their Negro male friends
and acquaintances between the ages of 15 and 30. A 47-item open-ended
questionnaire was used, covering actions, opinions, and thoughts about
a number of issues. The interviewer was supposed to record the entire
answer to each question. From August 1-20, 1967, 222 interviews
were completed. The sample consisted mainly of unmarried, urban,
Negro men. A good number of students and intellectuals between the
ages of 15 and 30 were included. For analysis, the sample was divided
into 76 participants and 146 nonparticipants.

Results
    1. The participants (Ps) included a few less married men, high
school and college graduates, and active churchgoers. They had a little
more unemployment than the nonparticipants (NPs). The occupational
level of the Ps was clearly inferior to that of the NPs.

2.   21% of the Ps and 35% of the NPs were married, divorced, or separated.

3.   52% of Ps and 64% of NPs were high school graduates, including 8% and 13% college graduates respectively.

4.   21% of the Ps and 33% of NPs were active Catholics or Protestants.

5.   51% of the Ps and 37% of the NPs were unemployed or laid off in the week before the disturbance.

6.   57 Ps and 99 NPs listed an occupation other than student.

7.   71% of the Ps and 30% of the NPs had positive feelings about the riot; 10% of the Ps and 39% of the NPs were negative.

8.   The teen-age Ps and those in their early twenties felt good about the uprising (73% and 80% respectively) twice as often as the Ps over 25 years (44%).

9.   Choosing between Rap Brown and Martin Luther King, 92% of Ps but only 42% of NPs favored Brown; 8% of Ps and 58% of NPs favored King. The Ps under 26 preferred Brown to King twice as often as those 26 and over.

10.   93% of Ps and 68% of NPs felt negative and critical about the behavior of the police; 4% of Ps and 22% of NPs approved police behavior.

11.   53% of the Ps and 40% of NPs felt the Vietnam war affected the uprising. Among the Ps, those 20-25 years old felt this twice as often as younger and older respondents.

12.   When asked whom the riot was against, half of the 84 replies said "whites" as did 35% of the 156 answers given by the NPs. The Ps between 15-25 were twice as likely to say "whites" as the 26-30 year-old NPs.

13.   71% of the Ps and 48% of the NPs felt the crowd made a distinction between white- and black-owned stores.

14.   92% of Ps and 85% of NPs felt another riot would occur.

DeFleur, M. L. "Occupational Roles as Portrayed on Television."
Public Opinion Quarterly XXXVII, 1 (Spring, 1964), 57-64.

Purpose: To analyze the portrayal of occupations on TV during the prime television viewing hours of children.

Method: An analysis was made of TV content for a six-month period in a mid-western community with four TV channels, during the hours most heavily viewed by children (3:30 - 11 p.m. on weekdays and 10 a.m.- 11 p.m. on weekends). Then 250 half-hour time segments were selected randomly from a universe defined as programs that depicted people interacting in a modern setting. Excluded were cartoons, commercials, news, westerns, historical shows, and other shows not portraying occupations. An occupational portrayal was defined as the appearance of a person on the screen for at least three minutes performing some kind of recognizable occupational duty. The data obtained for each portrayal was grouped by type of occupation; background settings; characteristics and traits of workers portrayed; and power analysis. Occupational type

was coded into categories suggested by census breakdowns. Background
settings were classified according to spaciousness, degree of decoration
and repair, modernity, adequacy of furnishings, and level of luxury implied. Results were then grouped into three types: glamorous, ordinary,
and humble. Characteristics and traits coded were speech patterns,
neatness of dress, intelligence, physical beauty, friendliness, eccentri-
city, and morality. Power was measured by coding orders given and
taken; permissions asked and granted; and titles of respect used. A
power index was computed by subtracting submissive acts from dominant
acts and dividing this figure by the total number of acts. As an adjunct
to the power analysis, a survey was conducted of 237 children in the
community from 6-13 years old. Children were asked to name the job
they believed most desirable among jobs that are respected, pay highly,
supervise other people, assist other people, and include travel to interesting places. A paired comparison technique was used.

Results
     Characteristics of the labor force
     1. Of the 436 portrayals analyzed, nearly one-third of the jobs
were associated with the enforcement or administration of the law.
     2. The distribution of occupations on TV varied greatly from the
actual distribution in the labor force; upper-status occupations were
greatly overrepresented and lower-prestige occupations were greatly
underrepresented.
     3. Female workers especially were overrepresented in TV jobs
in comparison to the proportion of female workers in the actual population.

     Characteristics of setting. Personal servants, lawyers, butlers,
theatrical agents, and bartenders were shown in glamorous settings;
judges, clergymen, and educators were shown in ordinary or humble
settings.

     Characteristics of workers portrayed
     1. In general, the higher the prestige, the more favorable the
portrayal. For example, physicians, educators, and executives were
not only well dressed, socially skilled, and intelligent, but also hand-
some.
     2. Stereotyped portrayals were common. Lawyers were clever;
artists were temperamental and eccentric; police were hardened and
brutal; private investigators were resourceful and more capable than
the police; and nurses were cold and impersonal.
     3. Character portrayals tended toward the atypical. For example,
a physician was seen as more exciting if implicated in an abortion.

     Power analysis of characters. The analysis of TV characters indi-
cated that the ranking was not unduly biased in terms of power. The
most powerful characters were those whose occupations required more
education or involved some form of management. Foremen, ranch
owners, and judges were ranked as the top three; personal servants,
bank tellers and clerks, and enlisted military personnel were ranked
as the bottom three. The field survey, however, indicated that

regardless of background, most children found jobs with power most desirable. Power jobs were followed by those involving money, prestige, travel, and aiding others, respectively. The author points out that the jobs portrayed on TV as most powerful (a characteristic desired in jobs by most children) are the jobs that young people as well as most employed people are least likely to have.

Disaster Research Center. "The Los Angeles Riot Study." Unscheduled Events I, 3 (Fall, 1967). Department of Sociology, Division of Research, College of Commerce and Administration, Ohio State University, 4-5.

Purpose: To summarize the results revealed in the 1965 Watts riot study executed by The Institute of Government and Public Affairs at the University of California at Los Angeles and administered by Nathan Cohen. This study surveyed 2,070 rioters, nonparticipant blacks, and members of the Los Angeles white community regarding their attitudes toward the community, established government, the riot, race relations, and each other.

Results
    The riot
    1.   About 15% of the Negro adult population (22,000) were active during the riot, that is, they went beyond being mere spectators. However, some 35-40% of the Negro adult population were spectators.
    2.   Demographically, young people were much more active than the old, and men more than women; both the educated and relatively uneducated took part; and long-time residents as well as new arrivals from the South participated.
    3.   About 34% of the Watts sample were in favor of the riot. Though a majority disapproved, the disapprovers often had empathy with the motives of those who participated. About 38% thought the riot would help the cause of civil rights; 20% thought it would do damage; 23% of the Watts sample thought the riot would augment the gap between the races, in contrast to 71% in the white community.
    4.   Most Watts respondents believed police malpractice occurred regularly in their community: a third of Watts males interviewed and 15% of Watts females claimed they were subject to malpractice; 50% of Watts males and 30% of Watts females reported witnessing such incidents.

In summation, although the black community generally was ambivalent toward the riot, a majority saw it as useful in bringing attention to their problems as a means toward eventual help.

    Division in Watts
    The riot revealed a growing polarization of three groups in the black community--the "traditionalists," "militants," and "survivalists." The traditionalists view individual success as a way to escape from such problems as poverty and bias. The poorest of the three, the survivalists, are less interested in status than in economic survival. And

between these two lie the militants who seek various new solutions.
They believe that the black can solve his problems only by collective
action. The core members of this group are educated and from educated families. These are also less religious and do not identify themselves with the lower class. They want to build ethnicity or a sense of
racial pride.

Watts respondents were asked if they approved of militant groups.
Those who did were classed as militants (30%); those who did not as
"conservatives" (35%); and the balance as uninvolved (35%). Factors
such as birthplace, sex, education, length of residence in Los Angeles,
political affiliation, and declared social class did not distinguish the
three groups. However, more of the militants (70%) and the conservatives (63%) were employed than were the uninvolved (55%).

Attitudinal differences

1. Militants were significantly less favorable than the conservatives
toward the news media unfair in their presentation of the black and his
problems. The uninvolved fell midway between the militants and the
conservatives in their evaluation of the mass media.

2. The militants also took a less favorable view of the political
institutions than did the conservatives. The uninvolved again fell in-
between.

3. Political figures were viewed in a similar fashion by the three
groups.

4. Civil rights groups were favored strongly by all factions; the
uninvolved were less favorably disposed than the others.

The militant ideology. The militant is an activist, more willing than
the conservative to engage in demonstrations. He tends to be politically
active and sophisticated. In the survey, the militant was more likely
to charge the police with brutality. He said he believed merchants
victimize the ghetto resident, and charged greater discrimination in
schools and jobs. Further, he tended to give more support to the riot,
and was more likely to believe that rioting produces positive results.
He was also more likely to forecast riots in the future.

The militants, no longer impressed with the upward mobility philosophy of the traditionalists--which they see largely as Uncle Tomism--
are in competition with the traditionalists for leadership of the survivalists. To obtain the support of the survivalists, the militants feel they
must develop a program of economic and political power, i.e., black
power. The militant's drive against both status and economic frustration
is more appealing to the survivalist because the traditionalist's offer of
status-frustration reduction alone does not fill empty stomachs nor promise to do so in any direct way. Therefore, the traditionalists, the
only group in which the whites and the political bureaucracy have any
confidence, seem to be in a questionable position in the black community.

The traditionalist seems dependent on the ability of the government
to deliver economic relief in far greater amounts than are presently
forthcoming. The militant hopes to keep before the survivalist the image
of the white as his enemy as a means of creating unity and generating
a power base. Slow integration into the social stream is not their goal;
they hope to quickly deliver political and economic power to the black.

The militant strategy is to induce fear in whites. The black refuses to have the benefits doled out to him by a white-dominated, colonialistic bureaucracy. The militant seems intent on fighting the white ambivalence that is manifested by encouraging black progress while simultaneously erecting barriers when it becomes operational.

Donohew, Lewis, and Singh, B. K. "Poverty 'Types' and Their Sources of Information About New Practices." Paper presented at the International Communication Division, Association for Education in Journalism, Boulder, Colorado, August 27-31, 1967.

Purpose: (1) To determine what typologies of individual life styles could be formed in a poverty community (in Appalachia) and whether such typologies were consistent across communities; and (2) to compare information sources of these various types concerning innovative practices introduced into their communities.

Method: The authors employed Cattell's Q-factor analysis to identify clusters of individuals who ranked similarly on 41 study items, including exposure to various media, basic demography, aspiration level, political knowledge, dogmatism, condition of living unit, level of dissatisfaction, degree of empathy, and feelings of powerlessness and social isolation. Basic variables tapped fell into three groups: (1) communication--contact with potential change stimuli; (2) S's receptivity to change--level of exposure to modernizing forces; and (3) sources of information. In addition, the researchers had to determine what constituted a poverty type. Basically, those respondents with life-style patterns falling far below national norms were designated as poverty types. Two sample areas, one with 84 respondents, and the other with 73, were chosen since both were impoverished and had active, long-standing community action programs. Interviewers were local school-teachers trained by the authors. Households were sampled randomly from each community. Questionnaires were administered in two waves, the first in 1965 followed by a second in the summer of 1966 in order to determine the level of adoption of selected practices.

Results: Three clusters of Ss were discovered from analysis in the two communities.
    1. Outgoing. Individuals with high scores on variables indicative of direct physical contact with the outside world, e.g. trips to the big city and acceptance of Head Start and other community action programs. These individuals were more likely to participate in organizations such as churches, visit others, possess automobiles, be educated, and have empathy. Females predominated in this type.
    2. Isolated. These Ss were most isolated from the forces of modernity. They were less exposed to the media, organizations, and other people. They tended to be less dogmatic as well as low in empathy, educational aspirations for their children and income. They were younger, more geographically isolated, and tended to live in delapidated

houses. However, they were found to be the most proficient adopters of Office of Economic Opportunity (OEO) community action program innovations.

    3.   <u>Mass media users</u>. These Ss were most exposed to the mass media, viewing news and public affairs programs more often. They possessed higher aspirations, income, and employment. They were older and seemed more dogmatic. They also tended to have a greater sense of powerlessness and feel socially isolated. (Actual differences in powerlessness and isolation from the other two groups were slight, however.) One would expect these Ss to be the highest adopters. However, this was not the case.

    The basic finding of communication consequence is that the data do not support the proposition that mass media exposure is related to the rate of innovation adoption. Adoption was most characteristic of the "isolated" individual rather than those more in touch with media and neighbors. The isolated individual also tended to be the least dogmatic. Those exposed to the mass media were the poorest adopters and empathizers, making them perhaps the poorest prospects for change.

    Ss were relatively similar in type of sources approached or used for information about new practices, despite the apparent differences noted above. For all three types, friends and neighbors were most frequently mentioned as sources, followed by more expert sources such as change agents, OEO staff, and radio. Print media rarely were mentioned as a source. TV also was used little as a source of information on OEO programs.

Donohew, Lewis and Singh, B. K. "Modernization of Life Styles. An Appraisal of the 'War on Poverty' in a Rural Setting of Southeastern Kentucky." Lexington, Ken., University of Kentucky, August, 1968.

<u>Purpose</u>: To analyze changes which took place in individuals with different levels of exposure to programs of the Office of Economic Opportunity (OEO) and Community Action Programs (CAP) in a region in rural Appalachia. Prior to their exposure to OEO, the respondents ranged from traditional to modern. For the authors, this traditional-modern continuum has essentially three bases: (1) the number of potentially modernizing instruments available to respondents, e.g., automobiles, TV; (2) the extent of receptiveness to change as indicated by social-psychological orientations, e.g., empathy, alienation, political efficacy; and (3) the extent of exposure to stimuli for change, e.g., mass media, schools, the outside world.

    The authors seek to answer three main questions: (1) what changes took place in the life styles of people?; (2) were there differences in the extent of modernization of persons in OEO communities versus non-OEO communities?; and (3) what kinds of persons adopt what kinds of ideas and practices supported by OEO after exposure to what sources of information?

Method: In consultation with OEO-CAP representatives in Knox County, Kentucky, six neighborhoods were selected. In two neighborhoods, community centers had been established before the study began. In two others, centers were to be established after the pre-measure data was gathered. And in the last two neighborhoods, centers were not available during either the pre- or post-measures. A census was conducted in each neighborhood and a random sample of households was made. At each house in the sample, a male interviewer interviewed the head of the household and a female interviewer interviewed the homemaker. In the spring and summer of 1966, benchmark data were gathered from 504 heads of households and homemakers. In the spring of 1968 409 of these same people were available for post-measures. Data was gathered on 58 aspects of the life styles of the respondents. These aspects were grouped into five major areas:

1. Communication behaviors. Data were gathered on exposure to print and broadcast media and to news and public affairs content within these media. At the interpersonal level, respondents were asked the number of persons with whom they visited and the frequency of their visits. They also were asked to identify their sources of information for each practice under measurement. Source credibility was measured in five dimensions--personal usage, utility, use by friends or family members, trustworthiness, and knowledge.

2. Social-psychological orientation. Data were gathered on perceptions of such items as self-worth, effectiveness in society, empathy, aspirations, political knowledge, and attitudinal and behavioral modernity.

3. Participation and contact. Variables indexed included the number of organizational memberships, degree of church participation and frequency of visits to the community center, trips to town, and visits to a big city.

4. Diffusion-acceptance of new ideas. Knowledge and use of the following were measured: community centers, early childhood programs, model homes, work-study, landscaping and home beautification, neighborhood youth corps, birth control, adult education, and Head Start.

5. Demography. Variables included age, education, level of employment, family income, source of income, sex of respondent, size of family, condition of dwelling, yard appearance, access to a highway, availability of a car, and distance from a community center.

Correlational analysis and factor analysis of the R-type were used to examine the relationships among variables. The extent of differences within neighborhoods between pre- and post-measures were tested with t-tests. Q-type factor analysis was used to locate clusters of people having the same styles of life.

Results
1. Where the CAP program had been operating long enough to demonstrate its effectiveness, the modernization process had been set in motion. There was a greater shift to more modern configurations in OEO-CAP communities, and a shift in the opposite direction in non-OEO-CAP communities. Although there were extensive differences between pre- and post-measures, no discernable pattern of change emerged.

2.   Factor analysis yielded three types of individuals in each neighborhood--least modern, semimodern, and most modern.

3.   The adoption of practices tended to appear as a characteristic of the more isolated individual rather than the person more in touch with stimuli presumed to be working in the service of modernity.

4.   For all types of individuals little change had occurred between pre- and post-measures on variables tapping demographic characteristics, especially income and mobility.

5.   For all three types there were considerable changes and some unexpected regression from modernity.

6.   The most frequent type of change appeared to be in the social-psychological area, indicating the development of a psychic mobility or readiness to change and become a more active participant in society. These changes occurred for all three types of individuals in community center areas more than they did for individuals in non-community center areas.

7.   All three types of individuals in community center areas showed an increase in exposure to mass media, television in particular, and to news and public affairs programs.

8.   The least modern typology of individuals (those with the fewest modern instruments and less receptive to change and exposure to change stimuli) were the best adopters of new practices; the most modern typology persons were the poorest adopters.

9.   The life styles of the least modern persons changed toward modernity faster in areas with community centers than in areas without. In non-OEO-CAP areas, changes toward modernity among the least modern appear to be related to OEO-CAP activities (primarily through innovations introduced by OEO-CAP that have spread to these communities).

10.   Personal sources were the favored sources of information in almost all the communities. There was more use of personal and media sources in the non-center areas than in the center areas. The areas that had had centers longest showed more diversified sources of information and more use of institutionalized sources as well. The results also indicate that a high level of acceptance of ideas is likely to generate more use of sources of information.

Epstein, Lenore A.   "Some Effects of Low Income on Children and Their Families." Social Security Bulletin XXIV, 2 (February, 1961), 12-17.

Purpose: To show the effects of low income on a child's future and on family harmony. Possible applications of this information in child welfare programs is discussed.

Method: Low-income families were defined as four-member households with incomes of less than $2,500. The article is based on compilations of existing data, including census and social security information.

Results: Some one-fifth of the nation's families are in the designated
low-income bracket, including 16 million of the nation's children under
18 years of age. These families are primarily: nonwhite; supported
by a household head working only part-time; broken by separation or
divorce; and extended families in which relatives beyond the nuclear
family live in the household.

Analysis of existing data reveals the following:

1. Families with higher incomes visit doctors and dentists four
times as often as families with incomes below the poverty level.

2. Families with incomes below the taxable limit have barely
enough money for an adequate diet and are often undernourished.

3. Poverty families also live in overcrowded housing and run-
down neighborhoods were both privacy and adequate play space are
often nonexistent.

4. The major reason for dropping out of college is lack of money.
When college students with average intelligence are considered, the
completion rate for children with family incomes of $2-3,000 is only
3%. The college completion rate is 12% at incomes of $3-5,000; 25%
at incomes of $5-7,000; 28% at $7-9,000; 55% at $9-11,000; and 65%
at $11-13,000.

5. Mothers of preschool children were in the labor force three
times as often when the husband earned $3,000 as when he earned
$10,000. One out of 12 children under 12 years of age in such families
is left to care for himself. Often, when the father loses his job the
teen-ager in the family must work.

6. Divorce rates are related to education and poverty levels. For
example, divorce rates are lowest for women with one to four years
of college and highest for women with only one to three years of high
school.

7. Single-parent families are much more likely to have relatives
outside the nuclear family living with them. In 1959, 25% of all one-
parent families lived with relatives compared to 2% of two-parent
families.

Fannin, Leon F., and Clinard, Marshall B. "Differences in the Con-
ception of Self as a Male Among Lower and Middle Class Delinquents,"
Social Problems XIII, 2 (1965), 205-214.

Purpose: To determine the differences in self conceptions between
lower- and middle-class delinquent boys and relate these differences
to actual delinquent behavior.

Method: Informal depth interviews were conducted. Forced-choice
scales were also administered. Ss were a random sample of 16- and
17-year-old lower-and lower-middle-class white, urban delinquents
in a midwestern state training school.

Results
1. Self-conceptions were found to be quite similar across class
lines.

2.   Lower-class boys conceived of themselves as tougher, more fearless, powerful, fierce, and dangerous. Middle-class boys felt they were more clever, smart, smooth, bad, and loyal.

3.   Differences in self-conceptions were found to relate significantly to specific types of behavior. "Tough" guys more often committed violent offenses, carried weapons, and stressed toughness in desired reputations and in sexual behavior.

Feldman, Laurence P., and Star, Alvin D. "Racial Factors in Shopping Behavior." In A New Measure of Responsibility for Marketing, edited by Keith Cox and Ben Enis. Conference Proceedings, Series No. 27. Philadelphia: American Marketing Association, June 17-19, 1968, pp. 216-226.

Purpose: To determine whether there is a separate Negro market or whether differences in Negro/white shopping behavior are manifestations of economic or social level.

Method: The authors used data collected by the Chicago Tribune. Some 1,000 Chicago residents (with and without phones) were randomly sampled, including 240 nonwhites (predominantly Negro) and 760 whites. Suburbanites were excluded. Data was available on income, race, nonstore and store shopping, and price influences.

Results
   Non-store shopping
1.   30% of the whites had shopped by mail order or phone within the preceding 12 months compared to 13% of the nonwhites. Whites also did more catalog buying than nonwhites.

2.   Despite these racial differences, however, controls for income produced no differences between the races. Higher income meant increased buying by mail order, phone, and catalog.

   Store shopping
1.   35% of the nonwhites had credit at department stores compared with 44% of the whites. This difference disappeared with controls for income.

2.   Both lower- and higher-income groups went outside their own neighborhoods to shop, but this tendency was greater for high-income groups. Differences between races on this variable were small.

3.   More whites than nonwhites had shopped at several different shopping centers in the 12 months preceding the study. But again income was a major factor. Higher income meant more shopping areas visited. However, there was some evidence of a racial difference on this variable.

4.   Whites shopped more frequently than nonwhites. Income controls depressed this relationship, but did not eliminate it.

5.   About 50% of both races shopped at discount stores 1-9 times a year; 30% shopped there 10-29 times.

6.   More whites than nonwhites visited downtown State Street stores. Again, income tended to depress this relationship. However, there was a difference as to what income level had to be attained before respondents began shopping on State Street. For whites, such shopping began at incomes above $3,000; for Negroes, at incomes above $5,000.

Price influences
1.   Whites with incomes under $3,000 were concerned primarily with price. Whites at the $5,000 level were concerned with value. Nonwhites at all income levels were concerned primarily with price. However, the greater nonwhite concern for price was significant only for respondents with incomes of $3-4,999 and $7-9,999.
2.   More nonwhites used discount stores more often than department stores. This difference persisted despite controls for income. However, results were significant only with the lowest-income groups. As income rose, differences decreased.

Fogelson, R. M., and Hill, R. B. Who Riots? A Study of Participation in the 1967 Riots. Mimeographed. Bureau of Applied Social Research, Columbia University, July, 1968.

Purpose: To test the "riffraff" theory of riot participation. According to this theory: (1) only an infinitesimal fraction of the black population actively participated in the riots; (2) the rioters were the riffraff and outside agitators; and (3) an overwhelming majority of the Negro population unequivocally opposed and deplored the riots.

Method: Survey research interviews were undertaken on samples of Negroes from riot areas. Standard survey research techniques were applied. The official reports on the riot arrestees prepared by the California Department of Justice (4,000 sheets on the Los Angeles riots of 1965) and the Governor of New Jersey's Select Commission on Civil Disorder (1,500 sheets on the Newark riots of 1967) were analyzed. In addition, the arrest data from the National Commission on Civil Disorders was used extensively. The authors computed a riot ratio: the number of potential rioters among the residents of the riot areas (Detroit, Newark, and Los Angeles) defined as Negro residents between the ages of 10 and 59 inclusive, divided by the number of arrestees for age intervals. This ratio was applied to other cities to determine how many Negros in a community might have joined in the riots.
The sample included 600 Negros from South Central Los Angeles, interviewed by David O. Sears of Institute of Governmental and Public Affairs at UCLA; 393 Negroes 15 years and older from the Detroit ghetto; and 233 Negro males between the ages of 15 and 35 from the Newark ghetto. Both the Detroit and Newark samples were interviewed by Nathan Caplan and Jeffry Paige of the University of Michigan's Survey Research Center. In addition, a Harris poll from 1966 that interviewed Negroes across the nation and government census data were employed.

Results
   1. <u>Extent of participation</u>. On the average, about 18% of the riot
area residents took part in the disorders. About 80% were not appre-
hended.
   2. <u>Composition of the rioters</u>. The sex ratio of arrestees was
nine males to one female, but survey research indicates female participation was higher. More than 60% of the arrestees were 18 years
or older; eyewitness accounts indicate juveniles and young adults (15
to 34 years old) constituted the great majority of the arrestees.
Arrestees were more likely to be single, northern-born, residents of
the area, and hold unskilled jobs. The overwhelming majority of rioters
were employed and the criminal element was not found to be overrepresented.
   3. <u>Arsonists and looters</u>. Such individuals were more likely to
be older, southern-born, and employed. The younger and native-born
were more likely to take part on the first day of rioting.
   4. <u>The sentiment of the community.</u> Although the overwhelming
majority deplored the violence in the riots, a majority felt that the
riots would help in improving the Negro's social and economic position.

Frazier, Franklin E. <u>Black Bourgeoisie</u>. New York: Collier, 1965.
(Original ed. in French, 1955.)

Purpose: A sociological study of the Negro middle class, the book
includes data gleaned largely from existing sources, e.g., census
material. The analysis deals with two characteristics of the group:
(1) its actual economic conditions and social status; and (2) its standards
of behavior and values. Little data are used to support the author's
contentions, which are the product of interviews, reviews of publications,
and personal insight. Given their questionable initial validity, the
author's conclusions may be seriously dated in light of the black power
movement, increased militancy, and a probable rise in racial pride.

Results
   First taking a historical approach, the author traces the differentiation of the black middle class and describes its current economic
position. Much attention is given to the status of Negro business and
the influence of segregated schools on aspirations and social and political outlook. This first section ends with the author's hypothesis that
the separation of the middle-class Negro from his traditional folk background has left him rootless, without a place in the black or the white
world.
   The second part of the book is devoted to the social behavior of the
black middle class as it exists in isolation from black and white communities. Much attention is paid to the myths and presumed inferiority
complex of the group. The balance of this abstract will be devoted to
examining the points of these two sections that might be particularly
relevant to communication.

Power and political orientation. Traditionally, organizational focuses for blacks have been churches, fraternal organizations, and Greek letter societies. The power of these groups is not inconsequential. They seem to reinforce a relatively conservative, business-oriented outlook. The author roughly equates the Negro intelligentsia with Uncle Tomism since those Negroes serve at schools run by whites or conservative blacks or at the pleasure of northern philanthropic groups. Traditionally, this intelligentsia has had to espouse optimistic views of integration or run the risk of being blacklisted or disfavored as leftist. Emerging political leaders are seen as portents of the middle-class outlook. Black politicians with underworld connections are noted as most effective since by largely unexplained means they are best able to organize the blacks and wring concessions from the whites. The author seems to assert that the black politico is ultimately dependent in some way on the white power structure, largely for funds and influence.

Break with traditional background. Here the author advances his principal thesis that the black bourgeoisie is caught in a cultural gap between the white and soul (black) worlds. He notes a change in the attitudes of the black bourgeoisie, largely in the form of a break away from the straight-laced mores of older upper-class blacks. Genteel virtues have been displaced by a premium on mobility and money. In support of this contention Frazier points out the reputed great effect of black entertainers on blacks as opposed to the presumably lesser effect of white entertainers on the white community. Black bourgeoisie religious efforts seem motivated more by concern with public relations than with salvation. In summary, many blacks who once compensated for feelings of inferiority by citing their white heritage (values secured by association with whites), education, and puritanical sex and family mores were forced to resort to other means when urbanization and increasing occupational differentiation blunted the effects of these means. Because of increasing white hostility, the new black middle class has sought solace in consumer items. The balance of the report is devoted to a description of the present make-believe world of the black middle class.

The world of make-believe. Studies in 1930 and 1943 sought to uncover why the Negro has failed to be involved in or carry out successful business ventures. Neither study revealed much because they overlooked the fundamental sociological fact that over the years the black has lacked the business tradition that others have built up through generations of buying and selling. Many stories circulate about the successes of Negro businesses but these seem to be largely exaggerations by the Negro press.

The Negro press and wish fulfillment. The Negro newspaper came into being as an organ of black protest, growing in importance because the white press ignored what was news to the black community. One of the aims of the Negro press was to provide the world with a proper picture of the Negro. But the Negro press gives much attention to the achievements of the race and the author feels these claims have been exaggerated to compensate for feelings of inferiority in the black middle class. Further, the press exaggerates or makes trivia newsworthy

merely because black participants are involved. This form of news
provides gratification for an insecure, opportunistic black middle class.
The press lacks a consciousness of the broader issues facing the modern world and serves instead as superficial gratification for the black
bourgeoisie. Further, foreign news in these publications is tantamount
to fantasy in its concern over princes and African potentates.

"Society"--status without substance. Initially, light complexion
was the key to attaining the Negro social elite. This criterion was re-
placed by occupation and income and their educational implications.
The present prerequisite for attaining status is conspicuous consumption
(Cadillacs and minks). Debutante balls and other social fetes are other
prominent manifestations of social climbing. Wide participation in
gambling, partially as a consequence of bankrupt philosophy and religious life, is another.

Conclusion. Despite the attempts of bourgeoisie parents to protect
their children from the hatred of whites, sufficient hatred is felt to
create feelings of inferiority. Inferiority brings about insecurity--fear
of white competition for jobs, fear of potentially higher white "standards," and fear of losing status in the Negro hierarchy. Frustrations
abound because of female dominance over men; females can find work
more easily and rule the family. These problems bring on guilt and
self-hatred which is manifested in the black bourgeoisie's scornful view
of lower-status blacks and other minorities. Thus, there is little cooperation among middle-class blacks, only fierce competition. The pan-
acea for these problems is escape into delusions of wealth and success
or excessive drinking, gambling, and sex. The bourgeoisie's mask of
a free and easy life hides its true frustrations and unhappiness.

Freeman, H. E., and Lambert, Camille, Jr. "The Influence of Community Groups on Health Matters." Human Organization XXIV, 4
(Winter, 1965), 353-357.

Purpose: To examine the differential influence of various volunteer
associations on individual opinion formation about health matters.

Method: Trained social workers using a pre-coded questionnaire conducted household interviews with the mothers. The questionnaire listed
12 organizations. Respondents were asked if they were members of
the groups. They were also asked to name two groups on the list from
which they would be most likely to accept advice and two from which
they would be least likely. The sample consisted of 289 lower-income
families with at least one child between the ages of five and eight years.
These families had been living in a census tract in Brookline, Massachu-
setts for a period of at least three years. If the families had bread-
winners, they were of lower-status occupations. Interviews were completed with 265 mothers.

Results: The Brookline Health Department ranked first in number of times mentioned and number of times mentioned positively. Only two other organizations had a positive net influence--the PTA and the Catholic church. Other organizations listed included the Chamber of Commerce, Better Business Bureau, Veterans of Foreign Wars, Protestant church, Jewish Federation, AFL-CIO, Democratic Party, Republican Party, and American Legion. These nine organizations had negative net scores.

Members of volunteer groups were much more likely to view them positively than were nonmembers. However, unions had a negative net score even among members and the PTA had a higher positive score among nonmembers.

Among families on the lower end of the socio-economic continuum, public agencies rather than groups with a membership base appear to be the key source of influence.

Friedman, M. "Television Program Preference and Televiewing Habits of Children As Related to Their Socio-Economic Status." PhD dissertation, Yeshiva University, 1957.

Purpose: To obtain information about the TV viewing habits and program preferences of children from three socio-economic levels.

Method: A pre-tested questionnaire was administered to 160 sixth grade children and each student kept a seven-day television diary. The subjects investigated were: (1) amount of viewing; (2) type of programs preferred; and (3) whether children watched programs classified as suitable by the National Association for Better Radio and Television and Junior Scholastic magazine. The children were from three socio-economic levels--high, middle, and low.

Results
1.   High-status children viewed 15 hours per week; middle, 23 hours; and low, 29 hours.
2.   Bedtime for all three groups was related to time TV viewing ceased.
3.   In all three groups, few parents prohibited specific programs.
4.   Viewing during dinnertime was prevalent in all groups.
5.   Situation comedies, westerns, and adventure programs were favorite programs for all groups.
6.   Peak viewing time for low-status children was 5-7 p.m.; for high-status children, 7-9 p.m.
7.   Few children viewed programs recommended by the two reviewing organizations.

Gans, Herbert J. The Urban Villagers: Group and Class in the Life
of Italian Americans. Glencoe, Ill.: The Free Press, 1962.

   Chapter 1--The West End: An Urban Village. Two major types of
neighborhoods exist in low-rent areas--the "urban jungle" which absorbs
criminals, deviates, and the mentally ill, and the "urban village" which
is a settling area for recent migrants. The West End is of the latter
type. At its height in 1910, the neighborhood held 23,000 inhabitants.
But today the number is down to 7,000 (in some 3,000 households)
primarily due to a decrease in dwelling units. Ethnic composition is
primarily of first- and second-generation Italian immigrants (42%),
Jews (10%), Polish (9%), and Irish (5%). Traces of other ethnic groups,
bohemians, students, artists, middle-class professionals, and "pathological households" constitute the balance. A fifth of the sample were
in their twenties, half were middle-aged, the rest were past 50. Some
70% were married and living with their spouse; 10% had never married.

   Chapter 2--The Italians of The West End: Place, Class, Culture,
and Social Structure.
   Class divisions. If usual criteria are applied (such as skill of
occupation and income), most West End residents are clearly working
class. Most have finished elementary school or the first two years of
high school. High school graduates are in the minority. Median
income is about $80 per week with the majority employed in manual
occupations. However, on the basis of behavioral styles it is possible
to distinguish four classes:
1.   The routine seekers. Their life aim is the establishment of a
     stable living pattern.
2.   The action seekers. Their life is a continual search for action,
     which is primarily a male prerogative.
3.   The maladapted. They are unable to control their behavior be-
     cause of alcoholism or other personal problems.
4.   The mobiles. Those who strive to advance themselves and/or
     their children into the middle class. These Ss have to model
     themselves after outsiders because they lack any such model in
     their own environment.

   Generally, the action and routine seekers are not mobile socially.
In terms of numbers, the routine seekers predominate, followed by the
action seekers, the middle-class mobiles, and the maladapted.
   The structure of West End society. The life of The West Enders
takes place within three interrelated sectors: the primary group, the
secondary group, and the outgroup. The primary group is the combination of family and peer relationships. The secondary group, also called
the community, refers to Italian institutions, voluntary organizations,
and other social bodies that support the workings of the peer group society. The outside world covers a variety of non-Italian institutions.
The primary group is a peer society because most of the West Enders'
relationships are with peers--among people of the same sex, age, and
life cycle status. The peer group society dominates the life of The West
Ender from birth to death and the mainstay of the adult peer society is
the family circle.

Chapter 3--The Family.
1.   Family types. West Enders fall between two types of families:
the nuclear family (husband, wife and children) and the extended family
(a group of nuclear families).
2.   Male-female relationships. Women sit together in one room,
the men in another. At social gatherings, whenever women initiate
conversations with men the men escape as quickly as possible and return to their group. The men fear their own ability for self-control.
As a result, the barriers between the sexes are high and are crossed
mainly by deviant types.
3.   Husband-Wife Relationships. The barriers between male and
female are translated into a marital relationship that can be best described as segregated as distinguished from joint relationship that characterizes the middle-class family. The husband's main role is bread-
winning and the wife is responsible for all functions concerning the
home and child. The segregation of functions is clearly visible in the
emotional aspects of the husband-wife relationship.
4.   Child Rearing. The West End family is adult-centered. Since
children are not planned, they are not at the center of the family.
Children are expected to behave like adults at home. The predominant
method of child rearing is punishment and reward as well as impulsive-
ness (non-purposive child rearing).

Chapter 4--The Peer Group and The Individual.
Peer group life. The basis of adult West End life is peer group
socializing. Membership in the group is based on kinship and friendship and is limited to people of similar ethnic background and class.
The group meets regularly in kitchens and living rooms. There are no
formal invitations. Conversations cover a relatively small number of
topics: accounts of activities since the last gathering; news of acquaintances, and plans for special events such as weddings. Much conversation is devoted to gossip. Peer group life also extends beyond the
family circle and some residents participate in informal cliques and
clubs made up of unrelated people.
The individual and the group. Social relationships within the peer
group follow a narrow path between individualistic display and strictly
enforced social control. The group is set up to provide its members
with an opportunity for displaying, expressing, and acting out their
individuality, as long as this does not become too extreme.

Chapter 5--The Community.
The nature of the community. The term "community" is used in a
nonspatial, limited sense. The institutions that constitute the community are the church, the parochial school, some commercial establish-
ments, and formal social, civic, and political organizations (some of
them church-related). These institutions, predominantly Italian, exist
outside the peer group society but are linked with it if they can be used
to meet group and individual needs. The peer group society so dominates West End life that the community is relatively unimportant.
Patterns of community participation and leadership. Middle-class
people are viewed as participating in community activities. Community
participation also provides an entree into the peer group society.

Leadership is sought because it provides opportunity for individual expression. Leaders always labor under some suspicion.

The Church. The most important formal institution is the Roman Catholic Church. West Enders do not closely identify with the church although they are religious people. The male attitude toward the church is based in large part on lack of respect for the priesthood.

Chapter 6--The Outside World: Work, Education, and Medical Care. The world of employers, professionals, middle class, city government, and the national society are external to the peer group society. They differ both in function and the way in which West Enders relate to them. The worlds of work and health care, are vital to both the individual and the peer group society. The services that social agencies from outside offer are treated with a mixture of curiosity and suspicion. In-between is education, which most West Enders now accept as necessary. At the other extreme are the law, the police, and the government. Conceived as agencies to exploit West Enders, they are viewed with hostility. The mass media constitute a major tie to the outside world. Attitudes toward the outside world are not entirely homogeneous. Action seekers are more suspicious and hostile than routine seekers. Men are more hostile than women. Even so, a basic gulf exists between all members of the peer group society and the outside world.

Chapter 7--The Caretakers: Missionaries from the Outside World. External caretakers include governmental and private agencies, such as the Department of Public Welfare, the Visiting Nurses Association, the Salvation Army, the settlement houses, nursery schools, and the public library. Although the external caretakers approach the West Enders with the best of intentions, the latter do not respond in kind. Cultural barriers, a mixture of lack of understanding, resignation, and fear of clients, seem to hover over most caretakers in the West End. One reason for the natural barrier between the West Enders and the external caretakers stems from the fact that the West Enders have their own internal caretakers (relatives, neighbors, church, store owners, and politicians). The internal caretaker functions most successfully when the client needs for group support.

Chapter 8--The Politicians: Ambassadors to the Outside World. By government, West Enders mean city government. There is almost no interest in state government. Government agencies have no reality. Since the government is viewed as consisting of individual actors, West Enders evaluate it on the basis of the same code that they apply to each other. The major functions of the "pol" (politician) is to do favors for his constituency, to keep them informed of what is going on, and to represent their point of view in the legislative and executive branches. Political life has traditionally served as a function for social mobility, although this was not true of all West End politicians. In many ways the politician's view of the power structure coincides with the peer group society's person orientation.

Chapter 9--Consumer Goods and Mass Media: Selective Acceptance of the Outside World. Adult West Enders make highly selective use of

popular culture. Among the variety of consumer goods, movies, TV
programs, and reading matter, their choices are structured to filter
out themes that do not support or enhance the life of the peer group
society.

The mass media. Of all the ideas that come from the outside
world, the most avidly received are those transmitted by the mass
media. West Enders read little but adolescents and young adults frequent movies and adults keep the television set on all evening long.
However, preferences in mass programming and performers are highly
selective. West Enders accept themes that mirror their own values
and reject others as illustrating the immorality and dishonesty of the
outside world. Thus, the media can be used to justify both peer group
society and its rejection of the outside world. Among the men, the
favorite movies or TV programs are those containing action. The women prefer the opposite, musical programs and soap operas. News
and other informational programs that deal with the outside world are
ignored: since TV does not cover local news, West Enders prefer to
get their information from peers.

Values and the mass media. The consistent choice of content and
performers suggests that West Enders are careful to select themes
that support their values, many of which originate within the peer group
society. The people who grew up in immigrant households are American
and not Italian in culture. That this change can be traced to the mass
media is doubtful, however.

Chapter 10--The Peer Group Society in Process. This chapter
looks at the immigrant generation and its ancestors and at changes now
taking place in the second and third generations. Most of the southern
Italians who went to America were day laborers and peasants. Data
suggest that the society and culture of the West Enders are quite similar
to those of the southern Italians, past and present. The southern Italians
who migrated to America came to better themselves. Studies of the
immigrant generation suggest that the move to America resulted in little
change in the pattern of adult life. The major changes took place among
children, especially as a result of their contact with American public
schools. The children who became adults of the second generation retained little of the Italian culture but they did retain most of its social
structure. The environment that the immigrants and West Enders have
encountered in America has differed in degree rather than kind; there
has been no radical change in the position of the working class vis-à-vis
other classes or in the position of minority ethnic groups vis-à-vis the
majority. As a result, there has been no strong pressure or incentive
among the West Enders for any radical change in their basic social
structure.

Chapter 11--The Subcultures of the Working Class, Lower Class,
and Middle Class. A hypothesis advanced in this book is that the peer
group society is a working class phenomenon and that class differences
separate the West Enders from the middle class (as opposed to the idea
that the peer group society is an ethnic phenomenon). The working-
class sub-culture is distinguished by the dominant role of the family
circle. The lower-class sub-culture is distinguished by the female-

based family and the marginal male. The middle-class sub-culture is
built around the nuclear family and its desire to make its way in the
larger society.

These sub-cultures are responses that people make to the opportunities and the deprivations that they encounter. These responses can
be seen as functions of the resources that a society has available and
the opportunities it can offer. Opportunities can increase or decrease
rapidly but the sub-cultures described are relatively slow in changing
their basic structure and content.

The culture of the West Enders is working-class. One distinguishing mark of a working-class group is its detachment from the larger
society. Because working-class culture is different from middle-class
culture, the move from one to the other is a difficult one, requiring
behavior and attitude change of considerable social and emotional mag-
nitude. The most important changes are cutting the attachment to the
family circle and the peer group society and a concurrent shift from
person to object orientation.

Gentile, Frank, and Miller, S. M. "TV and Social Class." Sociology
and Social Research XLV, 3 (April, 1961), 259-264.

Purpose: To test two theories: (1) that working-class individuals are
underrepresented as characters in network television shows; and (2)
that when they are portrayed, certain negative stereotypes are applied
to them.

Method: The characters appearing on 26 programs were analyzed. The
programs were the top 10 Nielsen-rated shows, plus 16 others broadcast in the evening on the two leading New York City network stations
during the period December 10-22, 1956.

Results: Some 122 characters were seen in this period, only seven
of whom were working-class people. An intensive analysis made of
these seven characters revealed that they were: (1) all males, (2)
did not speak proper English, and (3) were seldom portrayed positively.

Gerbner, George. "The Social Role of the Confession Magazine."
Social Problems VI, 1 (1958) 29-41.

Purpose: To establish the link between people of lower income levels
and the role of the confession magazine in fulfilling their needs.

Method: Not a survey but a report on limited conversations with publishers of confession magazines and some readers.

Results

1. Publisher reports indicate that the majority of the readers of confession magazines are women of families with young children and with household incomes under $4,000 per year. Most readers have a high school education or less and are working-class people. In contrast, the women who read McCalls or Good Housekeeping are middle class, live in households with incomes over $4,000, and are more likely to have attended college (30%).

2. According to the publishers, the confession magazine is printing material at the reading level of working-class readers. The content is earthy, descriptive, and concerns topics familiar to the working-class woman. The characters in the stories look like working-class women and perform the same daily tasks. The publishers point out that the magazines are designed to help readers in their daily lives. The format of the stories is always the same: some wrong is committed by the woman, followed by suffering, and then by repentance.

Gerson, Walter M. "Mass Media Socialization Behavior: Negro-White Differences." Social Forces XLV, 1 (September, 1966) 40-50.

Purpose: To examine the differences between blacks and whites in their utilization of the mass media as a means of socialization regarding relations with the opposite sex.

Method: The primary instrument for gathering data was a pretested questionnaire calling for anonymous responses. The questionnaire was administered to 638 adolescent boys and girls in four communities in the San Francisco area. The final sample included 272 whites and 351 blacks. The average age of respondents was 15.2; 49% of the respondents were male. The two criterion measures tapped two socializing functions of the mass media--reinforcement and norm-acquisition. Reinforcement was measured by asking respondents if they ever tried out their ideas about dating by watching to see if their ideas really happened in TV, movies, books, or magazines. Norm-acquisition was measured by asking respondents if they ever got any ideas on dating from the media. Control variables included: age (dichotomized as 15 and under, 16 and above); sex; non-daters versus noncompetitive daters versus competitive daters; middle class versus working class; and integration into peer culture.

Results

1. More black respondents used the media for socialization than white respondents: 39.4% of the blacks were high users of media for reinforcement compared with 29.8 of the whites; 47.1% of the blacks were high in media norm-acquisition compared to 36.4 of the whites. A four-type typology was developed combining the two socialization functions. A total of 53% of the whites used media for socialization compared with 66% of the blacks. Results are summarized below.

	Negro	White
High mass media socialee (used media for both reinforcement and norm-acquisition)	22%	14%
High mass media (reinforcement only)	18%	16%
High mass media (norm-acquisition only)	26%	24%
Mass media non-socialee	34%	47%

    2.   Analysis using control variables upheld the Negro/white difference reported above:

        a.   Media use for reinforcement increased with age for white teens; media use for norm-acquisition increased with age for black teens.

        b.   Black males were more likely to use media for socialization than black females; the reverse was true of white respondents.

        c.   Use of media for socialization was lowest for those black respondents actively involved in competitive dating in contrast to the whites where use of media for socialization was lowest for nondaters.

        d.   The working-class respondents among both whites and blacks indicated higher use of media for socialization but this difference was larger for whites.

        e.   It was expected that high integration into the peer culture would reduce the need for media socialization but the data support this expectation for blacks only.

The author emphasizes that race alone is not an explanation for the differences cited above, for race is a socially visible variable cloaking other factors. These other factors must be analyzed in order to explain differences. The author suggests that all teen-agers strive for social acceptance and the media play an important role in this process. Black teens live for the most part in a "black" world, but they have high mobility, and recently they have felt increased pressure for aspiring for success in the larger society. These three factors might intersect, leaving the black teen with a high need for information on the social rules of the white world--information which he can obtain through the media.

Gieber, Walter. "How the 'Gatekeepers' View Local Civil Liberties News." Journalism Quarterly XXXVII, 2 (Spring, 1960) 199-205.

Purpose: To examine conditions affecting how reporters and news-papers select stories about civil rights events.

Method: The author intensively interviewed 17 news sources and received comments from 12 others. These sources designated 12 reporters

for interviewing. Ten other reporters added their comments as well.
The survey was conducted with three medium-sized city dailies and
two metro papers in four California cities. News sources and reporters
were considered "gatekeepers." The sources were asked questions
about the progress of civil rights, the activities of their groups, and
their attitudes toward and relationships with newspapers. The reporters
were asked about their newspapers' policies regarding civil rights news
and their experiences in this area as well as about working conditions
and other relevant factors (e. g. , craft and environmental conditions)
that might affect the reporting of civil rights events.

Results
        1.   Gieber found source attitudes toward the media ranging from
hostile to uneasy; no source was favorable toward the media. He also
found that sources were rather ignorant about the nature of the mass
audience and journalistic techniques. Some sources were public relations people for their groups; others were just volunteers. In general,
legally-oriented groups used the press little; groups seeking to influence
legislation or "educate" the populace used the press more. Sources
were found to disagree with the media on what is news and how it should
be treated.
        2.   Gieber found that reporters were generally sympathetic to the
civil rights cause; some were even active in the drive for civil rights.
However, reporters noted that civil rights news was just one type of
news that they had to report. They were sensitive about their right to
report events as they saw them. Generally, they were resentful of
sources who said reporters needed to be "educated. "
        3.   Freedom and policy on civil rights news differed from paper
to paper. Some papers were more authoritarian. Policy was usually
unclear; it was lacking in the case of three of the papers studied.
Probably only one paper was negative toward civil rights. A reporter's
personality also had much to do with how he reported news. Initiative
and interest were important. Some reporters did not seem to care what
happened to a story after they were through writing it. Reporters also
suffered from a lack of understanding of the audience's wants.

Gottlieb, David. "Goal Aspirations and Goal Fulfillments: Differences
Between Deprived and Affluent American Adolescents. " American
Journal of Orthopsychiatry XXXIV, 5 (1964), 934-941.

Purpose: To identify differences in the social systems of adolescents
at varying socio-economic levels and to relate these differences to
perceptions, aspirations, and values.

Method: Information was obtained by questionnaire from: (1) all students in a segregated Negro high school in a southern rural community
of 14, 000 people; (2) all students in a segregated Negro high school in
a southern city of more than 100, 000 people; (3) all students in a segregated white high school in the same community as (1); (4) all students

in a segregated white high school in the same community as (2); (5) a
25% random sample of Negro and white students in an integrated high
school in an industrial midwestern community; and (6) a 25% Negro
sample in a segregated high school in a northern city of more than one
million people. Variables included: occupational level of father as
a measure of socio-economic status; parental education level; family
disorganization; aspirations toward college; expectations of attending
college; importance placed on academic activities; perceptions of
teacher desire to help students; and perceptions of teacher goals and
own goals.

Results
          1.   Lower-class background meant a lower level of parental edu-
cation, a higher incidence of family disorganization, and a higher incidence of residential mobility. These relationships held for all groups
of lower-class adolescents and were even more prevalent for Negro
adolescents.
          2.   In terms of aspirations for going to college among white stu-
dents (either southern or northern), the lower the class, the lower the
aspiration. However, the relationship between class and aspiration did
not hold among Negroes. About 80% of Negroes of all classes expressed
a desire to go to college. Female blacks were more likely to express
this desire than male blacks, and southern male blacks were more likely
to do so than northern. The lowest aspirations were found among blacks
in the integrated northern school. The blacks were also less likely than
whites to aspire to go beyond four years of college.
          3.   The discrepancy between college aspirations and expectations
among white students appears related to socio-economic class; the
discrepancy lessens as one goes up the status scale. Again, social
class had less importance among blacks. In class group of blacks,
20% who expressed a desire to go to college did not expect to do so.
Blacks in segregated southern schools were most likely to match expectations with aspirations and blacks in the northern integrated school
were least likely.
          4.   The higher his class background, the less discrepancy the
respondent saw between his goals and those he believed were held by his
teachers. However, Negro students regardless of class saw greater
discrepancy.
          5.   There was little difference between racial and class groups in
their perceptions of the teacher's ability to help students attain certain
goals.
          6.   The class groups did differ, in their perceptions of the teacher's
desire to help; the lower classes saw less desire to help. This was particularly true among Negroes. Negro perceptions also were related to
the teacher's race.

Gottlieb, David. "The Neighborhood Tavern and the Cocktail Lounge: A Study of Class Differences." American Journal of Sociology CXII, 6 (May, 1967), 559-562.

Purpose: To study the basic differences between a tavern and a cocktail lounge by stratifying clientele on a class basis and by examining the social climate of each institution.

Method: A sample of cocktail lounges and taverns was selected in Chicago and its suburbs. The sample was considered representative of various racial, income, and residential conditions. Interviews were conducted in 24 taverns and 22 cocktail lounges. In all, 60 respondents were interviewed in taverns and 48 in cocktail lounges.

Results: Basic class differences were found in the use of taverns and cocktail lounges. Upper-middle-class people mostly patronize the cocktail lounge (96%) and very rarely the tavern (4%). On the other hand, lower-middle-class people largely frequent the tavern (72%) rather than the cocktail lounge (28%). The tavern crowd is a highly cohesive group of generally lower societal standing. Usually a TV is present. Clients find friends of the same social status present. The primary drink is draft beer. On the other hand, the cocktail lounge is irregularly visited by members of higher classes. They visit for personal gain, not to converse with other patrons. Therefore, they are a low-cohesive group. Patrons are not usually from the immediate vicinity. They are generally entertained by something other than TV, usually live entertainment. Patrons are usually from a more heterogeneous group than the tavern regulars. They drink liquor rather than beer.

Grosser, Charles F. "Local Residents as Mediators Between Middle Class Professional Workers and Lower Class Clients." Social Service Review XL, 1 (March, 1966), 56-63.

Purpose: To analyze the discrepancies between middle-class professionals and their lower-class clients and the possible role of indigents in social service programs.

Method: Three groups of respondents were questioned on their perceptions of the lower east side slum community in New York City. One group consisted of professional staff members of the Mobilization for Youth (MFY) program. Another group was a stratified random sample of community residents. The third was a group of indigents hired to work with MFY. Respondents were asked to give their perceptions of the community in which they lived or worked. In addition, the MFY staff members--both professionals and indigents--were asked to predict answers the poor would give. Sample sizes are not given.

Results
   1.   Professionals and residents had quite different perceptions of
the community.
      a.   The professionals were a great deal more optimistic about
           whether the social order can be changed.
      b.   However, the low-income residents were more optimistic
           about current conditions. For example, 80% of the low-
           income residents said everyone had an equal chance to get
           ahead or that any male could earn $10,000; 80% also said
           that slum children were treated equally in school, that
           teachers understood the children, and that the schools
           weren't bad. Professionals were a great deal less opti-
           mistic on these subjects.
   2.   Indigent staff members had predicted low-income responses
better than the professionals.
      a.   The indigent workers were more likely to score in the top
           third of a prediction scale than were the professionals--52%
           of the indigents had high scores compared to 26% of the
           professionals.
      b.   However, the indigents' own perceptions of the community
           (as opposed to his predictions of the residents' perceptions)
           were actually closer to those of the professionals.
      c.   The correlation of staff performance ratings and pre-
           diction ability was not significant for either professionals
           or indigents, although there was a positive trend for pro-
           fessionals and a negative trend for indigents.

   The author raises a number of questions in discussing these results. Indigents are used in programs because it is felt that they can
serve as liasons to local residents. Yet the above results suggest that
they may be less effective as staff members and actually may have
attitudes closer to the professionals than to the residents.

Hazard, William R. "Anxiety and Preference for Television Fantasy."
Journalism Quarterly XLIV, 3 (Autumn, 1967), 461-469.

Purpose: To explore the possible relationships between viewer anxiety,
cultural isolation, and social position of adult television viewers and to
specify the causal nexus of these variables in relation to fantasy program choices.

Method: Interviews of 90 minutes were held with 430 adult viewers in
Austin, Texas, in the summer of 1963. Respondents were chosen on
the basis of a multistage sample employing probability and matching
procedures. Three independent variables were measured: (1) anxiety,
measured on the Taylor Manifest Anxiety 28-item short form scale and
then divided into three levels (low, medium, and high); (2) social position,
measured on the Holingshead scale combining occupation and education
and categorized into high and low; and (3) cultural activity, measured on

the Iowa Culture scale, which taps such community and cultural activities as participation in musical events, art galleries, and book reading
(this variable was also dichotomized). The dependent variable, use of
fantasy TV, was measured using a fantasy viewing scale. The scale
has a 10-point continuum on which 1 =.a news program; 4 = realistic
fiction; 7 = non-realistic fiction; and 10 = purely fantasy shows. This
scale was pretested on a sample of TV shows by a team of 40 viewers.
As measured by Kendall's Coefficient of Concordance, reliability
equaled .86. This scale then was applied to respondent answers from
the field survey question: "If you could plan a perfect evening's viewing,
what shows would you be most likely to see?" This question elicited at
least two TV show names from 97% of the respondents and the median
shows mentioned was 6. Each of these shows subsequently was scored
on the fantasy viewing scale and a respondent's fantasy viewing score
equaled the median score for all shows he mentioned. Validity of this
measure of fantasy viewing was checked by comparing the results with
results from actual viewing.

Results
        1.   The results support the hypothesis that high anxiety leads to
low cultural participation and also to more preference for fantasy TV
fare. The corollary is also true since persons low in anxiety tend to
be participants in cultural activities and to avoid fantasy programs.
This suggests that fantasy viewing is a functional alternative to cultural
participation.
        2.   Persons of low social position tend to be more likely to seek
out fantasy shows.
        3.   Low social position is correlated with low cultural activity.
        4.   Thus, a four-variable chain was identified suggesting that fan-
tasy TV has a primary audience of persons who are anxious, avoid
cultural contact, and have low social status.

Henry, Jules. "White People's Time, Colored People's Time."
Trans-Action II, 3 (March/April, 1965), 31-34.

        Middle-class observers studying a large St. Louis housing develop-
ment inhabited almost exclusively by very poor Negroes noticed a
pronounced tendency of the tenants toward random, unrealistic behavior.
Their attitudes toward space, time, objects, and persons seemed to
lack organization, predictability, and sometimes even sense.
        The families themselves seemed aware of the differences. They
made a strong distinction between colored people's time and white
people's time. They believed that an event occurs when scheduled in
the highly organized world of whites but that in the colored people's
world a scheduled event may occur at any moment over a wide spread
of hours or perhaps never.
        Illusion is their way of life, fancy their only possible achievement.
Unemployed men talk of jobs they do not have. Women speak of husbands who never existed. Young and old spend money they do not have,

brag of their "influence," and concentrate on getting the better of each
other.

For the children, survival takes precedence over all other considerations. Their home backgrounds lack the elements of order necessary to achievement and do not operate on schedules that adhere to
school concepts of time. The children lack the belief in achievement
and the fear of no achievement. A desire to "show off" rather than to
"accomplish" interferes with learning and facing school realistically.
Peer group pressures are very strong. Gaining the approval of white
students or of students of the opposite sex can be more important than
gaining teacher's approval. In short, the children lack the structure
on which conventional education can build.

Herzog, Elizabeth. "Some Assumptions About the Poor." Social Service Review XXXVIII, 4 (December, 1963), 389-402.

Purpose: To look at some assumptions about the poor and review some
studies that support and refute them.

Method: The article is a review and compilation of existing studies.
Studies examined dealt mostly with urban areas, considered both blacks
and whites, and paid particular attention to family and sexual patterns.

Results
        1.   There is a poverty culture. This contention is supported by
much of sociological research. The poor usually marry into equal
status, have very poor education, have a constant fear of the environment, and feel they have little control over it. Because of their socio-
economic level, their fears are very real. They are locked into a
vicious circle of poverty which they rarely can escape.
        2.   The poor have different family structure and sex patterns. In
the impoverished household, the father is looked upon much as an animal
and often an inadequate provider. The children usually are raised by
the mother. She dominates the household, causing problems in the
emotional development of the children. Sex is experienced at a relatively
early age and illegitimate births are considered unfortunate but not
calamitous. Thus, sexual impulse control is apparently not an important norm in poverty areas.
        3.   Family and sex patterns of poor blacks do not differ from those
of poor whites so long as whites and blacks examined are of the same
socio-economic level.

Hirsch, Paul M. "An Analysis of Ebony: The Magazine and Its Readers."
Journalism Quarterly XLV, 2 (Summer, 1968), 261-270 & 292.

Purpose: To describe and assess the editorial content and readers of
Ebony magazine from its inception in 1945 through the spring of 1966.

Results

Ebony's readers. As of spring, 1966, Ebony had 900,000 readers,
almost 5% of the 19 million Negroes in the U.S. (1960 Census). Ebony
is the only national Negro magazine of its kind. Its readership is 96%
Negro and mostly middle class. A comparison of Ebony readers with
the total U.S. Negro population shows that they are significantly better
educated, hold more white-collar jobs, and have higher mean incomes.
In addition, the median age of the Ebony reader is 32.2 compared with
21.6 for the general Negro population. Some 86% of Ebony readers are
married compared with 60% for the general Negro population; 52% own
homes compared with 38% for the general Negro population.

Despite heavy middle-class readership, the circulation still
includes a sizable number of non-middle-class Negroes--31% of its
readers earn less than $5,000 a year and 41% did not complete high
school. The author suggests that these lower-class subscribers are
undergoing anticipatory socialization or expressing a positive orientation to a nonmembership reference group.

Ebony's policy. Ebony's initial stated editorial policy was to mirror the
happier side of Negro life and present a true and accurate picture of
Negroes. The author sees a conflict here and suggests that Ebony
solves it by primarily emphasizing the positive. Ebony has tried to
serve the needs and interests of all its readers. Since its readers are
highly variable, this has resulted in some conflicting policies.

The prevading approach of the magazine up until the civil rights
movement of the 1960's can be summed up as follows: emphasis on
recognition of Negroes, success achieved by hard work, and "making
it." This emphasis may be a positive one, for the presentation of
success fantasies may motivate readers to make them realities. Until
the 1960's, the magazine's approach to civil rights was to work within
the status quo and avoid references to militancy. This approach toward
civil rights changed in the 1960's, due to: (1) the increasing number of
college graduate Negroes with a new philosophy; and (2) the increased
involvement of middle-class Negroes in the protest movement and their
increased identification with the Negro masses (particularly by Negroes
with some acceptance within the white community). Because of these
trends, Ebony became more militant but has never accepted the extreme
militant approach of such groups as SNCC and CORE. The author posits
that the reason is that middle-class Negroes have not supported these
groups. Despite a trend toward more militant content, the main message
of Ebony has continued to be "self-help."

The magazine does have a conflict in that some of its middle-class
readers have disinterest or hostility toward the Negro lower classes.
The "black bourgeoisie" Negro generally gains his status within the
Negro community (e.g., as a merchant to Negroes). He is ambivalent
toward Negro progress because he has much to lose if the closed system
becomes more open.

The Negro middle class consists of several factions that disagree
over a variety of questions. Ebony's ambivalence and self-contradiction
is a response to its desire to serve all readers. Currently, the magazine shows a basic conflict between the protest versus self-help
philosophies. If the Negro achieves by effort, then he fails by lack of

effort. But he doesn't fail by lack of effort because society won't let
him succeed. Another basic conflict is the conspicuous consumption
versus savings and sacrifice dilemma. The magazine treats these as
opposing orientations and emphasizes the acquisition of middle-class
status goods as well as the need to save.

Ingram, Jim. "What Blacks Read--and Who They Believe." Detroit
Scope Magazine I, 39 (January 4, 1969), 6-8.

Purpose: To review the reading habits and preferences of Detroit
blacks.

Method: Surveys (of unspecified nature) of Detroit blacks, personal
interviews, and opinions are presented. The Scope survey included
interviews with doctors, lawyers, businessmen, factory workers, construction laborers, housewives, and unemployed blacks.

Results
    1. According to a recent Scope magazine survey, Detroit blacks
read many conventional periodicals (e.g., Life, Look, Newsweek, and
Time) but these publications are not high in their preferences. Blacks
prefer black magazines (e.g., Ebony, Jet, Tan, and the Michigan
Chronicle, the leading black weekly newspaper in Michigan).
    2. A recent survey by the Michigan Chronicle reports that whites
as well as blacks are disturbed by the biased picture of blacks presented
by the major daily papers.
    3. The Scope survey indicates that blacks see the Detroit Free
Press as more liberal and truthful than the Detroit News in reporting
the news. References from personal interviews suggest that blacks
are particularly disturbed by majority newspaper efforts to make the
blacks' charges seem ridiculous or far-fetched as well as the use of
racial designations in crime stories.
    4. The Scope survey shows that more blacks read Ebony than its
white counterpart, Life. Although militants say that Ebony is aimed
primarily at the black middle class, poor Negroes enjoy reading
glamorous presentations of black accomplishments. The ads are also
attractive to many black readers.
    5. Reader's Digest ranked highest on the list of national white
publications read by Detroit Negroes--80% of Scope's respondents said
Reader's Digest had a good reputation and contained interesting reading.
The black counterpart to Reader's Digest, Negro Digest, is read primarily by black college students, intellectuals, and professionals.
Most lower-income blacks had never heard of Negro Digest.
    6. The article emphasizes the problems of black publishers.
Ghetto Speaks, a bi-weekly black power newspaper in Detroit, is read
by both blacks and whites but has very little advertising. The problem
is too little staff to solicit ads. Another black newspaper, Epic News,
has too much advertising; a recent issue was 70% ads. The problem
is not enough qualified black journalists to support the paper. Tuesday

magazine, a newspaper supplement for blacks appearing in the <u>Detroit News,</u> has been in existence for more than three years. Its editors report that initially they had advertising problems because whites failed to see Negroes as a separate market. <u>Tuesday</u> magazine is published in both Chicago and Detroit and has two million readers.

    7.   The <u>Scope</u> survey indicates that most respondents read at least four newspapers, one magazine, and one-half a paperback novel each week.

Irelan, Lola M. , and Besner, Arthur. "Low Income Outlook on Life. " <u>Welfare in Review</u> III, 9 (September, 1965), 13-19.

<u>Purpose</u>: To summarize from numerous prior studies the approach to life of the poor and the connection between poverty conditions and life styles.

<u>Results</u>: According to these studies, the poor show the following characteristics:

    1.   <u>Comparative simplification of the experience world.</u> The poor have little opportunity for change in social and cultural settings. Daily routines become rigidified and are seldom discarded. Few leaders are found in the community. Socially, the poor seldom leave their kinship and neighborhood groups.

    2.   <u>Powerlessness.</u> The poor have little actual power. They have few bargaining agents within the social structure. They are unskilled, uneducated, and easily replaced in the employment structures. They have little opportunity to change their conditions and are unable to acquire information and training to improve their skills. They also see themselves as powerless: as individuals who strongly doubt the possibility of controlling their own lives and see no possibility of changing society.

    3.   <u>Deprivation.</u> The poor feel deprived because the large gap between their own attainment and that of the rest of society is all too evident to them. Even their own realistic expectations of attainment fall well below that of the majority society.

    4.   <u>Lack of security.</u> The poor constantly are subjected to sickness, injury, loss of work, and legal problems. Their meager resources are wiped out by even small emergencies. They are unable to get help from agencies because they are usually unaware that such agencies exist.

    5.   <u>Meaninglessness.</u> The poor are so accustomed to being moved around that they feel no sense of control over their own destinies and they cannot grasp the structure of the world or their own place within it.

    6.   <u>Isolation.</u> Isolated from the majority society and many of its information sources, the poor know less about current life than others. They often feel detached even within their own social stratum and consider the world indifferent to them.

    7.   <u>Fatalistic.</u> Their life approach assumes that they cannot influence what is going to happen to them. Resignation is the most realistic approach; anything good that happens comes from luck.

    8. Present-orientation. Since the poor cannot see the chance of controlling their own futures, they do not plan ahead. Children are raised in terms of immediate reward and punishment; resources are too meager to save.

    9. Authoritarianism. People are classes as weak or strong and strength is the basis for authority. Authority rather than reason is the basis of decision-making. Simple solutions are preferred. Deviance and disobedience are punished severely.

    10. Concreteness. Verbal communication is characterized by few abstractions, generalizations, or concepts. Reference more often is made to direct observation and concrete objects.

Despite the general picture of powerlessness presented above, research supports the notion that the poor have the same goals and values as other Americans--they want the same luxuries and comforts, better jobs, educated children, security, to escape everyday routine, and stable marriages. However, their reasons for wanting these things may often differ from the middle class. They value education, for example, not for self-improvement or worth but because education is a way out of the slum. In addition, although they have the majority societal values, they do not ostracize those who do not fit the picture.

Kean, George G. "A Comparative Study of Negro and White Homeless Men." PhD dissertation, Yeshiva University, 1965.

Purpose: To study the sociological and psychological predictors of homelessness. The author suggests that sociological factors predominantly cause homelessness for Negroes, but psychological factors are the cause for whites.

Method: A comparative study of three groups of males, matched for age and intelligence. Group 1 consisted of 30 native American Negro homeless men; group 2 consisted of a matched set of 30 native American white homeless men; and group 3 (control group) consisted of 30 native American Negro domiciled men. Evaluations were made of the family, environmental, educational, vocational, social, and economic background of each subject. Psychological tests were administered to determine the intellectual status, personality characteristics, and levels of adjustment of each group of respondents. The psychological tests included the Revised Visual Retention Test, Grassi Block Substitution Test, Visual Motor Festalt Test, Rorschach Psychodiagnostic Test, and Thematic Apperception Test. Kean's hypotheses were:

    1. The Negro homeless men came from families that were significantly more likely to have the following characteristics: more disorganization, lower social and economic levels, and less education and vocational training.

    2. The Negro homeless men would demonstrate significantly higher performance on the battery of psychological tests than the white homeless men but lower than the Negro domiciled men.

Results: Families of the Negro homeless men were more disorganized than those of either the white homeless men or the Negro domiciled men. However, the Negro and white homeless men did not differ significantly on any of the other characteristics suggested by the first hypothesis.

Few differences on the psychological tests were found between black and white homeless men. Generally, the only differences found were between homeless and domiciled men, e.g., the Negro domiciled men had faster reaction times, better emotional adjustment, and better contact with reality.

Keller, Susanne. "The Social World of the Urban Slum Child: Some Early Findings." American Journal of Orthopsychiatry XXXIII, 5 (1963), 823-831.

Purpose: To compare selected aspects of the after-school and home activities of a sample of poor Negro and white children attending first and fifth grades in New York City public schools. Discussion centers on factors that distinguish the family life, self-image, and recreational activities of these children from those of the middle-class schoolmates with whom they must compete.

Method: The 46 children studied were from the poorer sections of New York City. The children might be considered somewhere near the top of the lower-lower class or at the bottom of the upper-lower class. A number of tests tapped their verbal, intellectual, and conceptual abilities. The parents received questionnaires by mail and the children gave accounts of typical weekend activities and life at home.

Results
    1. Social and economic background. One out of six breadwinners was unemployed at the time of the study. These families were receiving welfare assistance. Two out of three families were supported by the father's paycheck for such low level jobs as porter, short-order cook, and unskilled or semiskilled factory work. A few were bus or taxi drivers, clerks, or self-employed. They had held the same or similar jobs for six or more years. On the average, the parents did not have more than one year of high school education. The mothers had somewhat more schooling than the fathers. Significantly, less than three-fifths of the families conformed to the typical American family of two parents and two or three children. These families were much larger, including eight or nine persons. When asked to classify themselves in terms of projected success, fully two-thirds said they were moving up in the world, three-tenths said they were at a standstill, and only 2% stated they were going downhill. The author finds this quite striking, since their chances for upward mobility, objectively speaking, are quite low.
    2. Life outside school. All 46 children lived in homes containing both radio and TV sets and all utilized both media regularly and

frequently. The majority society seems to come to these children via
entertainment and escapist TV stories. Even in the first grade, children
were familiar with the names of programs and leading characters.

There was a clear lack of sustained interaction with adult members
of their families. For example, only about one-half regularly ate one
meal with one or both parents; the rest ate alone or with brothers and
sisters only.

3. Self-perceptions. The children typically had low self-esteem,
drawing unfavorable comparisons between themselves and their schoolmates. When asked to complete this sentence, "When I look at other
boys and girls and then look at myself, I feel . . ," 60% of the children
answered unfavorably; "I feel ashamed, sad, heartbroken." Only 30%
responded: "I feel good, happy, the same."

4. Parental aspirations for their children. These parents, like
most parents, hoped for a better life for their children. Some 80%
wanted their children to obtain a college degree. Fully two-thirds hoped
that their sons would become professional men, e.g. doctors, lawyers,
or teachers.

5. Racial differences. Lower-class Negro children come from
larger families than lower-class white children. In addition, three
times as many Negro children lived in families where the adults
currently were unemployed and receiving welfare and other types of
aid. Only one-half of the Negro families were supported by the father
compared to 90% of the white families. Three-fourths of the Negro
parents were mobile geographically; two-thirds were native to the
south; and one-tenth were immigrants to the U.S. None of the white
children came from mobile families. Both their parents were born in
the north. Negro parents were more likely to have held their present
jobs six years or more; more than half of the whites had held their present job for less than six years. Negro parents had less education
than the white parents but indicated more concern for their children's
schooling.

Kohn, Melvin L. "Social Class and Parental Values." The American
Journal of Sociology LXIV, 4 (January, 1959) 337-351.

Purpose: To see if there are class differences in the values that parents deem important for their children. Knowledge of this type could
help explain class differences in child and family behavior.

Method: Two samples of Washington, D.C., families were selected
from census tracts. All families had children in the fifth grade. The
first sample consisted of 200 white working-class families and the second of 200 white middle-class families. Parents were asked what
values they would most like to see expressed in their children's behavior; the parents selected three most important characteristics for
a fifth grade child from a list of 17 characteristics. In all 400 homes,
the mother was interviewed. In every fourth family, the father and the
fifth grade child also were interviewed (82 families). Interviews were

held in the home. Parents were interviewed separately, in different rooms at the same time. A male interviewed the father, a female questioned the wife. The first person to complete interviewing a parent questioned the child.

Results
    1. Mothers of both social classes agreed that standards of conduct such as honesty, consideration, obedience, dependability, manners, and self-control are highly desirable for both boys and girls of this age. Popularity, being a good student (especially for boys), neatness, cleanliness (especially for girls), and curiosity are highly desirable in both classes but somewhat less so than the first group of values. Few mothers chose ambition, ability to defend oneself, being affectionate, being liked by adults, ability to amuse oneself, or seriousness as highly desirable for children of this age, although they could be desirable traits of children of other ages.
    2. Some class distinctions were apparent. Generally, the higher a mother's social status, the more likely she was to select consideration, self control, and curiosity as desirable characteristics for both boys and girls. In addition, the higher-class mother was more likely to cite happiness as desirable for boys than were lower-class mothers. The desirability of the "happiness" characteristic differed by social class for boys only. The lower a mother's social status, the more she chose obedience, neatness, and cleanliness as most desirable. Further, mothers of lower status valued honesty in their children more than those at higher levels.
    3. The father's choices agreed with those of the mother, except that fathers were less likely to value happiness for their daughters regardless of social class. Middle-class fathers placed high value on dependability in their children; working-class fathers placed more value on the ability to defend oneself.
    4. All parents were concerned that their children conform to their conception of proper age and sex roles.

Kurtz, Norman R. "Gatekeepers: Agents in Acculturation." Rural Sociology XXXIII, 1 (March, 1968) 63-70.

Purpose: To describe the gatekeepers who provide urban minority members with access to the resources needed to solve their problems. The setting of the study is Denver, Colorado, where Spanish-Americans (mostly low-income) make up about 9% of the population. Acculturation is defined as the process of acquiring skills to solve living problems in an urban setting. Gatekeepers are defined as those who help people with Spanish surnames gain access to resources.

Method: A list of gatekeepers was acquired through organizations active in the Spanish community by asking known gatekeepers to name other gatekeepers and asking residents of the Spanish community to name gatekeepers. The final list of gatekeepers numbered 73; 57 were

of Spanish descent; one was Negro; and 15 were Anglos. A cluster
analysis based on a 73 x 73 matrix then was developed. A scoring
method was used to indicate each gatekeeper's relationship to every
other gatekeeper; a zero score indicated that a gatekeeper did not cite
and was not cited by another gatekeeper; a score of one indicated a
gatekeeper cited or was cited by another; a score of two indicated a
gatekeeper cited and was cited by another. The resulting matrix was
analyzed to determine the structure or network of relationships that
formed the framework of the informal gatekeeping system.

Results: Six different principal types of clusters emerged from the
analysis:
    1. Public patrons. Three clusters of gatekeepers who were
public employes and seemed involved primarily due to their occupational
positions.
    2. Local churches. Three clusters of gatekeepers for whom the
local church provided the social context for gatekeeping activity.
    3. Political parties. Two clusters of this type consisted of gate-
keepers actively involved in political parties; the key member of each
cluster was a politician.
    4. Political rebels. Two clusters of people who had political
power in the community, but were not committed to any party.
    5. Do-gooders. Three clusters, composed primarily of the
Anglo gatekeepers who were primarily middle class, moderate in their
views, and ready to help out the "poor who wanted to get ahead."
    6. Poor people. One cluster composed primarily of poor people
who helped other poor people and a few social workers who supported
the poor gatekeepers in their gatekeeping functions. Social workers
did not seem to have access to resources unknown to the poor but they
were more adept at using formal channels for acquiring resources from
community agencies.

    Several gatekeepers did not fit into any of the clusters. Seven
showed very limited exchange of resources with other gatekeepers and
confined their activities to areas in which they had direct access to
resources. The remaining eight unassigned gatekeepers, seven of
Spanish descent, were omitted from clusters because they had too many
contacts with other gatekeepers and therefore had equally strong ties
to all cliques. They also had strong ties to each other, so in a sense
they formed the superstructure of the network. These eight contacted
the most members in the clusters and were contacted most often by
members of the clusters.
    Other key findings were:
    1. Gatekeepers used informal channels to transfer resources to
people in trouble.
    2. One major problem in the informal system was inefficiency.
Individuals were spending too much time and effort looking for resources
to which they had very limited or no access. For instance, doctors were
using unlikely channels to find inexpensive housing while real estate
agents struggled to help people who were ill.
    3. The burden on active gatekeepers was great. The eight "cos-
mopolite" gatekeepers, for example, were contacted directly by people
in trouble as well as by other gatekeepers.

Lambert, Verdelle. "Negro Exposure in Look's Editorial Content."
Journalism Quarterly XLII, 4 (Autumn, 1965), 657-659.

Purpose: To examine issues of Look for their treatment of blacks.

Method: Content analysis was performed for two sampling periods,
November-December 1959-60 and 1963-64. The inferences derived
are drawn from very small samples since only 13 articles in these
time periods included blacks.

Results
    1. Only one black appeared on the cover of the magazine during
the two time periods considered.
    2. During the 1959-60 period, a black generally was not the
subject of a story unless he was a nationally known figure or a criminal;
over half of the 1959-60 articles in which blacks appeared could not
properly be called racial type stories. In 1963-64, blacks did not
appear unless presented in some racial context.
    3. In general, the 1963-64 articles were more favorable in their
treatment of blacks.

Lang, Kurt, and Lang, Gladys Engel. "Racial Distrubances As Collective Protest." The American Behavioral Scientist II, 4 (March-April),
11-13.

Purpose: To analyze the causes and psychological functions served by
the urban race riot by an examination of prior reports on urban disturbances. In particular, to find out how rioting becomes an acceptable
means of protest.

Results
    1. The potential for riot violence depends on: (1) adequacy of
other channels of protest; (2) acceptability of violence; (3) size of crowd,
including bystanders who seem to lend tacit support for the rioters;
(4) perceived police action and policy, i.e., the extent to which police
appear to impose upon a racial minority; (5) clarity of reasons for police
action; (6) injury to minority self-esteem by police impersonality; and
(7) moral sentiment and the acceptability of violence in the riot community.
    2. The extent to which the riot spreads depends upon: (1) abstrac-
tion of the degree to which the riot is perceived as an attack on the
establishment; (2) level of sympathy for the riot among the nonviolent
majority that might inhibit them from calling on the law; and (3) the
youth of the rioters. The typical black rioter is in his late twenties;
a quarter are under 21. Most are employed, largely in unskilled jobs.
Though instigators of the riots may have been criminals and agitators,
the criminal element seems insignificant. The number of criminal
records among the rioters did not differ significantly from similar
people in a non-riot area.

3.   Potential for repetition of the riot seems largely a function
of: (1) recognition given to the rioters; (2) hot weather; (3) extent of
violent reaction by the white power structure; (4) the level of dramati-
zation afforded ghetto conditions by civil disobedience and the extent to
which peaceful protest evolves into violence; (5) level of destruction
wrought upon targets, e.g., white stores; and (6) the extent to which
negotiations deal only with riot "leaders" rather than the entire ghetto
community.

Larson, Carl M. "Racial Brand Usage and Media Exposure Differentials." In A New Measure of Responsibility for Marketing, edited by
Keith Cox and Ben Enis. Conference Proceedings, Series No. 27.
Philadelphia: American Marketing Association, June 17-19, 1968,
pp. 208-215.

Purpose: To determine what brands Negroes prefer and whether these
brands differ from those preferred by whites.

Method: Random sampling procedures were used to select 210 Negro
and 200 white households in Chicago. Respondents were asked which
products they had purchased for 30 days prior to the interview. An
inventory of products in the household was also taken. Demographic
information was collected. Interviewers were college students matched
to respondents by race.

Results
     1.   Car preference seemed more the result of income level than
race. More blacks than whites owned lower-priced cars--61% of
blacks owned Chevrolets or Fords compared with 44% of whites.
     2.   Blacks preferred premium gasoline more than whites did.
     3.   Blacks bought their food in national chains, contrary to the
belief that they prefer the corner grocery store.
     4.   Blacks bought more grains and cooked cereals than whites.
     5.   Other items which blacks bought more than did whites included
vitamins, laxatives, pork sausage, and packed luncheon meats.
     6.   Whites purchased more shampoo, hair spray, cosmetics,
soups, diet beverages, and regular coffee.
     7.   Some 21% of the black families used hair straighteners; 17%
used skin bleach.
     8.   Whites bought a variety of alcoholic beverages; the main choice
of blacks was scotch.
     9.   Among blacks, national brands were more popular than local
ones.
     10. Producers who have appealed to the black consumer were re-
warded with patronage.
     11. Companies with unflattering black symbols were not the choices
of blacks.
     12. Radio use
     a.   Both races preferred to listen to the radio in the morning
          rather than the afternoon or evening.

    b.   Stations aimed at the mass market drew many black
        listeners. However, a black-oriented station (WVON)
        drew more black listeners than the mass stations.

Larson, Richard B., and Sutker, Sara. "Value Differences and Value
Concensus by Socio-Economic Status." Social Forces XLIV, 4 (1966)
563-569.

Purpose: To examine the effects of socio-economic status (SES) and
ethnicity on health, knowledge, values, and practices. The emphasis
of the study was on discovering variations in values.

Method: A sample of 142 adults was selected randomly. Subjects first
ranked occupations (such as businessman, doctor, or waiter) according
to importance. Then they ranked desiderata (values) according to
which were most important for them (such as being clean, possessing
life insurance, and having good health). The sample was divided into
five SES levels. Four hypotheses were tested:
    1.   Upper SES respondents will differ in their values from lower
SES respondents.
    2.   There will be fewer high versus low SES differences in ranking
occupations according to importance than in ranking desiderata according to importance.
    3.   There will be less variation across all Ss in ranking occupations
than in ranking desiderata.
    4.   Consensus in ranking the two items will vary according to
social class.

Results
    1.   All four hypotheses were supported. In the case of the first
hypothesis, upper and lower SES respondents gave different rankings
to occupations and desiderata. The high SES people ranked good education and health as most important; their low SES counterparts ranked
cleanliness, owning a home, and having insurance as most important.
Concerning occupations, businessmen rated higher with the high SES
group and police, plumber, and waitress scored higher in the low SES
group.
    2.   Regarding the fourth hypothesis, there was more consensus in
ranking the two items among the higher than among the lower SES levels.

Levenstein, Phyllis, and Sunley, Robert. "Stimulation of Verbal Interaction Between Disadvantaged Mothers and Children." American Journal of Orthopsychiatry XXXVIII, 1 (January, 1968), 116-121.

Purpose: To determine whether the verbal intelligence of socially disadvantaged preschoolers (two-year-olds) can be increased by encouraging

verbal interaction--playing and talking--between the children and their mothers.

Method: Subjects were twelve Negro mother-child dyads living in a low-income public housing project in a New York City suburb. Prior to the experiment, each mother and child was given the Peabody Picture Vocabulary Test to determine pre-verbal IQ level. After matching the dyads on pre-IQ, the dyads were assigned randomly to treatment and control groups. The experiment consisted of 15 visits to the experimental dyads' homes over a four-month period. For each visit, the social worker brought one or two new Verbal Interaction Stimulus Materials to demonstrate to the mother and child. The mother and child were encouraged to work with the toys and books together. At the end of the four-month period, the experimental control dyads were tested for verbal IQ with alternate forms of the Peabody test.

Results
    1.   On the pretest, the mean IQ of the experimental children was 75.8 and of the control children 80.8. After the four-month period the mean of the experimental children was 89.5, a gain of 13.7. The mean of the controls dropped .4 to 80.4.
    2.   The verbal IQ scores for both experimental and control mothers did not change significantly over the four-month period. The experimental mothers' mean rose from 83.5 to 87 and the control mothers rose from 86 to 89.8.
    3.   Experimental subjects showed high and lasting interest in the Verbal Interaction Stimulus toys and books.

Lewis, Oscar. "The Culture of Poverty." Scientific American CCXV, 4 (October, 1966), 19-25.

Purpose: To find out if membership in a group with a history of poverty constitutes membership in a separate culture.

Method: Some 100 families from four representative slums of San Juan, Puerto Rico, were compared to 50 families of their descendants living in New York City. A battery of tests and questionnaires requiring some 12 hours of the respondent's time was employed to assess residential and employment history; family relations; income and expenses, possessions; medical history; friendship patterns; views on politics, religion and the world in general; and degree of cosmopoliteness. A battery of psychological tests including open-end interviews and various standard projective tests also was administered to some of the families.

Results: The author concludes that one can isolate a culture of poverty. Principal characteristics of this culture include the following:
    1.   High incidence of common law marriage and matriarchial households.

2. Chronic unemployment or employment in minimal, low-paying jobs. Since income is small, food is frequently purchased in small quantities at high prices.

3. Low rate of membership in political parties, labor groups, and other similar organizations.

4. Awareness of but rejection of middle-class values, especially the importance placed on marriage.

5. Hostility toward the institutions basic to the maintenance of the middle class, e.g., the police and government.

6. The poverty community is highly gregarious but low in organization beyond the limits of the extended family.

7. The poor family does not cherish childhood as a prolonged and protected stage of life. Further, despite emphasis on family solidarity, there is much sibling rivalry for the limited supply of goods and affection available.

8. Poor Ss in this culture generally have strong feelings of fatalism, dependency, and inferiority as well as weak ego structure and confusion in sexual identification.

9. There is widespread belief in masculine superiority and a consequent preoccupation among males with their masculinity.

10. The characteristics mentioned above transcend nationality and appear to be common throughout the western world.

Liebow, Elliot. Tally's Corner: A Study of Negro Streetcorner Men. Boston: Little, Brown, and Co., 1967.

Chapter 1--Introduction. Adult Negro males are studied to determine their life patterns and relationships within the Negro family. The great bulk of the material is drawn from participant observation of two dozen Negro men who shared a corner in Washington D. C.'s second precinct as a base for their operations. These men were unskilled construction workers, casual day laborers, menial workers in retailing and service trades, or unemployed. They ranged in age from the early twenties to the mid-forties. Some were single, some were married, some lived with their wives and children, some did not. The main body of the data consists of a day-by-day record of the routines of these men as they frequented the street corners, alleys, hallways, poolrooms, beer joints, and private homes in the immediate neighborhood.

Chapter 2--Men and Jobs. Tally's Corner was a job recruiting station for employers needing laborers by the day. To the casual observer or the white employer looking for laborers, it appeared that most of the men at the Corner did not work or want to work. The white truck driver recruiting men, for example, was successful with only 2 or 3 men in every 35 or so contacts he made. But as Liebow notes, surface impressions are deceptive for most of the men on the Corner had jobs: some worked at night, some were on their day off, some worked shifts starting at odd times. Liebow did not argue that some were unemployed and did not want to work. These men, he suggests, are especially significant because their values are the strongest representation of the attitudes toward work found throughout the streetcorner world. However, the nonworking men differed from the workers only in degree not in kind.

The middle-class values of acquiring a job, maintaining a job, and performing well have low priority in the streetcorner world. For example, getting a job may be subordinate to maintaining relations with women or other nonwork considerations. Attitudes toward jobs fit into a complex of values, attitudes, and beliefs drawn from experiences and assessments of objective reality. As an example, Liebow reports one of the major conflicts he observed: although job regularity is an important aspect of a job's benefits, the most regular jobs often pay less than non-regular jobs. On the other hand, the regular job does offer the opportunity for stealing. The employer expects the men to steal and the men cooperate. However, some men do not steal or are unable to steal their worth, so they do not take regular jobs. If a man gets caught stealing, the tacit recognition of both labor and management that the men may steal is not honored.

As Liebow also observes that the built-in low self-esteem of the streetcorner men operates in job attitudes. Fear of being tested or accepting responsibility often prevent a man from accepting a job.

Chapter 3--Fathers Without Children. The absence of the father is one of the chief characteristics of the father-child relationships of the men in this study. The father-child relationship seemed to be stronger when the child was being cared for by the father's family rather than the mother's family. When the child was cared for by the father's family, he usually carried his father's name and his father provided at least partial financial support. The father was often informed of the child's well-being and even when separated by great distances, father and child visited at least one or more times a year. Father and child also exchanged gifts frequently and meetings were marked by affectionate displays.

In contrast to this type of father-child relationship is that of the father living with his children. This father seemed to take no pleasure in his children and gave them little time and attention. He seldom mentioned his children in casual conversation, and rarely was seen with them in public. When the father returned home, the child might not even look up and the father would take no more notice than he received.

Liebow suggests several explanations for this paradox in which the fathers who lived with their children appeared less warm than those who did not. The most obvious explanation is that the separated father is not charged with day-to-day responsibility for the child and can afford to be-attentive and affectionate.

Chapter 4--Husbands and Wives. Liebow reports that the men and women in streetcorner society are careful to distinguish between marriage ("having papers") and consensual unions ("common law, shacking up, living with"). Marriages have clear-cut rights and duties which are not denied even though they may not be adhered to. Consensual unions have rights and duties patterned after marriages but are more ambiguous. First, consensual unions have less public force behind them. Secondly, the rights and duties of consensual unions are less clearly defined. For these respondents a marriage implies exclusive sexual access to one's spouse but a consensual union does not necessarily imply the same.

To the outside observer, of course, marriage appears to be the superior type of relationship. The men on the streetcorner do not agree. For them, marriage as it is experienced day in and day out does not work.

Chapter 5--Lovers and Exploiters. The men and women of this neighborhood often talked of themselves in exploitative terms. Generally, the men preferred to see themselves as the exploiters and the women as the exploited. Often, a woman's desirability was assessed in terms of her wealth or earning power or in equating "being nice" with "having a job." Whenever a woman was present, the men were encouraged to portray themselves even more flamboyantly as ruthless exploiters as proof of their prowess.

Although exploitation was the major theme of the verbalized talk on the streetcorner, the actual practice of the male-female relationships was not purely exploitative. In most relationships, exploitative and nonexploitative (loving and liking) impulses operated concomitantly. The men often found that they were lovers as much as they had hoped to be users.

Chapter 6--Friends and Networks. Perhaps, more than most social worlds, this streetcorner world took its shape and color from the structure and character of the face-to-face relationships of the people living there. Unlike other areas of our society where a large portion of the individual's energies are invested in self-improvement and career, each man on the streetcorner had his own network of personal relationships.

At the edges of these networks were those persons with whom the man's relationship was neutral, area residents whom he had "seen around" but did not know except to say "Hi" to. Toward the center of the network were those persons the man knew and liked best, those with whom he was "up tight," e.g., his walking buddies and girl friends. He had more or less daily contact on a face-to-face basis with these people. He turned to these people for aid, comfort, and support in times of crisis.

In general, close friendships tended to develop out of associations with those in a man's network of personal relationships. One of the most striking characteristics of these friendships was the use of kinship ties as a model. Most of the men and women on the streetcorner were unrelated to one another and only a few had kin in the immediate area. Nevertheless, kinship ties were frequently manufactured to account for and validate friendship relationships. The most common form of this pseudo-kinship relationship between two men was known as "going for brothers," meaning that two men agreed to present themselves as brothers to the outside world. In the "going for brothers" relationship, the usual claims, obligations, and the expectations of friendships were publicly declared to be at their maximum.

However, friendships on the streetcorner, lacked depth in both
past and present and were easily uprooted by the tug of economic forces
or self-interest. The recognition of this weakness, coupled with the
importance of friendship as a source of security and self-esteem,
seemed to be a principal source of the impulse to romanticize relationships and elevate what others saw as a casual acquaintanceship to
friendship and friendship to close friendship.

Luchterland, Elmer, and Weller, Leonaval. "Social Class and the
Desegregation Movement: A Study of Parents' Decisions in a Negro
Ghetto." Social Problems XIII, 1 (1965), 83-88.

Purpose: To study the relation of social class to the desire of Negro
parents to keep their children in segregated schools or to transfer
them. Other factors considered were basic demography of the parents,
organizational membership, and characteristics of the decision-making
process.

Method: The study was conducted in 1962 in New Rochelle, New York,
and involved 252 families: 169 completed interviews were obtained.
Only two of the incomplete interviews were due to refusal; most were
due to moves away from the area or inability to locate the intended
respondent.

Results
     1.   Most parents who desired to transfer were relative newcomers
to town. More of them had attended racially mixed schools than the
"stayers" (those who wished their children to remain in the segregated
school). Transfer families had more family discussions, more agreement between husband and wife, and more advice seeking than the stayers. More transfer parents also belonged to groups taking an active
role in the desegregation movement.
     2.   Interestingly, most transfers occurred among those of lower
social class and with less education.
     3.   Neighborhood parents defeated a bond issue for construction
of a new school on the location of the old segregated building. In doing
so, they voted against present convenience, the present emotional
security of their children, and a possible increase in real estate values
accruing to them through a new school building. In short, the desire to
promote integration seemed stronger than the comforts of the status quo.
It is likely that increased national publicity concerning desegregation
awakened the discontent of the lower-class Negro and set it in motion.

Lyle, Jack. "The Negro and the News Media." In Jack Lyle, The News in Megalopolis. San Francisco, Calif.: Chandler Publishing Co, 1967, Chapter 9, pp. 163-182.

Purpose: To broaden the relatively limited scope of research on the Negro press. In the past such research has focused on content, circulation patterns, and advertising revenues. This study focuses on reader behaviors--use of newspapers in general and black papers in particular as well as reader attitudes toward these newspapers.

Method: A sample of 165 Los Angeles area Negroes was interviewed by Negro interviewers. The sample was stratified on the basis of income, geographic proximity to the ghetto area, and degree of integration, i.e., concentration of Negroes. Sampling included respondents living in the heart of the ghetto, in higher-income black areas close to the ghetto, in predominantly white higher income neighborhoods close to the ghetto, and in areas roughly 20 miles from the ghetto. The author acknowledged a strong interviewer bias in actual house-hold selection toward better-educated respondents and an over-sampling of women. Respondent use of and attitudes toward four newspapers were measured. The major metropolitan paper was the Los Angeles Times. The three Negro weekly newspapers studied were The California Eagle, The Herald Dispatch, and The Los Angeles Sentinel. Of the three Negro papers, the Sentinel is considered the most professional and politically moderate and is the only one with audited circulation figures. It also carries the most local news.

Results
    Use of the Los Angeles Times and Herald Examiner (the daily metropolitan papers).
    1.   All of the respondents read one daily paper at least occasionally.
    2.   30% subscribed to the Times, and 32% to the Herald. Subscription levels for college-educated respondents were not different from the general sample. The proportion of subscribers did increase as distance from the ghetto increased.

    Attitudes toward treatment of news in the metropolitan dailies.
    1.   A plurality of the respondents gave negative answers to all questions: one-fourth said that Negro churches or organizations had an equal chance of getting stories published in metropolitan papers; one-third said a Negro candidate would get equal treatment; and 13% said that both sides of the issue were always printed when blacks and whites were involved--11% said both sides were never printed.
    2.   83% said these papers did not give enough news on Negroes; 50% said the daily papers were unfair to Negroes.

    Readership of the Negro weeklies. 70% of the respondents regularly read the Sentinel; 10%, the Eagle; 6%, the Herald Dispatch.

    Attitudes toward Negro papers
    1.   Generally, the Negro weeklies were seen as relatively accurate and complete but sensational and biased toward certain persons. (For

90% of the respondents, the Sentinel was the referent for these attitudinal items.)

2.   80% felt the paper usually was accurate and comprehensive;
80% also felt that it frequently tried to make events sound more exciting
than they were.

3.   Education was a significant factor in evaluations of sensationalism. Those with more college objected more to sensationalism
than did those with less college.

4.   Education was also related to perceptions of preferential treatment: the less educated objected more often. This, of course, is
highly related to actual treatment of less educated Negroes in the press.
When asked whether they had ever had their own names in the weekly
Negro press, 74% of the respondents with only an elementary education
said "never" compared to 33% of the college educated respondents.

5.   Respondents were also skeptical about the paper's independence
from advertisers; 60% said they felt the paper would suppress a story
if an advertiser so requested.

6.   Most of the respondents (78%) felt that the papers gave preferential treatment to certain people and that local people hardly ever got
into print in the Negro weeklies.

Reasons for using newspapers
1.   When asked their main sources for various topics, respondents
indicated that the Negro paper was used primarily for civic affairs and
entertainment (named by 11% and 14%, respectively). The Negro paper
was named by less than 2% of the respondents for all other information
areas.

2.   The daily metropolitan newspapers were used much more for
information. Some 51% of respondents used them for national and
international news, 52% for sports, 44% for food shopping, 43% for
household shopping, 42% for entertainment, 40% for civic affairs, and
30% for school information.

3.   The weekly shopper newspaper was used by 36% for grocery
shopping, 23% for household shopping, 19% for clothes shopping, 14%
for school information, and 10% for civic affairs. All other responses
were below 5%.

4.   TV was named as a main source for national and international
news by 18% of the respondents and as a main source for sports by 14%.
All other response categories were under 10%.

Specific reasons for reading the Negro papers. 52% of the respondents read Negro papers for Negro news and 14% for local news. All
other categories had low response frequencies.

Media comparisons
1.   When asked which was more reliable, the daily paper or TV,
78% of the respondents said TV, 12% said the Times, and the rest said
"neither" or "don't care."

2.   When asked which was more trustworthy, the daily paper or
the Negro weekly, 36% said the daily, 25% the weekly, and the rest
said "neither" or "don't care."

3.   When asked which was more important, the daily newspaper
or TV, 56% said TV and 35% said newspaper.

Need for Negro paper. The hypothesis that reliance on the Negro paper drops as respondents become more integrated was tested and supported. Perceived need for the Negro paper was highest in the central ghetto and lowest in the geographic area farthest from the central city: 47% of those in the central ghetto needed the paper very much compared with 42% in the suburbs who found no need for it.

Use of other media
1.   Exposure to TV and radio was high for the respondents. Regular radio news listening was reported by 55% and regular viewing of TV newscasts by 84%.
2.   Most respondents stated that they read some magazine regularly; only 10% said they read none. The median number of magazines read regularly was three. Negro magazines together with general magazines scored highest and were named by 60% of the respondents. In addition, 20% said they read a news magazine, 50% said they read Ebony, and 30% said they read Jet.

News interests and knowledge
1.   Knowledge of local civic officials was comparatively high: 90% named the mayor of Los Angeles and 50% knew the city councilman for their district and the incumbent congressional representative.
2.   There was a strong relationship between frequency of discussion of news topics with others and educational level, particularly on national government, international affairs, business affairs, and crime. Among those with college education, 70% reported frequent discussion on national and international news compared to 20% of those with elementary education.

McCabe, Alice, R. "Re: Forty Forgotten Families." Public Welfare XXIV, 2 (April, 1966), 159-171.

Purpose: To present an in-depth study of the characteristics of mothers receiving Aid to Dependent Children in East Harlem.

Method: Respondents were randomly selected from a list of welfare recipients meeting the following criteria: no father in the home; a mother under 40 years of age as head of the household; two or more children in the home; and the eldest child being a school-aged child under 10 with a record of anti-social tendencies. Twenty-one of the mothers were Negro and 19 were Puerto Rican. In-depth personal interviews were conducted with each mother.

Results
1.   Most of these mothers had dropped out of school before graduating because of work, marriage, or pregnancy. They grew up in broken homes, overwhelmed by loneliness and poverty.
2.   Three basic marital patterns were found: (1) legal marriages with children born within the marriage; (2) no marriage with children

fathered by one to four men; and (3) a combination of both. The 40
mothers in this study had 148 children, ranging in age from 6-10 years.
The Negro mothers had fairly even numbers of boys and girls; the
Puerto Rican families had more boys.

    3. Most of these mothers hoped for a permanent relationship with
a man. However, they exhibited enormous economic and emotional
deprivations which caused them to make poor judgments and brought
a series of unsatisfactory relationships.

    4. These mothers tended to be overprotective, underprotective,
or competitive with their children. Most acknowledged their responsibility for the physical care of their children. But they were rated poor
in developing emotional stability in their children.

    5. The energy level for most of the mothers was judged to be
very low.

    6. The children were very much the product of their environment
and their mothers' childhoods. They were wistful, showed a wide range
of anti-social behaviors, lacked impulse control, exhibited pervasive
anxiety, had unsatisfactory and fragmented inter-personal relationships,
and showed a diminished capacity for learning. They lacked self-
identity and coped with their environment in ways necessary for survival.
Their devotion to the family was based on their perception of the family
as a defense against a hostile world.

McCombs, Maxwell E. "Negro Use of Television and Newspapers for
Political Information, 1952-64." Journal of Broadcasting XII, 3 (Summer, 1968), 261-266.

Purpose: To measure black participation in the most universal means
of participation--the mass media. Several studies have indicated a significant increase in black political participation since the 1954 Supreme
Court school integration decision. Using 1952 (prior to the Supreme
Court decision) as a baseline date, studies show that between 1952 and
1960, black voting turnout rose 21% from 32% turnout to 53%, while
white turnout remained stable at 70%. Indeed, other studies suggest
that despite the demographic characteristics that place blacks as primarily lower in status, their participation is often higher than would
be expected. For example, 45% of blacks with grade school education
or better belong to one or more organizations in comparison with 30%
of whites and 12% of blacks with incomes under $4,000 belong to a
political organization in comparison with 2% whites.

Method: University of Michigan survey research data from the Presi-
dential elections of 1952, 1960, and 1964 were used. In each survey,
about 10% of the respondents were Negro. Two questions from each
survey were utilized--amount of newspaper use and amount of TV use.
Respondents were dichotomized on each variable and four typologies
were developed: (1) high media users (high on TV, high on newspaper);
(2) low media users (low on both); (3) TV specialists (high on TV, low
on newspaper); and (4) newspaper specialists (high on newspaper, low
on TV).

Results
   1.   In 1952, the majority of Negroes (63%) were low media users.
By 1964, only 41% were low media users, a decrease of 22%. In the
same time period, whites increased 12% in the low media use category.
   2.   Blacks had increased 10% in the high media use category between 1952 and 1964 (9% to 19%). During the same period whites did
not increase in this media use category, remaining at 23%. In addition,
blacks increased from 17% to 27% in the TV specialist category, while
whites decreased from 30% to 18%.
   3.   The pattern outlined above remained when educational level was
held constant. The pattern showed up even stronger at the low educational level. Controlling for age and sex, the trends still appeared
strong and were even more pronounced for those 40 years of age and
older.

McCord, William, and Howard, John. "Negro Opinions in Three Riot
Cities." The American Behavioral Scientist II, 4 (March, 1968), 24-27.

Purpose: To examine similarities and differences in the opinions of
blacks in Houston, Oakland, and Watts on such items as jobs, police,
schools, and violence.

Method: Formal interviews were held with 572 randomly selected
Houston blacks before the violence of 1967. Similar interviews were
conducted with 187 Oakland blacks immediately after the violence in
that city. In Watts, so-called "Natural dialogues" were held with 426
randomly selected blacks in 1967. Only black interviewers were used.

Results: A great deal of variation in attitudes was found from city to
city. Some of the more striking of these were:
   1.   In Houston and Oakland, jobs were considered the main problem for blacks. In Watts, the police were the principal difficulty.
   2.   Both Oakland and Watts respondents were strongly against the
low quality of their schools.
   3.   When asked if violence helped or hurt the black cause, more
people in post-riot Oakland believed it would help than in pre-riot
Houston.
   4.   Watts' Negroes were the most inclined to use violence as a
means of achieving their ends.

McIssac, Hugh, and Wilkinson, Harold. "Clients Talk About Their
Caseworkers." Public Welfare XXIII, 3 (July, 1965), 147-154.

Purpose: To learn through interviews what welfare recipients thought
about the attitudes and activities of caseworkers.

Method: Forty Los Angeles recipients of funds from the Aid to Families of Dependent Children program were interviewed. These included 36 women and four men: 19 were black; 18, white; 2, Mexican-American; and 1, American Indian. These families had a history of 2-13 caseworkers. Results were described qualitatively rather than quantitatively.

Results
    1.   The majority of the recipients had only vague ideas about the purpose of caseworker visits. Many of the respondents who could give some reasons for caseworker visits gave no indication they saw part of the caseworker's task as rehabilitative. The usual response was that the caseworker came to check on whether families still were eligible for welfare. Beyond this, recipients expected little of the caseworkers.
    2.   Despite this lack of clarity on the caseworker's role, most clients responded to social workers who took a personal interest in their welfare. Recipients seemed particularly responsive to nonverbal cues indicating caseworkers' attitudes.
    3.   Reactions to caseworkers were most often extreme. Either the caseworker was seen as a supporter in the recipient's life or the worker was feared and hated and the bi-monthly casework visits negatively affected the recipient's total life functioning.

McLeod, Jack; Ward, Scott; and Tancill, Karen. "Alienation and Uses of Mass Media." Public Opinion Quarterly XXIX, (Winter, 1965-66), 583-594.

Purpose: To examine two principal hypotheses:
    1.   The alienated person should spend more time using the mass media to compensate for a lack of satisfaction with more personal communication. This should be particularly true for the more fantasy oriented electronic media.
    2.   Within a given medium, the alienated person should select content that agrees with his image of a hostile and unpredictable world. That is, he should prefer news about accidents, violence, and disruption over news about government and institutions.

Method: Personal interviews were conducted with a random sample of 180 adults selected from Madison, Wisconsin census tracts. The Ss level of alienation was computed by summing across 13 items taken from various psychological tests of alienation of the Likert type.

Results
    1.   No support was found for the hypothesis that alienation would be positively correlated with mass media exposure time. The best predictor of consumption was education.
    2.   No basic support was found for the second hypothesis. However, alienation was significantly associated with lower interest in non-sensational news.

Middleton, Russell. "Alienation, Race, and Education." The American Sociological Review XXVIII, (December, 1963), 973-977.

Purpose: To determine the interrelationships between various types of alienation and the relationship of alienation types to disabling social conditions.

Method: Alienation was broken down into six major types as identified by consensual agreement of 14 sociology graduate students. The types of alienation and the statements that measured them were: (1) power-lessness: there is little that one man can do about most of the important problems that we face today; (2) meaninglessness: there is no way for the average man to really understand the events that take place in the world; (3) normlessness: in order to get ahead, you are almost forced to do some things that are not right; (4) cultural estrangement or isola-tion: indexed by little interest in mass media; (5) social estrangement: indexed by items on loneliness; and (6) work estrangement: indexed by items tapping whether the respondent dislikes his job but keeps it in order to buy things he needs. A sample was drawn randomly from a list of all residents in a Central Florida town of 18,000 in the summer, 1962. From this original list, 256 completed interviews resulted. The number of blacks in this sample was too low so 50 additional black cases were added by sampling from a list of all Negro adults in the com-munity. Final sample count was 207 whites and 99 blacks. Generaliza-tions to the overall community were based on the original sample of 256 but black-white comparisons are based on the augmented sample. The relationship of alienation to social conditions was tapped by relating alienation types to race and education levels.

Results

Relationship between the types of alienation
1.   Estrangement from work most highly correlated with other types, suggesting it may be a useful index of estrangement generally.
2.   If cultural estrangement is excluded, the remaining five types of alienation all intercorrelate above .45 and form a Guttman scale with a reproducibility coefficient of .90.

Relationship of alienation types to race and education
1.   For all types of alienation except cultural estrangement, blacks were more likely to be alienated than whites. The difference was greatest for work estrangement. These alienation results agree with demographic records indicating that 72% of the blacks but only 14% of the whites in this community hold semi-or unskilled jobs.
2.   Some respondents (6% of the blacks and 28% of the whites) in-dicated alienation on only one scale; some showed alienation on all six (28% of the blacks and 1% of the whites).
3.   When race is considered in terms of education levels (less than 12 years versus 12 years or more), results show that increased education depresses degree of alienation for both whites and blacks, although the effect of education is stronger for whites.

Miller, S. M. "The American Lower Class: A Typological Approach."
Social Research, XXXI, 1 (Spring, 1964), 1-22.

Purpose: The article is not a formal research study but rather a
proposal. The author suggests that the difficulty in solving problems
of the poor stems from the fact that the lower classes exhibit a poverty
syndrome, a combination of causes that must be recognized in order to
provide effective aid. It is often assumed that the poor are homogeneous
in their characteristics. Some classifications of the poor emphasize
social and psychological problems; others emphasize economic deprivation; some class the poor skilled and semi-skilled regular worker
with the poor unskilled irregular worker. The author suggests the use
of a typological approach to begin to tap the variability within the poor.

Results: Miller recognizes two criteria for classifying the lower classes:
economic security and familial stability. The former taps the economic
deprivation aspect of poverty; the latter taps the social and psychological
aspect of poverty. If each aspect were cross-tabled against the other,
the minimum typology produced would be:

FAMILIAL

		Stable	Instable
ECONOMIC	Stable	Stable Poor	Strained
	Instable	Copers	Unstable

This approach suggests four types:
   1.   The stable poor. Regularly employed, low skill, stable, poor
families. In this category, the majority would be white, rural, and
southern. Many aged poor would be included. Negro families with higher social status in their communities would be here. Children of these
families would be most likely to be educationally and occupationally
mobile.
   2.   The strained. Families that show regular employment but
unstable family patterns.
   3.   The copers. Here may be found a large number of Negroes,
those hardest hit by extensive layoffs and changing employment conditions.
   4.   The unstable. This typology would represent unskilled irregular
workers, those in broken and large families, the aged, the physically
handicapped, and the mentally disturbed.

   The author suggests that action programs be adapted for the different
poverty types. He sees three basic strategies: (1) direct economic
change, e.g., minimum guaranteed income, steadier employment;
(2) direct services, e.g., casework, homemaker aids; and (3) indirect
change of neighborhoods, whether political, psychological, or social.

Minuchin, Salvador, et al. Families of the Slums: An Exploration of
Their Structure and Treatment. New York: Basic Books, 1967.

Purpose: To study in an exploratory fashion the structure and characteristics of disorganized, low-income families that had each produced
more than one delinquent child in an attempt to develop by experimen-
tation new therapeutic procedures to resolve problems in such families.
The authors, acknowledging the high failure rate of traditional therapy
aimed at the individual delinquent child, saw that the pathology of the
entire immediate family needed treatment in order for any given member
of it to be effectively helped. The authors' prime concern was fighting
the stereotyped, dysfunctional characteristics of the deprived, ghetto
delinquent, which are manifested in the following kinds of behaviors:
(1) a diffuseness of experience--participation in a situation without
sharply experiencing one's own participation; (2) peaks of reaction to
stimuli followed by a rapid loss of interest in or effect from the stimuli;
(3) the inability to recapture and explore an event or experience when
asked to do so; and (4) sullen, projective responses to inquiries by
counselors.

Method: Experiments were done in conjunction with Wiltwyck, a
private treatment center for deprived, delinquent children. Twelve
"delinquent-producing" families were selected for an experimental
group on the basis of having more than one troublesome child in the
family. Delinquents were designated as children so judged by the court,
children who had been institutionalized, and children who had been tru-
ant to an extensive degree. Wiltwyck children were between 8 and 12
years of age and were often the youngest delinquent members of their
families. Ten "no-delinquent" control families were selected to closely
match the ethnic background, occupation, family size, education, income, and family composition of the experimental group.
     The authors were impressed by the lack of a stable father figure
in the families of delinquent children. Even when the father was present, the task of raising the children was often relegated to the mother.
Unfortunately, the mothers seemed to see themselves as powerless and
overwhelmed by their children's demands. Guidance was lacking--the
parents relinquished their executive role, forcing the child to look to
his siblings for guidance. As a result, children often became socialized
by a "gang" value system. Consequently, therapy was planned in the
following stages: (1) restoration of executive functioning of the family;
(2) increase the communicative effectiveness between parent and child;
and (3) modify the sibling's value system and functions. Therapy sessions lasted about 1-1/2 hours and involved both the delinquent child
and his family, sometimes in joint sessions and sometimes in individual
sessions.

Results
     Communication characteristics of the delinquent's family. Communi-
cation patterns in impoverished homes often cause severe developmental
delay or other serious difficulties in the children concerned. Disadvantaged children are particularly handicapped in school performance because of their atypical language, verbal, and perceptual skills. Motor,

physical, perhaps aggressive methods rather than verbal channels are used to relate to others. Deficiencies in introspective, empathic skills as well as memory difficulties, poor time orientation, and lack of reward expectancy also interfere with school success. There is also evidence of diminished auditory skills in such children as compared with middle-class peers.

The deprived child is lacking in good powers of self-observation since the environmental consistency that this process requires is denied to him. Self-esteem is stunted because the child's competence in controlling and mastering his world prove to be highly limited. The impoverished family shows defects in knowledge of the implicit rules that regulate the flow of communication. In overcrowded conditions, parents pay little attention to the requests of individual children and the children, in turn, accept the fact that they will not be heard. Conflict among siblings is resolved by a series of escalating threats and counterthreats. The result is a style of communication where people assert themselves by yelling; a style where loudness is more important than message content. Conflicts do not have closure; there is a restricted range of emotional expression, an inability to focus on a specific subject matter sufficiently to carry it to conclusion, and a lack of training in the elaboration of questions to gather information. In the poverty situation, the child is trained to pay attention to the person with whom he is dealing rather than the content of the message received. Constant defining of relationships between members of the family outweighs the comprehension of the message content.

In view of the above background, communication in the sampled "delinquent families" may be summarized as follows:

1.   Listening. Subjects did not expect to be heard; if heard, they did not expect a response. If a response was uttered, it was not necessarily along the lines of the preceding communication. Any irrelevant response was likely to be accepted.

2.   Development of themes. A topic rarely was carried to any conclusion: a small number of interactions on one topic generally were discontinued by the unrelated intervention of another family member who started a new topic.

3.   Noise. Intensity of sound frequently displaced the topic of discussion and was frequently accompanied by such behavior as disruption, movement, or the throwing of objects. Members of the family not involved frequently withdrew, answering questions only by monosyllables or "I don't know."

4.   Pathways. The mother was the central pathway for transactions among family members. Her functions ranged from being the target for anger to regulating the flow of transactions. Many of the children's disruptions seemed aimed at activating the mother's role as controller. Spouses rarely talked to each other and the children's sustained talk was mostly with the mother.

5.   Content. Discussion themes centered on aspects of a dangerous, violent, anti-social world. Addiction, crime, and the unfairness of police constituted prime topics. Among the children, discussion of power predominated in an attempt to rate each other's relative power. The mother's messages to the children were mostly restrictive "don'ts".

Thus, the irrelevance of content in negotiating and clarifying inter-
personal positions was of major importance in freezing family roles
into an unchangeable structure. This inability to develop sufficient rules
for adequate inter-personal transactions was perhaps the principal characteristic distinguishing the experimental from the control families.

Experimental Results. Families were measured along three principal
dimensions: communication, "executive behavior," and affective
relations.

Pre-treatment comparison of experimental and control families

1.   Communication.   Compared with controls, experimental
families were at extremes. Experimental families were either very
talkative or very silent. Children addressed mothers frequently or
ignored them. A positive relationship was found between the talkative-
ness of the mother and the frequency with which she was addressed.
Experimental families communicated with greater difficulty: they mis-
understood, misinterpreted, confused issues, and denied each other's
communications. Experimental parents seemed more egocentric in
expressing their attitudes to their children. Similarly, experimental
children were less able to express their attitudes in an objective fashion.

2.   Executive behavior.   Experimental mothers were more extreme
in their use of behavior control. However, more control parents appeared to be effective leaders in family discussion and they were more likely
to exert behavior control in family disputes. The control parents offered
more concrete rules and examples of acceptable or unacceptable behavior, perhaps providing a better learning experience than the experimental parents. Further, control parents were more likely to use
nonphysical means to enforce their executive function; the experimental
parents were more liable to use force. Control children's requests for
leadership, control, and guidance were responded to with greater frequency by parents. Finally, control children supported their mothers'
executive behavior in proportion to the level of such behavior manifested
by the mother.

3.   Affective relations.   In the experimental group, themes of
aggression were prominent in discussions of family disputes and in
attitudes toward siblings. In contrast, control children focused more
on their siblings' cooperativeness or competitiveness.

Changes in experimental Ss as a result of therapy

1.   Communications.   No changes were observed in the formal
variables, e.g., quantity of verbalization of mother and extent she was
addressed. Some families had improved insight into the nature of their
family conflicts and were better able to verbally express their attitudes
about other family members. The objectivity of parents' responses to
questions or requests for control as well as the children's responses
remained relatively unchanged.

2.   Executive behavior.   Mothers spent less time in leadership
activity, but appeared to be more effective. Results suggest that experimental parents played a greater part in behavior control and guidance
than they had previously. Parents appeared to be more responsive to
their children's requests for leadership and guidance and the children
showed more support for their parents' executive guidance. Unfortunately,
parents still relied heavily on physical punishment.

3. Affective relations. There were fewer fights and fewer themes
of agression in discussion of family fights and attitudes toward siblings.
However, few families were able to conceive integrative family activities
other than eating.

Moles, Oliver C. "Child Training Practices Among Low Income
Families--An Empirical Study." Welfare in Review III, 12 (December,
1965), 1-19.

Purpose: To determine whether there is any significant difference in
the ways welfare recipients report rearing their children. Earlier
studies have indicated that very poor parents become resigned to a loss
of control over their children at an early age. In this study, comparisons
were made between public assistance recipients, usually the poorest of
the poor, and low-income nonrecipients regarding their child training
practices.

Method: The basic data were collected in 1963 from 800 families with
children in 12 inner city schools in Detroit, Michigan. The children
were selected at random from the upper fifth and sixth grades of each
school and 87% were 11 or 12 years of age. Child training questions
were largely asked in interviews with the mothers of low-income
families but there were also some questionnaires filled out by the sample
children. Of the 800 families studied, 422 had received public assistance
in the previous three years. They were divided into low and high recipient groups. The 208 low recipients had 1-29 months of assistance and
the 214 high recipients had 30-36 months of assistance. There were
378 who had not received any local public assistance in this three-year
period.
    All families in the three sample groups reported incomes of less
than $6,000 for 1962. (4.5% of welfare recipients and 34.2% non-
recipients were deleted from the original sample of 1,021 families to
meet this income criterion.) The independent variable of prime interest
was the receipt of welfare assistance. In some cases, income and
"father presence" were controlled.

Results: Differences in child training practices between the high recipients and the nonrecipients did not occur as often as the researchers
expected. Only 28% of the questions showed meaningful differences
(significant at the .05 level) between these types.
    A great number of questions revealed no meaningful differences
between the studied types. The parents' education, the mother's help
with the school work, and reading stories to the children were about
equal. Likewise, husband-wife disagreements over child punishment,
the relative power of husbands and wives in deciding how much schooling
their children should have, the relative frequency of the husband or wife
disciplining the child, and the husband's relationship to the children
regarding free time spent with them showed no substantial difference
between nonrecipients and low and high recipients.

Mugge, Robert H. "Aid to Families with Dependent Children: Initial Findings of The 1961 Report on the Characteristics of the Recipients." Social Security Bulletin XXVI (March, 1963), 3-15.

Purpose: To determine the characteristics of those receiving welfare and the conditions that brought about their dependency. Characteristics examined included nature of residence, occupation of parents, education, health problems, and length of time on aid.

Method: In 1961, the Bureau of Family Services conducted a national survey. The states were required to complete schedules on a probability sample of 500 cases in November-December 1961.

Results
    1. Individuals receiving aid. 54% were white, 44% were Negro, 2% were Indian or other nonwhites.
    2. Conditions bringing on dependency. Two-fifths received aid because of broken homes, one-fifth due to disability of father, and one-fifth due to children born out of wedlock. The most frequent applicant was a mother with two children.
    3. Residence. Most lived in a "housing unit," a room or rooms intended for single occupancy. More than half lived in overcrowded conditions. Some 70% rented; 22% owned or were buying a home.
    4. Duration of assistance. The median time for receiving aid was 2.1 years for the most recent continuous period. Two-thirds had never received aid prior to this time; 20% had been on the rolls once before; 7% twice before; and 5%, three or more times.
    5. Occupation of parents. Of the fathers, 3% were white-collar workers compared with a national average of 35%. Only 7% held good industrial jobs compared with the national average of 20%. More than a third were unskilled compared to 7% for the nation. The mothers' occupations were concentrated heavily in areas requiring minimal training with high turnover and minimal job security. Only 14% of mothers worked.
    6. Education. Most were school drop-outs. The average unemployed father had attained eighth grade.
    7. Health. Of those receiving aid, 9% had dental problems, 6% had visual defects, 3% had emotional or nervous disorders, 3% were retarded, and 4% had orthopedic difficulties.

Muir, Conal E., and Weinstein, E. A. "The Social Debt: An Investigation of Lower Class and Middle Class Norms of Social Obligation." American Sociological Review XXVII, 4 (1962), 532-539.

Purpose: To compare attitudes of lower- and middle-class women toward social obligations.

Method: Intensive interviews in which subjects were asked to report their behavior and attitudes concerning favors and social obligations

as well as situational interviews in which respondents were asked to
predict the behavior of characters in a series of typical situations involving favors and social obligations. The sample consisted of 120
white adult female residents of Louisville, Kentucky, of whom 60 were
classified in the lower socio-economic class and 60 in the upper-middle
socio-economic class as defined by census tracts.

Results
1.   Higher-class Ss more actively exchanged favors with acquaintances, and lower-class Ss exchanged more favors within the family.
2.   Ss from both groups liked to do favors for others but only 8.9%
of all Ss liked being obligated to others. All Ss felt obligations should
be voluntarily repaid where possible and disapproved of debtors who
did not repay.
3.   Despite disapproval, lower-class Ss were unlikely to cut off
social credit but higher-class Ss were more likely to do so.
4.   Higher-class Ss were likely to feel especially willing to do
favors "in return." Most lower-class Ss reported that "this made no
difference."

National Advisory Commission on Civil Disorders. Report of the National Advisory Commission on Civil Disorders New York: Bantam
Books, 1968.

Purpose: To find the conditions and causes of the violent urban riots
that occurred in major U.S. cities in the summer of 1967. The emphasis of this abstract will be upon: (1) the patterns of disorder; (2)
basic riot causes; (3) the formation of racial ghettos; (4) unemployment, family structure, social disorganization, and other conditions
of life in the ghetto; and (5) the relation of the news media to the disorders. The reader should note that the report covered other areas
which are substantially omitted from this abstract.

Method: The members of the riot committee drew heavily on existing
research, interviewed many experts on riots, urban slums, and racial
strife, and visited the troubled cities themselves. Other data came
from records of FBI officials, various prosecutors, courts, police departments, and other witnesses. Some surveys of riot participants,
i.e., police, fire departments, residents, were conducted.

Results
Basic riot causes. These may be enumerated under the following
classifications which do not presume to include the many minor variations or account for many of the complexities of the riot but are
acknowledged to be relatively clear, fundamental causes.
1.   Pervasive discrimination and segregation. These conditions
exclude blacks from the benefits of economic progress and have a
corrosive and degrading effect on the Negroes' morale. The result is
a deep bitterness which is at the core of racial disorder.

2.   Black migration and white exodus.   The rapid influx of the
southern black to northern cities is matched by an exodus of middle-
class whites to suburbia.   The result is an increased burden on the
already overworked resources of the city, creating a crisis of deterior-
ating facilities, services, and unmet human needs.

3.   The black ghetto.   Poverty and segregation intersect in the
ghetto to destroy opportunity and hope and enforce failure.

4.   Frustrated hopes.   The hopes aroused by civil rights legislation and desegregation movements have led to frustration, hostility,
and cynicism in the face of the gap between promise and fulfillment.

5.   Legitimization of violence.   White terrorism in the south,
police brutality in the north, and legal evasion of integration by authorities all over the country have reduced the effectiveness of and respect
for authority.   Community standards and restraints on violence have
slipped.

6.   Powerlessness.   Many blacks have come to believe that they
are exploited politically and economically by the white power structure.
Their seeming inability to escape the confines of the ghetto has fostered
the impression that violence is the only practical expression of movement and redress.

7.   Incitement and encouragement of violence.   The preachings of
black militants echoed and disseminated by the mass media could have
encouraged violence by heightening tensions, legitimizing, and creating
an expectation of violence.

8.   The police.   Invariably, events triggering the riots were routine
arrests of blacks by white police.   Called upon to maintain order in
the combustible atmosphere of the ghetto, the police have come to
symbolize white authority, racism, and repression.

Formation of racial ghettos.   In 1910, 2.6 million blacks lived in
cities--27% of the black population at that time.   Today, 15 million or
67% of the black population lives in cities.   About half of the black
population lives in cities of the north or west.   These population shifts
result from three prime causes: (1) a rapid increase in black population;
(2) a continuous flow of blacks from the rural south to cities primarily
in the north and west; and (3) an increasing concentration of these metropolitan blacks within racially segregated neighborhoods, accompanied
by an exodus of whites to suburbia.

Unemployment, family structure, and social disorganization.   There
are between 2 and 2.5 million disadvantaged blacks living in urban U.S.
ghettos.   Although this group comprises only about 1% of the U.S. population, it represents about 16 to 20% of the black population of all central
U.S. cities and a much higher proportion in certain cities.   The ability
to secure and hold a good job is the traditional test of participation in
American society.   Steady employment at constructive work yields both
purchasing power and social status, developing capabilities, confidence
and self-esteem needed to be a responsible citizen and provide a stable
family life.   Unfortunately, the urban Negro poor have become increasingly immersed in a poverty cycle of social, economic, and psychological disadvantages that are passed on in the environment from generation
to generation.   Despite recent declines in black unemployment, black

joblessness is still double the rate for whites in every category, including married men. Of more importance is the often menial and degrading
nature of work relegated to the employed black, involving substandard
wages, low status, instability and uncertainty of tenure, little chance
for advancement, and often exhausting duties. The Negro man particularly is affected by this employment stigma, causing him to lose self-
respect and often flee from his responsibilities to his family. Families
with female heads are much more common among blacks at all income
levels than among whites. Furthermore, the number of fatherless
black families is on the rise, imposing severe handicaps on the children
involved.

The news media and the disorders
1.   Despite incidents of sensationalism, inaccuracy, and distortion,
the mass media generally made a sincere effort to give a balanced,
factual account.
2.   Despite this effort, the portrayal of violence failed to reflect
accurately its scale and character. In short, the events were exaggerated, as was the mood, with too much time afforded emotional events
and militant leaders.
3.   Most importantly, the media generally have failed to report
adequately on the causes and consequences of civil disorders and the
underlying problems of race relations.

The members of the commission addressed much attention to the
question of exaggeration of riot conditions by the media. Their initial
impression upon reviewing the evidence caused them to condemn the
press for exaggeration. However, in order to test their suspicions
they ordered that a systematic analysis be made of the media for the
time of the riots. The analysis did not confirm the commission's
suspicions; the majority of TV sequences examined were relatively
"calm" or "normal" in their presentations. Only a small proportion
showed mob action or looting. Moderate leaders appeared with greater
frequency than militants in newscasts. Newspapers focused more on
legislation and other measures that would prevent future riots than on
any other topic. However, the commission found instances where violence was staged for news cameras and where unreliable sources were
used to obtain information about the scale of the disorders, e.g.,
injuries and property damage. The local officials who were often asked
for such information were frequently inexperienced in making such
estimates and consequently were not always able to sort the truth from
rumor.
Coverage of the events on TV tended to define events as black-
white confrontations, losing sight of the fact that most rioting occurred
in all-black areas. People became sensitized to riots, making it
possible for relatively minor events to precipitate strong emotional reactions in media consumers. In summation, the commission's main
complaint against the media was that coverage was not as representative
as it could have been.
A second prime complaint was that the media generally have failed
to analyze and adequately report on U.S. racial problems or to meet
the Negroe's legitimate expectations in journalism. In general, the

media have failed to communicate to both black and white Americans a sense of the problems the country faces and the sources of potential solutions.

The media cannot be singled out as the cause of riots, although they very undoubtedly had some effect. No doubt, TV coverage lowered the violent inhibitions of some or awakened their sense of excitement. It is likely that the reaction of Detroit authorities to riots was in some respects shaped by earlier events in Newark publicized by the media.

The reactions of blacks to media riot coverage was of great interest to the commission. Basically, the ghetto black distrusts the media, particularly the press, frequently viewing the media as instruments of the white power structure which rely on police for information during disorders and disregard instances of blacks trying to maintain order, police brutality, and false arrests. A prime recommendation was that more blacks be involved in the news media, so that the media become representative of minorities as well as the white majority society.

O'Shea, Robert M., and Gray, Shirlene B. "Income and Community Participation." Welfare in Review IV, 4 (April, 1966), 10-13.

Purpose: To study the relationship between degree of community participation and income.

Method: The National Opinion Research Center interviewed 1,520 U.S. adults in October, 1965, for a study sponsored by the U.S. Public Health Service's Division of Dental Health. Among the questions, which were primarily concerned with dental health, were items relevant to community participation and income. Variables measured included: (1) self-perceived leadership, indexed by respondent indications that he was a leader in the community, active but not a leader, an ordinary citizen, or alienated from the community; and (2) kind of participation in community, e.g., gave money or time, collected money for charity, called friends on an issue or candidate, signed petitions, or wrote letters to officeholder or newspapers.

Results
    The relationship of income to self-perceived leadership
    1.   Income made no difference in proportion of respondents seeing themselves either as leaders or alienated.
    2.   However, income was related to proportion of respondents seeing themselves as active non-leaders or merely ordinary citizens. The proportion of active non-leaders rose with income, while the proportion of ordinary citizens dropped with income.
    3.   In the overall sample, 4% identified themselves as leaders, 19% as active non-leaders, 71% as ordinary citizens, and 5% as alienated.

    The relationship of income to kinds of community participation
    1.   The proportion of respondents indicating they had done each type of community participation activity rose with income: 38% of

those with incomes under $3,000 had collected money for charity compared with 75% of those with incomes over $10,000. Percentages for the extreme income groups on the other activities were: contributing time and money, 38%, low-income, 66% high-income; writing letters, 8% low-income, 30% high-income; making calls, 16% low-income, 38% high-income; signing petitions, 31% low-income, 67% high-income.

2. An analysis was made of the effect of education on participation in these activities for the two lowest income groups -- those with incomes under $3,000 and those with incomes between $3,000 and $4,999. Results showed that as education rose within income groups, participation in these activities rose.

Rainwater, Lee; Coleman, Richard P.; and Handel, Gerald. Working-man's Wife. New York: Oceana Publications, 1959.

Chapter 1. The authors define the blue-collar worker as one who usually has had no more than a modest education (high school or less) and lives in modest housing in neighborhoods occupied by other blue-collar workers. Although a wage earner, his lot has changed drastically since 1941. He has participated dramatically in the economic and social changes in the country, yet little is known about him. This class has had a concentration of delinquency and mental illness. The main purpose of the study then, was to better understand this class, which makes up from 60-65% of the urban families in the country. The study concentrates particularly on the young working-class housewife.

Interviews were conducted with 480 working-class housewives, 120 each from Chicago, Louisville, Tacoma, Washington, and Trenton, New Jersey. In addition, 120 middle-class housewives and mothers were used for comparison purposes; 30 were interviewed in each city. These women were located by using census data to identify middle-to upper-middle-class neighborhoods from which 15 older residential blocks and 15 newer blocks were selected. One woman was interviewed on each block. Respondents in both samples were between the ages of 20 and 44. Qualitative interviews and data involving objective, projective, and directive techniques including TAT and Draw-A-Person tests were employed. An analysis of personality, social world, and consumption behavior was made.

Results
Chapter 2. The daily life of the working-class housewife is traced. Her life is found to be centered on three tasks: homemaking, child rearing, and catering to her husband. The other main activities in her day are TV viewing and visits to neighbors. The middle-class housewife refused to describe a typical day but reportedly she is not as restricted to the three activities in the working-class housewife's daily routine.

Chapter 3. A brief sketch of the concept of personality is given, followed by a discussion of the personality of the working-class housewife. Conclusions are made on the basis of central tendency. The

working-class housewife considers the world chaotic and dangerous
and feels she has no control over it. She fears loneliness, and basic
human events such as illness, births, and deaths concern her. The
working-class housewife's basic aims are to search for a stable
world and happiness in her life. Her resources are wishfulness, forti-
tude, practicality, determination, and realism; obstacles to realizing
her aims are negative thinking, psychological passiveness, lack of ex-
perimentation with new life styles, absence of faith in personal efficiency,
and acceptance of circumstances as givens. She also was found to be
emotionally unorganized and very concerned with morals and doing the
"right thing."

Chapter 4. The wife's view of herself, her husband, and children
is described. The husband plays a central role and the working-class
housewife's relationship with him seems to be of vital importance to
her emotional well-being. She is shy, acquiescent, retreating, and
admiring to him. She perceives marriage as meaning that she is a full
member of a wider society, mature and worthwhile as a person. She
sees her husband as dominant and controlling but he is her best antidote
to loneliness. She feels that if problems exist, she must either put up
with them or leave but changing the husband is not one alternative she
considers. Roles of husband and wife are isolated and demarcated;
separateness and not sharing is the rule.

Chapter 5. The working-class housewife's role as a mother is
described. Generally, she believes that having children proves to herself, and hopefully to others, her own worth. She wants her children
to grow up happy and good and especially wants to be needed and loved
by them. In contrast, the middle-class housewife wants her children
to be adjusted and successful. The working-class wife considers school
as a necessary evil and minimally relevant to later life. She sees
nothing wrong with her children growing up and remaining in the same
economic class. She wants reciprocated love; the middle-class wife
wants reflected glory.

Chapter 6. This chapter discusses the working-class wife's relations with people outside the immediate family. Relatives are of extreme
importance and non-relatives of little importance. The working-class
wife is a clannish, family-type person but this is by default. Outside
the family, the working-class housewife feels friendless and lonely. If
she does make friends with nonrelatives, they will be as similar as
possible to herself.

Chapter 7. In describing the working-class wife's relation to organizations (clubs) and churches, the authors note that she is not a club
woman and although she is deeply religious, she is not a church-goer.
She considers church (organized religion) like any other organization
she disfavors. She claims no time for it and considers people who go
to be snobbish and hypocritical.

Chapter 8. This chapter considers the working-class wife's reading of True Story and other romance magazines. Two-thirds of the
working-class wives who read any magazine read one of the romance
magazines; 80% of the readers of True Story are housewives; 75% of
housewives reading True Story are working class. In a 1955 study involving 300 interviews, 150 with True Story readers and 150 with non-
readers, i.e., middle-class women, the following conclusions were
reached:

1. Non-readers say the magazine is all sex and unrealistic;
readers say it deals with topics of human interest and importance and
that it is very realistic.

2. The magazine mirrors the working-class wife's conflicts and
standards. It reassures and accepts them, helps and encourages them,
reduces isolation and loneliness, reduces tension through fantasy, helps
organize life, and provides guidance and information about day-to-day
problems.

3. Advertising is well attended to: 61% of the readers remembered
brand names; 14% remembered products but not brands; and 25% remembered neither. The advertising appears to be appropriate for the working-class wife.

Chapter 9. The working-class wife's purchases and finances are
analyzed. The working-class wife was found to be discontented with
her financial status but her discontent is more absolute than the middle-
class discontent which is relative to other middle-class people. The
working-class wife sees no change in financial status in her future.
She has major financial control and makes most of the purchases for
her family. She uses a "tin can" accounting system and does not like
time payments or interest, nor does she understand them. She lacks
confidence in buying skills and distrusts the business community. She
likes door-to-door salesladies. Store fliers motivate her to buy more
often than other forms of advertisements.

Chapter 10. The working-class housewife's consumer priorities
and preferences are dealt with in this chapter. She wants, above all
else, an up-to-date house with a modern kitchen, whereas the middle-
class wife seeks aesthetic objects and luxuries. The working class wife
seeks comfort, utility, modernness and inexpensiveness. TV is important
for the working-class housewife; 94% of the working class homes have
TV, and 50% have automatic washers.

Chapter 11. What tastes and styles do the working-class housewife
prefer? Taste does not matter as much to the working-class wife as
it does to the middle-class housewife. Taste conforms to what the
working-class wife can afford and her self-conception as a plain and
simple person. Preferences do not seem related to any general pattern
of likes and dislikes aside from the wish for the current and modern.
Plain, simple and all-American is the rule for food and dress purchases.
New but ordinary is the working-class wife's general rule.

Chapter 12. How does one reach the working-class wife through
advertising? Appeals are often made in a glorified atmosphere as opposed
to a factual, practical presentation of a product. If advertisers can make
their products fit in with the working-class wife's more serious strivings
for common status, yet prove stimulating and gratifying emotionally, the
appeal should be strong.

Ransford, H. Edward. "Isolation, Powerlessness, and Violence: A
Study of Attitudes and Participation in the Watts Riot." American
Journal of Sociology LXXIII, 5 (March, 1968), 581-591.

Purpose: To test the hypothesis that isolated individuals are more prone
to extremism, that is, violence.

Method: A random sample of 312 black males between the ages of 18
and 65 was drawn after the Watts riot. All respondents were heads of
households in one of three areas in Los Angeles: (1) the integrated
middle-income Crenshaw district; (2) the segregated low-income Watts
district; and (3) the segregated low-income South Central district. Independent variables measured included: (1) isolation, a measure of the
amount of social contact respondents had with whites; (2) powerlessness,
measured by 12 forced-choice attitude items; and (3) dissatisfaction
with treatment as a Negro, measured by five items. The dependent
measure was willingness to use violence, e.g., "Would you be willing
to use violence to obtain Negro rights?"

Results: The table illustrates the results of pitting the criterion variable against the three predictor variables:

	Isolation		Powerlessness		Dissatisfaction	
	High	Low	High	Low	High	Low
NOT WILLING TO USE VIOLENCE	83%	17%	16%	84%	17%	83%
WILLING TO USE VIOLENCE	66%	44%	41%	69%	48%	52%

As predicted, respondents high in social contact, low in powerlessness, and low in dissatisfaction were significantly less willing to use
violence. Additional results indicated that these results were upheld
even with controls for high versus low income and segregated versus
non-segregated neighborhoods. Education level tended to wash out the
relationship between willingness to use violence and powerlessness and
dissatisfaction. Education did not affect the relationship of willingness
to use violence and isolation.

Riesman, Frank, "Low Income Culture: The Strengths of the Poor."
Journal of Marriage and Family XXVI, 4 (November, 1964), 417-421.

Purpose: To increase awareness of the strengths of the poor, which
hopefully will aid in the understanding of their motivations and consequently aid in dealing with them.

Method: This is not a study but a compilation of insights from prior research and action programs.

Results
    1.   Minority groups maintain ethnic traditions that the more affluent lose in an effort to become Americanized.
    2.   Many of the strengths arise from weaknesses: individuality from lack of formal training; closeness between siblings from lack of closeness with parents; and independence and self-education from lack of formal supervision.
    3.   Most keep a conservative attitude, cooperativeness, a sense of humor, and a democratic attitude toward life.

    The author suggests that the teachers and the schools should strive to understand the culture of the poor and develop ways of working with the poor in conjunction with this understanding. The Mobilization for Youth Program, implemented in large cities and designed to involve the ghetto in community affairs, particularly those of the school, was a very successful self-help program. The author attributes its success to its efforts to learn about the poor, understand their culture, and help them accordingly.

Roach, Jack L. and Gursslin, Orville R. "The Lower Class, Status Frustration, and Social Disorganization." Social Forces XLIII, 4 (1965), 501-510.

Purpose: To point out the weaknesses of the status-frustration hypothesis as a predictor of the social disorganization of the lower class. The lower class has the highest rates of various indexes of social disorganization: mental disturbance, suicide, homicide, delinquency, and adult crime. Contemporary sociology offers the status-frustration hypothesis as an interpretation for this deviant behavior. The hypothesis suggests that success goals are an important part of the lower-class value system. However, the existing society prevents the lower-class person from achieving success goals. The barriers cause frustration and therefore lead to aggressive and deviant behavior.

Method: Support for and against the status-frustration hypothesis in existing empirical research was reviewed.

Results: The authors' analysis of existing research offers little support for the status-frustration hypothesis. The research supports these empirical generalizations on the lower class: (1) low aspiration levels; (2) rudimentary and relatively unstructured cognitive processes; (3) weak ego-control and self systems; and (4) limited role behavior skills.
    These generalizations contradict the status-frustration hypothesis. As an alternative theoretical framework, the authors suggest that economic deprivation be treated as the independent variable. They see

material deprivation not status deprivation as the basic problem and
feel that material deprivation more adequately accounts for the lower-
class social disorganization. Their reasoning suggests that people who
exist in extended conditions of economic deprivation grow up with defi-
cient role systems, value systems, and personality systems. Their
environment prevents the development of skills in cognition, perception,
verbalization, role, and self-control. Thus, they have difficulty coping with the conditions of a modern, complex, industrial society and
manifest severe behaviorial disorganization.

Rosen, Bernard. "Attitude Change Within the Negro Press Toward
Segregation and Discrimination." Journal of Social Psychology LXII,
1 (1964), 77-83.

Purpose: To determine if the middle-class Negro press reflects the
changing attitudes of Negroes--their growing self-esteem and militancy.
Attitudes on civil rights were studied in Ebony for 1948 and 1960.

Method: 55 articles from 1948 and 60 articles from 1960 were chosen
randomly and subjected to content analysis as were 12 editorials printed
in each of the sample years. Five variables were tested: (1) frequency
of items on discrimination; (2) emphasis given these items; (3) frequency
of references to whites; (4) opinions on which race was responsible for
ending racial bias; and (5) ideological position, i.e., militant or grad-
ualistic.

Results: The following table includes a brief summary of the quantitative
results.

	1948	1960
Frequency of mention of discrimination		
Mentioned	79%	60%
Not mentioned	21	40
Salience of discrimination		
Direct mention	26%	56%
Indirect mention	74	44
Prevalence of whites		
Whites mentioned	81%	51%
Not mentioned	19	49
Agents responsible for integration		
Negroes	32%	79%
White	68	21
Ideology		
Gradualistic	85%	36%
Militant	15	64

These results show that although more articles in 1948 dealt with discrimination, 1960 references were more direct. Other changes included:
    1.   Significantly less mention of whites in 1960 articles.
    2.   A significant change in position on who must be responsible
for integration efforts. In 1948, integration was considered the responsibility of whites; in 1960, it was considered the responsibility of blacks.
    3.   The 1960 articles were significantly more militant.

Runciman, Alexander P. "A Stratification Study of Television Programs." Sociology and Social Research XLIV, 4 (March-April, 1960),
257-261.

Purpose: To study the different program selections made by TV viewers
and the relationship of these selections to social background, interests,
attitudes, and social class. The basic hypothesis was that different
social classes have different viewing selection patterns.

Method: The article reports the results of three studies. In the first,
data on the 1,200 homes in the A. C. Nielsen U.S. fixed panel was used.
Measures of age, sex, education, and family size were related to day
and evening program selections. In the second study, phone interviews
were conducted in Los Angeles with 306 adult respondents in the American Research Bureau's coincidental telephone survey. This study was
conducted between 8-9 p.m. on a Sunday night and investigated the relationship between social class (occupation and education of head of
household) and viewing selections at the time of the interview. The
measure of social class used was the Hollingshead Index. In the third
study, interviews were conducted with a purposive sample of 25 male
industrial and business leaders in Los Angeles. Respondents were
between the ages of 42 and 81 and had completed at least four years of
college. TV behaviors of the 25 men were used as a contrast to behaviors of respondents in the first two studies.

Results
    Study 1
    1.   Variety programs were selected equally by respondents at all
educational levels.
    2.   Suspense programs were preferred more by the younger house-
wives, larger families, and those with only elementary or high school
education.
    3.   Adult soap operas were equally popular with women of all ages
but preference for these shows decreased as education increased.
    4.   Quiz and audience participation shows were preferred more by
younger women.
    5.   Situation comedy preference rose with family size and was
fairly equally distributed across education levels. However, college
educated respondents showed less preference.
    6.   Dramas were preferred by women, especially middle-aged
women.

7.   Child program preferences increased with family size.

8.   Westerns were preferred more by those with less than a college education.

Study 2. An analysis of program selections within the five-position social class index (with class 1 the highest social class) indicated differences in preference by class. Variety programs were preferred mainly by classes 2, 4, and 5; general drama by classes 2 and 3; and westerns by classes 3 and 4.

Study 3. In contrast to most TV fans (studies 1 and 2) who watched TV 35 hours per week, these executives averaged only about 3-1/2 hours of viewing a week. Their top program preference was sports, followed by variety programs, public service, situation comedies, westerns and dramas, and quiz programs.

Sargent, Leslie W., and Stempel, Guido H. III. "Poverty, Alienation, and Mass Media Use." Journalism Quarterly XLV, 2 (Summer, 1968), 324-326.

Purpose: Prior research has shown both alienation and poverty to be related to mass media use. Both variables are associated with less use of news media and more use of escape media. However, poverty and alienation are also related to each other. The question asked here is whether one of these variables is spuriously related to mass media usage.

Method: Two samples of Ss in Athens, Ohio, (city of 16,000) were interviewed. One consisted of all 51 families on relief (39 completed); the other of a randomly drawn phone sample of 150 general population adults (115 completed). Ss were asked about mass media use and given the five-question Srole anomie scale, with increased alienation indexed by the conviction that community leaders are indifferent to the needs of individuals, goals are worthless in an orderless society, the individual is retrogressing, personal relationships no longer support the individual, and internalized social values are lost.

Results
      The relation of poverty to mass media use. (1) relief Ss used the newspaper less--67% read the daily newspaper 20 minutes or more compared to 75% of the general population Ss; (2) relief Ss listened to radio more--49% listened two or more hours compared to 34% general population; (3) relief Ss listened to radio news more--44% listened to radio news 20 minutes or more compared to 29% general population; (4) relief Ss watched TV more--51% watched five hours or more compared to 20% general population; (5) relief Ss watched TV news more--49% watched TV news 20 minutes or more compared to 33% general population. Findings (2), (3), (4), and (5) were significant at $p < .01$.

Relation of alienation to mass media use. Relief Ss were divided
into high and low anomie groups. Results show: (1) high anomie Ss
were equal to low Ss on newspaper use (67% for both groups read a
daily newspaper 20 minutes or more); (2) high Ss used the radio less--
43% listened two hours or more compared with 56% of the lows; (3) high
Ss listened to radio news less--38% listened to news 20 minutes or more
compared with 50% for the lows; (4) high Ss used TV less--38% watched
five or more hours compared to 67% for the lows; and (5) high Ss used
TV news more--52% watched TV news 20 minutes or more compared to
44% for the lows. Only finding (4) was considered significant by authors,
although no significance tests are reported and total N equaled 39.

Sargent, Leslie; Carr, Wiley; and McDonald, Elizabeth. "Significant
Coverage of Integration by Minority Group Magazines." Journal of
Human Relations XIII, 4 (1965), 484-491.

Purpose: To study magazines for two major minorities in the United
States--Negroes and Catholics--for their treatment of integration.

Study 1: Life and Ebony
      Hypothesis: Ebony, a Negro magazine, and Life, a general interest
magazine, were both expected to be understanding toward the Negro.
But Life was expected to be more conservative in its coverage of violence erupting from racial crises.

Method: A content analysis was made of all pictures including aspects
of integration or segregation in both magazines from January, 1962 to
December, 1963. The sample from Life included 235 pictures and that
from Ebony, 1,516 pictures.

Results: Forty-two of Life's pictures on the segregation-integration
issue were classified as showing "active violence," i.e., including violent
behavior, and 40 of the pictures were coded as depicting "passive
resistance" or nonviolent behavior. Ebony included 25 violent and 100
nonviolent pictures. Consequently, the hypothesis was refuted, since
Ebony included less violence than Life in its picture material.
      A study of pictures of the two races together also pointed out
major differences between Life and Ebony. Ebony gave racial association
more importance than Life and included 10 times as many pictures of
whites and Negroes together.

Study 2: America and Commonweal
Hypothesis: A papal encyclical by Pope John XXIII would influence the
treatment of civil rights by America and Commonweal, two Catholic
opinion magazines. The encyclical was concerned with the rights and
responsibilities of men in society.

Method: Seventy-three issues of America and 63 issues of Commonweal
were studied for 38 weeks before and 38 weeks after the issuance of the

encyclical on April 11, 1963. The researchers measured the total
number of inches printed relating to racial problems and computed percentages of this total in relation to the average "news hole." The researchers then made a content analysis of the magazines, using the
sentence as the coding unit. Categories were taken from topics in the
encyclical and included such items as social, economic, and political
rights.

Results: Items dealing with the Negro's struggle for civil rights had
received extensive coverage prior to the encyclical. However, the
encyclical seemed to boost this coverage further. America used 3%
of its news hole for racial news prior to the encyclical and 4% after-
ward. Commonweal gave such news 5% of its space before and 7%
following the encyclical.

Schatzman, Leonard, and Strauss, Anselm. "Social Class and Modes
of Communication." The American Journal of Sociology LX, 4 (January,
1955), 329-338.

Purpose: To determine whether thought and communication differ with
social class. The authors suggest that differences in actual communication modes (degree of preciseness, vocabulary use, and style) relate
to differences in the organization of perception and thought.

Method: Interviews from 340 disaster victims, giving their own experiences, were obtained from a random sample of communities struck
by tornadoes. Respondents gave unstructured reports of their experiences, that averaged 29 pages. This group was further sampled to obtain only respondents with the following characteristics: (1) extreme
income and education levels, classified as lower class if no high school
and income under $2,000 and classified as higher class if at least one
year college and income above $4,000; (2) white only; (3) between the
ages of 21 and 65; (4) Arkansas native and local resident for more than
three years; (5) near or in the tornado area; (6) cooperative; (7) required
fewer than eight probes per page during the original interview to avoid
rigid question-answer response style. These criteria yield 10 upper-
class cases and 10 lower-class cases.

Results: Differences between the lower and upper group were marked.
    1. Perspective. Lower-class respondents gave highly subjective
descriptions. Middle-class respondents, on the other hand, could
describe the situation not only from their own viewpoint but from the
perspective of another person, group, or the entire community.
    2. Imagery. Imagery used by lower-class respondents was
unclear. They seemed unaware that their listeners might not understand or might see events differently than they did. Precise details
and references were lacking. Middle-class respondents gave more detailed explanations and seemed aware of the possible diversity in imagery
between speaker and listener.

3.   Classifications. Lower-class respondents made references
mainly to the acts of particular people and became relatively inarticu-
late when asked to give information about classes of people or entire
organizations. Lower-class speakers used mainly particularistic or
concrete terms rather than class terms. Relationships between classes
were not spelled out. Middle-class respondents, on the other hand,
used class terms frequently. For them, conceptual terminology over-
shadowed the use of concrete referents.

4.   Organization and style. Lower-class respondents gave personal narratives, often wandering off on tangents. Their descriptions
lacked organization and unity. Their stylistic devices for connecting
thoughts were primitive, e.g., use of words such as "so" and "then."
Middle-class respondents had more organized accounts, sticking to the
topic at hand. They gave more detail and were less repetitive. They
used summary statements, transitions, and a wide variety of stylistic
devices.

5.   Intra-class differences. Despite the marked differences suggested between classes, the authors emphasize that there was also wide
variability within classes.

Shuey, Audrey; King, Nancy; and Griffith, Barbara. "Stereotyping of
Negroes and Whites: An Analysis of Pictures in Magazines." Public
Opinion Quarterly XVII (1953), 281-287.

Purpose: To determine what kind of discrimination, if any, exists
against Negroes in picture magazines.

Method: The first two issues of each month for Life, Post, Time, and
The New Yorker were examined for the years 1949 and 1950. In addition,
all issues of Colliers and the Ladies Home Journal for the same two
years were examined. In all, 292 magazine issues were examined.
Every picture in each issue showing a Negro was included in the analysis.
Pictures of whites were sampled by selecting the first picture after every
Negro picture. The final count on pictures was 213 advertising pictures
showing blacks and 213 showing whites; 513 non-advertising pictures
showing blacks and 513 showing whites. Pictures were classed by size
and the occupation of people shown. Occupational categories included
"above skilled labor," "skilled/clerical labor," and "below skilled
labor."

Results
1.   Only 5% of the 213 advertising pictures showing blacks could
be placed in the "above skilled labor" category; 86% of the whites portrayed could be so classed. Only 8% of the whites were pictured in ads
in the "below skilled labor" category with most of these portrayed as
farmers or cowboys. Over 95% of the blacks fell in the "below skilled
labor" category and 75% of these showed the blacks as servants. Some
15% showed scantily dressed African natives. No blacks were shown
in ads as "skilled/clerical labor;" 6% of the whites were so depicted.
2.   In editorial content, 81% of the whites were classified as being
"above skilled labor" in comparison with 38% of the blacks. Whites

rarely were seen as "below skilled labor" (13%) but most blacks were
(57%). Most of the portrayals of blacks as "above skilled labor" showed
sports personalities and entertainers.

Singer, Benjamin D. The Detroit Riot of July 1967: A Psychological,
Social, and Economic Profile of 500 Arrestees. Report prepared for
U.S. Department of Labor, Manpower Administration, Research Con-
tract No. 81-24-68-03. London, Ontario, Canada: Department of
Sociology, University of Western Ontario, n.d.

Purpose: To obtain information on persons arrested during the 1967
Detroit riot.

Method: 500 black male arrestees were interviewed via structured and
open-ended personal interviews at their places of detention following
the 1967 Detroit riot. Variables measured included demographic characteristics, attitudes toward various black leaders, attitudes toward civil
rights and riots, and media preferences and usage patterns. Interviewers were male Negroes, with at least a high school education.

Results
    Demography
    1. Causes for arrests. Of the 500 respondents, 39% were arrested
for breaking and entering; 11% for curfew violation; 9% for larceny; and
25% for other reasons, e.g., possession of goods, carrying weapons.
    2. Age. 67% of the respondents were below age 30; 20% were
between 16 and 19 years.
    3. Education. 81% of the respondents had at least some high
school; 12% had elementary school only; 5% had some college; less than
1% had completed college.
    4. Employment. 22% were currently unemployed. Of those who
worked, 30% made between $51-100 a week; 32% made between $101-150
a week.
    5. Marital status. 48% were unmarried; 38% were married; 11%
were divorced or separated.
    6. Voting. 85% of those more than 25 years of age had voted at
least once.
    7. Participation in retraining or anti-poverty programs. 17%
had participated in some government retraining or poverty program.
    8. Marital situation of parents. 59% reported that their own
parents were together; 32% reported their own parents separated or
divorced while they were growing up.
    9. Organization memberships. 72% belonged to no clubs or organ-
izations; 20% indicated organization memberships averaging one such
membership each. These memberships were primarily in social or
fraternal organizations, then unions, sports groups, and finally, political
and civil rights organizations.
    10. Favorite amusements. Spectator sports were the favored
amusement for 37% of the arrestees; participant sports, 28%; art, 16%;
and drinking and nightclubbing, 12%.

11. Employment record. About 50% had been out of work one or more times in the past year; 4% had not worked at all; 42% had had two or more employers in the past year.

12. Garnishments. 17% reported they had had part of their wages taken away because of debts; 78% had never been garnisheed. Only 1% reported they had been fired because of debts; 49% said they had not been fired for this cause; 50% gave no response.

13. Court orders to pay debts. 21% said they had had a judgment against them; 60% said they had not; 20% gave no response. Some 15% indicated they had had goods repossessed; 70% said no; 15% gave no response.

Communication

1. How respondents found out about riots in other cities. 54% said TV; 52% said newspapers; 28% radio, 12% personal communication. Respondents were allowed to give more than one answer.

2. Own TV and radio. 83% owned both; 7% radio only; 5% TV only; 2% neither; 2% no response.

3. Ever seen race riot on TV: 75% said yes, 22% said no; 3% gave no answer.

4. What action did respondents see in televised race riots: 35% said most people were destroying property; 21% said whites were agressing against Negroes; 11% said most people were just generally fighting. These were the most frequent response categories.

5. Kind of TV program watched most: 27% named detective-spy-mystery; 23% named westerns; 18% named variety or quiz shows; 17%, news or documentaries; 11%, movies; 11%, sports. All other program types received less than 10% mentions. Respondents were allowed to name more than one category.

6. Newspapers read regularly by more than 10% of the respondents: Detroit News, 47%; Detroit Free Press, 18%; Detroit News and Detroit Free Press, 15%; Michigan Chronicle, 16%; none, 7%.

7. Type of magazine regularly read: 58% read Negro magazines regularly; 42%, family magazines; 14%, news magazines; 16% said none.

8. Kind of radio program heard regularly: 98% said pop music; 8% said none. No other program type was mentioned by more than 10% of the respondents.

9. Feelings viewing race riot on TV: 43% said they disapproved or felt bad; 27% felt resentment toward whites and authority; 6% felt ambivalent, wondered how to prevent it, or worried about causes.

10. How respondents first heard of Detroit riot: 47% said they were at home; 23% said they were on the scene; other answers received low total mentions. Some 22% first heard by direct observation; 17% heard on the radio; 22% named people in general; 17% named friends; 9% named relatives; 8% named TV; 2% named fellow workers. In all, 49% learned via person-to-person communication; 25% by electronic media; 21% by direct observation. No mentions of newspapers were made.

11. How respondents informed others about riot: 39% of the respondents did inform others. Of these, 80% did so by face-to-face contact; 10% did so by telephone; 10% gave no response.

12. What respondents communicated to others about the riot: Most reported that they merely transmitted direct information (60%); 14%

said they told others they were worried; 6% said riots were bad; 2% said riots were good.

13.   Diffusion of riot news and response: Only 1% of the respondents reported hearing of the riot by Saturday night; 35% by Sunday morning; 47% by Sunday afternoon; 5% by Monday. Of those who heard, 9% went to the riot scene Sunday morning; 37% Sunday afternoon; 15% on Monday. Fifteen percent went to the scene less than 30 minutes after they first heard; 12% took from 30 minutes to two hours; 13% from two to six hours; and 18% took six hours or more.

14.   Whether respondents met friends at riot: 52% said no; 30% said yes; 18% did not respond.

15.   How respondent checked on seriousness of riot: 30% said they listened to radio; 25% watched TV; 26% went to see for themselves; 21% checked the newspaper; 10% called the police; 3% did nothing. Respondents were allowed multiple answers.

Singer, Benjamin D. Television and the Riots. Mimeographed. London, Ontario, Canada: Department of Sociology, University of Western Ontario, June 7, 1968.

Purpose: To critically evaluate the Kerner Commission's rather favorable treatment of TV and its relationship to riots.

Results: The Kerner Commission's treatment of TV was based on three arguments derived from an analysis of 837 TV sequences dealing with riots and racial problems in 15 cities. The analysis was done by the Simulmatics Corporation. This analysis lead to three fallacious arguments, Singer charges.

1.   The calm coverage argument. The analysis of the sequences yielded 58% classified as calm; 31% as emotional; and 10% as normal. In its report the Commission emphasizes the large proportion of calm sequences.

2.   The ratio argument. The analysis also showed that the ratio of white adult males to black males in the TV sequences was high (1.2) considering that the riots took place in predominantly Negro neighborhoods. This leads to the conclusion that the riots were racial rather than economic in nature.

3.   The balance argument. The analysis also showed that Negro leaders whom the commission considered "moderate" were depicted three times more frequently than "militants" in the TV sequences.

Singer challenges these arguments mainly on the basis that they assume that there is some direct correspondence between what is shown on TV and what is recalled or deemed important by viewers. He cites his own research. In his study of Negro males arrested after the Detroit riots, evidence indicated that: 77% of his 500 male respondents had seen riots on TV before the Detroit riot; 46% remembered seeing property destroyed or looted; 28% perceived whites aggressing against Negroes; 14% saw fighting in a general sense; and 9% reported Negroes fighting against law enforcement officials and soldiers.

These recall and perception reports are in direct conflict with the commission reports that only 5% of the actual TV scenes showed looting, mob action, sniping, arson, and injury or killing.

Swinehart, James W. "Socio-Economic Level, Status Aspiration, and Maternal Role." American Sociological Review XXVIII, 3 (June, 1963), 391-398.

Purpose: Findings from a number of previous studies justify the conclusion that the socialization practices of parents vary with their social class. To establish some probable basis for class differences in child rearing, this study investigates the relationship of socio-economic status (SES) and status aspiration (upward mobility orientation) to three other variables: mother's primary objective in rearing children; her major source of satisfaction from the maternal role; and her concern about effective fulfillment of this role. Swinehart's hypotheses were:
    1. Mothers of different SES levels differ in their primary child rearing objectives.
    2. Upper and middle class mothers are less accepting of the "service" aspects of maternal role.
    3. Mothers oriented toward upward mobility are less accepting of the "service" aspects of maternal role than mothers who are relatively content with their social status.
    4. Middle class mothers express greater concern than upper or lower class mothers about the adequacy of their maternal role performance.
    5. Upward aspiring mothers express greater concern than non-aspiring mothers about the adequacy of their maternal role performance.

Method: Personal interviews were conducted with 815 mothers of third grade children in St. Louis; 444 of these respondents met four criteria: (1) they had more than one child at home; (2) neither spouse had had a previous marriage; (3) there was no religious conflict at home; and (4) both parents were alive and in the home. Respondents then were divided into six SES levels (using the Warner scheme combining occupation, education, income, living conditions, wife's income, and education). Because respondents in the lowest levels of SES status were low in number, 192 respondents at other levels randomly were deleted to make cell Ns more equal. The resulting levels and Ns for SES were: upper class, 28; upper-middle, 28; mid-middle, 56; lower-middle, 56; upper-lower, 56; and lower-lower, 28. Respondents also were divided into two levels of status aspiration determined by three indices: occupational discrepancy (parent's occupation versus that desired for child); educational discrepancy; and satisfaction with neighborhood. The interview schedule was a combination of open-ended items, probes, and structured closed-ended items.

Results
    1. Hypothesis 1 was confirmed. Mothers on different SES levels clearly differed in their primary child rearing objectives. Upper-class

mothers felt best in meeting social and emotional needs of children; middle-class mothers emphasized character and morality; mothers at the two lower levels emphasized meeting physical needs.

2.   Hypothesis 2 was confirmed but results were not as clear as with hypothesis 1.   Lower-class mothers tended to accept "service" components of maternal role more than upper- and middle-class mothers. Results were significant but trends in the middle levels were not clear.

3.   Hypothesis 3 was not confirmed.   There was a nonsignificant trend in the opposite direction.

4.   For hypotheses 4 and 5 concerning the relationship of concern over maternal effectiveness to SES and aspiration, results were inconsistent.   Measures from open-ended versus structured items produced different results.

U.S. Government.   Recent Trends in Social and Economic Conditions of Negroes in the United States.   Current Population Reports, Series P-23, No. 26, BLS Report No. 347. Washington, D.C.: Government Printing Office, July, 1968.

Purpose: After the summer civil disturbances in 1967, the Bureau of Labor Statistics and the Bureau of the Census prepared statistical reports on the social and economic conditions of Negroes in the United States. This original report was published in October, 1967. The present report is a shorter version giving the most important new data available.

Highlights of the findings
    1.   The percentage of Negroes in the total population has remained about the same since the turn of the century. In 1968 there were 22 million Negroes in the total U.S. population of 198 million.

    2.   In the two years prior to 1968, Negro population in central cities leveled off and Negro numbers in the suburbs continued to increase. However, since 1950, most Negro population increases have occurred in central cities while most white increases have been in metropolitan suburbs. In 1968, 11.8 million Negroes lived in central cities; 3.2 million in suburbs, and 7 million in smaller cities, towns, and rural areas. in 1968 45.8 million whites lived in central cities; 64.9 million in suburbs, and 63.0 million in smaller cities, towns, and rural areas.

    3.   In U.S. central, cities Negroes today represent 20% of the population compared to 12% in 1950. Since 1960, the percentage of Negroes in metropolitan areas has leveled off, stabilizing at 12% in 1968 for both central city and suburban areas combined.

    4.   Median family income for Negroes in 1967 was $4,939 compared to $8,318 for whites. Negro median family income is now 59% of white family income.

    5.   The proportion of nonwhite families with incomes of $8,000 or more was three times greater in 1967 than in 1957. In 1967, 27% of nonwhite families had incomes of $8,000 or more compared with 53% of white families.

6. Negroes in the south are in a much worse financial position than Negroes in other regions. In 1967, median Negro income in the south was $3,992 compared with $5,764 in the northeast and about $6,500 in the north central states and west. Comparable figures for whites were: south, $7,448; northeast, $8,756; north central, $8,414; and west, $8,901.

7. In 1967, the proportion of nonwhites with incomes below the poverty level was 35% compared to 10% for whites. The 1959 figures were 55% for nonwhites and 18% for whites. The poverty definition is based on minimum food and other needs of families, taking account of family size, number of children, and farm or non-farm residence. As of 1967, the poverty threshold for a non-farm family of four was $3,335.

8. The percentage of nonwhite and white families receiving welfare in 1968 was 14% and 3% respectively.

9. Both white and nonwhite unemployment rates have been steadily decreasing since 1961. In 1961, the rates were 12.4% for nonwhites and 6.0% for whites. In 1968, the rates were 6.8% for nonwhites and 3.2% for whites. Nonwhite teen-agers had the highest unemployment rates in the labor force: 24.7% of nonwhite teen-agers were unemployed in 1968 compared with 10.9 of white teen-agers.

10. In 1967 for the first time, more than half of all nonwhite workers held white-collar, craftsmen, or operative jobs.

11. The number and percentage of nonwhite workers in most high skill and well paying occupation groups increased sharply from 1960 to 1967. For example, nonwhites had an 80% increase in professional and technical workers, a 17% increase in managers and officials, and a 77% increase in clerical workers. Nonwhite private household workers decreased 17%.

12. During the past two years, the proportion of nonwhites completing high school has increased sharply while the white rate has remained about the same. In 1960, the education gap between nonwhite and white young men was two years. Today, the gap is less than 1/2 year. The percentage finishing four years of high school or more was 60% for nonwhite males, 56% for nonwhite females, and 75% for white males and females.

13. The proportion of nonwhite households living in housing that was dilapidated or lacked basic plumbing decreased sharply since 1960--from 44% in 1960 to 29% in 1966 for nonwhites compared to from 13% in 1960 and 8% in 1966 for whites.

14. Life expectancy of nonwhites in 1966 was lower than for whites in all age groups.

15. Mortality rates among both nonwhite and white mothers and infants have dropped sharply in the past 25 years but nonwhite rates are still much higher than white.

16. In 1968, 89% of white families were two-parent (husband-wife) families compared to only 69% of nonwhite families.

17. Nonwhite unemployment rates are much higher than white rates both inside and outside urban poverty areas. In 1968, for example, 8% of nonwhites in poverty areas were unemployed compared with 5.2% of whites. For persons living outside poverty areas, the figures were 5.8% for nonwhites and 3.1% for whites.

Walters, James; Conner, Ruth; and Zunich, Michael. "Interaction of
Mothers and Children in Lower Class Families." Child Development
XXXV, 2 (June, 1964), 433-440.

Purpose: To examine how lower-class mothers behave toward their
children when told that their children are performing below their
potential.

Method: The sample consisted of 40 mothers whose behavior toward
one of their children was monitored and recorded in one of 17 categories
every 5 seconds for 30-minute periods. Mothers were lower-class,
white, American-born, full-time homemakers with husbands with no
more than a high school education. Two-thirds of the mothers had two
or more children. Children were of pre-school age and were observed
in a play session with the mother. Following the play session, half of
the mothers were told that their child was not performing up to par and
that the child would hopefully do better on the second trial. The remaining half was told nothing (control group). Interaction of mother and
child was observed again at a second play session and recorded according to the same category scheme. Categories noted such behavior as
whether the mother facilitated the current behavior of the child or tended
to restrict it and whether the mother taught the child or merely criticized him.

Results
    1. Control group mothers showed more helping behavior at the
second session than at the first. There were no significant differences
between the two groups of mothers at the first session.
    2. At the second session, the experimental group mothers showed
more contacting, directing, and structuring of behavior.
    3. Mothers with girls did more contacting and structuring and
mothers with boys did more restricting.
    4. By comparing the lower-class children and mothers' responses
in the present study to similar findings with middle and upper classes
from prior work, the following differences were pinpointed:
        a. There is much more interaction of mother and child in
            the middle and upper classes.
        b. Upper-and middle-class samples show much more
            directing, helping, structuring, teaching, and playing
            behavior than did the low class sample of the present
            study.
    5. Mothers at all social levels seemed sensitive to the criticism of
the child advice expert.

Zunich, Michael. "Attitudes of Lower Class Families." Journal of
Social Psychology LXIII, 2 (1964), 367-371.

Purpose: To determine if attitudes between parents and offspring are
related and how close attitudes are within the lower-class family.

Method: Sample was composed of 42 white lower-class family units,
each of which included a father, mother, son, and daughter (the children were of adolescent age). Families were tested with the Parental

Attitude Research Instrument in personal interviews. Control was
assured by eliminating interaction between parents and/or children by
interviewing the latter at school and each parent independently at home.
All interviews were made at the same time and on the same day.

Results
    1. Mothers and daughters shared more similar attitudes than
other members of the family.
    2. Parents and their children shared significantly similar and
favorable attitudes on these scales: comradeship, openness in family
communication, and problem sharing.
    3. Attitudes of parent and child on these scales were not related:
attitudes on treating children as equals (equalitarianism) and attitudes
toward punishment of children.
    4. Attitudes of parent and child were considerably closer in some
families than in others. Quite different attitudes were represented by
different family members in some families.

ALPHABETICAL LISTING OF PUBLICATIONS
IN THE BIBLIOGRAPHY

Allen, T. H. "Mass Media Use Patterns and Functions in a Negro
Ghetto." Master's thesis, University of West Virginia, 1967.

Barban, Arnold M. "Negro and White Reactions to 'Integrated' Advertising: Some Preliminary Findings." Paper presented to Division
of Advertising, Association for Education in Journalism, Boulder,
Colorado, August 27-31, 1967.

_____, and Grunbaum, Werner F. "A Factor Analytic Study of
Negro and White Responses to Advertising Stimuli." Journal of
Applied Psychology XLIX, 4 (1965), 274-279.

Barcus, F. Earle, and Levin, Jack. "Role Distance in Negro and
Majority Fiction." Journalism Quarterly XLIII, 4 (Winter, 1966),
709-714.

Bell, Endell. "Anomie, Social Isolation, and the Class Structure."
Sociometry XX (June, 1957), 105-116.

Bell, Robert R. "Lower Class Mothers' Aspirations for Their Children." Social Forces XLIII, 4 (May, 1965), pp. 493-500.

Berkman, David. "Advertising in Ebony and Life: Negro Aspirations
vs. Reality." Journalism Quarterly XL, 1 (Winter, 1963), 53-64.

Besner, Arthur. "Economic Deprivation and Family Patterns." Welfare in Review III, 9 (September, 1965), 20-28.

Blood, Robert O., Jr. "Social Class and Family Control of Television
Viewing." Merrill-Palmer Quarterly VII, 3 (July, 1961), 205-222.

Boyenton, William H. "The Negro Turns to Advertising." Journalism
Quarterly XLII, 2 (Spring, 1965), 227-235.

Broom, Leonard, and Glenn, Norval D. "Negro-White Differences in
Reported Attitudes and Behavior." Sociology and Social Research
L, 2 (January, 1966), 187-200.

Burma, John W. "An Analysis of the Present Negro Press." Social
Forces XXVI (1947), 172-180.

Caplan, Nathan S., and Paige, Jeffrey H. "A Study of Ghetto Rioters."
Scientific American CCXIX, 2 (August, 1968), 15-21.

Caplovitz, David. The Poor Pay More. New York: The Free Press,
    1963.

Carey, James W. "Variations in Negro/White Television Preference."
    Journal of Broadcasting X, 3 (1966), 199-212.

Carter, Roy E., Jr. "Racial Identification Effects Upon the News Story
    Writer." Journalism Quarterly XXXVI, 3 (Summer, 1959), 284-
    290.

Chilman, Catherine S. "Child Rearing and Family Relationship Patterns
    of the Very Poor." Welfare in Review III, 1 (January, 1965), 9-19.

_____. Growing Up Poor. U.S. Dept. of Health, Education and Wel-
    fare, Welfare Administration Publication No. 13. Washington,
    D. C.: Government Printing Office, May 1966.

Clark, Kenneth B. Dark Ghetto: Dilemmas of Social Power. New York:
    Harper, 1967.

Cloward, Richard A., and Jones, J. A. "Social Class: Educational
    Attitudes and Participation." In Education in Depressed Areas,
    edited by A. H. Passow. New York: Teachers College Press,
    Columbia University, 1963, pp. 190-216.

Cohen, Albert K., and Hodge, Harold M., Jr. "Characteristics of the
    Lower Blue-Collar Class." Journal of Social Problems X, 4 (Spring,
    1963), 103-134.

Columbia Broadcasting System. White and Negro Attitudes Towards
    Race Related Issues and Activities. Princeton, N. J.: Public Opin-
    ion Research Corp., July 9, 1968.

Darrow, Charlotte, and Lowinger, Paul. "The Detroit Uprising: A
    Psychosocial Study." Paper presented at the Academy of Psycho-
    analysis meeting in New York City, December, 1967.

DeFleur, M. L. "Occupational Roles as Portrayed on Television."
    Public Opinion Quarterly XXXVII, 1 (Spring, 1964), 57-64.

Disaster Research Center. "The Los Angeles Riot Study." Unscheduled
    Events I, 3 (Fall, 1967), Department of Sociology, Division of Re-
    search, College of Commerce and Administration, Ohio State Uni-
    versity, 4-5.

Donohew, Lewis, and Singh, B. K. "Poverty 'Types' and Their Sources
    of Information About New Practices." Paper presented at the Inter-
    national Communication Division, Association for Education in
    Journalism, Boulder, Colorado, August 27-31, 1967.

_____. "Modernization of Life Styles. An Appraisal of the 'War on
    Poverty' in a Rural Setting of Southeastern Kentucky." Lexington,
    Kentucky: University of Kentucky, August, 1968.

Epstein, Lenore A. "Some Effects of Low Income on Children and Their
    Families." Social Security Bulletin XXIV, 2, (February, 1961),
    12-17.

Fannin, Leon F., and Clinard, Marshall B. "Differences in the Con-
    ception of Self as a Male Among Lower and Middle Class Delin-
    quents." Social Problems XIII, 2 (1965), 205-214.

Feldman, Laurence P., and Star, Alvin D. "Racial Factors in Shopping
    Behavior." In A New Measure of Responsibility for Marketing,
    edited by Keith Cox and Ben Enis. Conference Proceedings, Series
    No. 27. Philadelphia: American Marketing Association, June 17-
    19, 1968, pp. 216-226.

Fogelson, R. M., and Hill, R. B. Who Riots? A Study of Participation
    in the 1967 Riots. Mimeographed. Bureau of Applied Social Re-
    search, Columbia University, July, 1968.

Frazier, Franklin E. Black Bourgeoisie. New York: Collier, 1965.
    (Original ed. in French, 1955.)

Freeman, H. E. and Lambert, Camille, Jr. "The Influence of Community
    Groups on Health Matters." Human Organization XXIV, 4 (Winter,
    1965), 353-357.

Friedman, M. "Television Program Preference and Televiewing Habits
    of Children As Related to Their Socio-Economic Status." Ph.D.
    dissertation, Yeshiva University, 1957.

Gans, Herbert J. The Urban Villagers: Group and Class in the Life of
    Italian Americans. Glencoe, Ill.: The Free Press, 1962.

Gentile, Frank, and Miller, S. M. "TV and Social Class." Sociology
    and Social Research XLV, 3 (April, 1961), 259-264.

Gerbner, George. "The Social Role of the Confession Magazine."
    Social Problems VI, 1 (1958), 29-41.

Gerson, Walter M. "Mass Media Socialization Behavior: Negro-White
    Differences." Social Forces XLV, 1 (September, 1966), 40-50.

Gieber, Walter. "How the 'Gatekeepers' View Local Civil Liberties
    News." Journalism Quarterly XXXVII, 2 (Spring, 1960), 199-205.

Gottlieb, David. "Goal Aspirations and Goal Fulfillments: Differences
    Between Deprived and Affluent American Adolescents," American
    Journal of Orthopsychiatry, XXXIV, 5 (1964), 934-941.

_____. "The Neighborhood Tavern and the Cocktail Lounge: A
    Study of Class Differences." American Journal of Sociology CXII,
    6 (May, 1967), 559-562.

Grosser, Charles F. "Local Residents as Mediators Between Middle
    Class Professional Workers and Lower Class Clients." Social
    Service Review XL, 1 (March, 1966), 56-63.

Hazard, William R. "Anxiety and Preference for Television Fantasy."
    Journalism Quarterly XLIV, 3 (Autumn, 1967), 461-469.

Henry, Jules. "White People's Time, Colored People's Time." Trans-
    action II, 3 (March/April, 1965), 31-34.

Herzog, Elizabeth. "Some Assumptions About the Poor." Social
    Service Review XXXVIII, 4 (December, 1963), 389-402.

Hirsh, Paul M. "An Analysis of Ebony: The Magazine and Its Readers",
    Journalism Quarterly XLV, 2 (Summer, 1968), 261-270, 292.

Ingram, Jim. "What Blacks Read--and Who They Believe." Detroit
    Scope Magazine I, 39 (January 4, 1969), 6-8.

Irelan, Lola M., and Besner, Arthur. "Low Income Outlook on Life."
    Welfare in Review III, 9 (September, 1965), 13-19.

Kean, George G. "A Comparative Study of Negro and White Homeless
    Men." Unpublished doctoral dissertation, Yeshiva University,
    1965.

Keller, Susanne. "The Social World of the Urban Slum Child: Some
    Early Findings." American Journal of Orthopsychiatry XXXIII,
    5 (1963), 823-831.

Kohn, Melvin L. "Social Class and Parental Values." The American
    Journal of Sociology LXIV, 4 (January, 1959), 337-351.

Kurtz, Norman R. "Gatekeepers: Agents in Acculturation." Rural
    Sociology XXXIII, 1 (March, 1968), 63-70.

Lambert, Verdelle. "Negro Exposure in Look's Editorial Content."
    Journalism Quarterly XLII, 4 (Autumn, 1965), 657-659.

Lang, Kurt, and Lang, Gladys Engel. "Racial Disturbances as Collec-
    tive Protest." The American Behavioral Scientist II, 4 (March-
    April, 1968), 11-13.

Larson, Carl M. "Racial Brand Usage and Media Exposure Differen-
    tials." In A New Measure of Responsibility for Marketing, edited
    by Keith Cox and Ben Enis. Conference Proceedings, Series No.
    27. Philadelphia: American Marketing Association, June 17-19,
    1968, pp. 208-215.

Larson, Richard B., and Sutker, Sara. "Value Differences and Value
    Concensus by Socio-Economic Status." Social Forces XLIV, 4
    (1966), 563-569.

Levenstein, Phyllis, and Sunley, Robert. "Stimulation of Verbal Interaction Between Disadvantaged Mothers and Children." American
Journal of Orthopsychiatry XXXVIII, 1 (January, 1968), 116-121.

Lewis, Oscar. "The Culture of Poverty." Scientific American CCXV,
4 (October, 1966), 19-25.

Liebow, Elliot. Tally's Corner: A Study of Negro Streetcorner Men.
Boston: Little, Brown, and Co., 1967.

Luchterland, Elmer, and Weller, Leonaval. "Social Class and the
Desegregation Movement: A Study of Parents' Decisions in a Negro
Ghetto." Social Problems XIII, 1 (1965), 83-88.

Lyle, Jack. "The Negro and the News Media." In Jack Lyle, The News
in Megalopolis, San Francisco, Calif.: Chandler Publishing Co.,
1967, Chapter 9. pp. 163-182.

McCabe, Alice R. "Re: Forty Forgotten Families." Public Welfare,
XXIV, 2 (April, 1966), 159-171.

McCombs, Maxwell E. "Negro Use of Television and Newspapers for
Political Information, 1952-64." Journal of Broadcasting XII, 3
(Summer, 1968), 261-266.

McCord, William, and Howard, John. "Negro Opinions in Three Riot
Cities." The American Behavioral Scientists II, 4 (March, 1968),
24-27.

McIssac, Hugh, and Wilkinson, Harold. "Clients Talk About Their
Caseworkers." Public Welfare XXIII, 3 (July, 1965), 147-154.

McLeod, Jack; Ward, Scott; and Tancill, Karen. "Alienation and Uses
of Mass Media." Public Opinion Quarterly XXIX, (Winter, 1965-
66), 583-594.

Middleton, Russell. "Alienation, Race, and Education." The American
Sociological Review, XXVIII, (December, 1963), 973-977.

Miller, S. M. "The American Lower Class: A Typological Approach."
Social Research XXXI, 1 (Spring, 1964), 1-22.

Minuchin, Salvador, et al. Families of the Slums: An Exploration of
Their Structure and Treatment. New York: Basic Books, 1967.

Moles, Oliver C. "Child Training Practices Among Low Income
Families--An Empirical Study." Welfare in Review III, 12 (December, 1965), 1-19.

Mugge, Robert H. "Aid to Families with Dependent Children: Initial
Findings of the 1961 Report on the Characteristics of the Recipients."
Social Security Bulletin XXVI (March, 1963), 3-15.

Muir, Conal E., and Weinstein, E. A. "The Social Debt: An Investi-
    gation of Lower Class and Middle Class Norms of Social Obligation."
    American Sociological Review XXVII, 4 (1962), 532-539.

National Advisory Commission on Civil Disorders. Report of the
    National Advisory Commission on Civil Disorders. New York:
    Bantam Books, 1968.

O'Shea, Robert M., and Gray, Shirlene B. "Income and Community
    Participation." Welfare in Review IV, 4 (April, 1966), 10-13.

Rainwater, Lee; Coleman, Richard P.; and Handel, Gerald. Work-
    ingman's Wife. New York: Oceana Publications, 1959.

Ransford, H. Edward. "Isolation, Powerlessness, and Violence: A
    Study of Attitudes and Participation in the Watts Riot." American
    Journal of Sociology LXXIII, 5 (March, 1968), 581-591.

Riesman, Frank. "Low Income Culture: The Strengths of the Poor."
    Journal of Marriage and Family XXVI, 4 (November, 1964), 417-
    421.

Roach, Jack L., and Gursslin, Orville R. "The Lower Class, Status
    Frustration, and Social Disorganization." Social Forces XLIII,
    4 (1965), 501-510.

Rosen, Bernard. "Attitude Change Within the Negro Press Toward
    Segregation and Discrimination." Journal of Social Psychology
    LXII, 1 (1964), 77-83.

Runciman, Alexander P. "A Stratification Study of Television Pro-
    grams." Sociology and Social Research XLIV, 4 (March-April,
    1960), 257-261.

Sargent, Leslie W. and Guido H. Stempel III. "Poverty, Alienation,
    and Mass Media Use." Journalism Quarterly XLV, 2 (Summer,
    1968), 324-326.

Sargent, Leslie W.; Carr, Wiley; and McDonald, Elizabeth. "Signi-
    ficant Coverage of Integration by Minority Group Magazines."
    Journal of Human Relations XIII, 4 (1965), 484-491.

Schatzman, Leonard and Strauss, Anselm. "Social Class and Modes of
    Communication." The American Journal of Sociology LX, 4 (Jan-
    uary, 1955), 329-338.

Shuey, Audrey; King, Nancy; and Griffith, Barbara. "Stereotyping
    of Negroes and Whites: An Analysis of Pictures in Magazines."
    Public Opinion Quarterly XVII (1953), 281-287.

Singer, Benjamin D. The Detroit Riot of July, 1967: A Psychological,
    Social, and Economic Profile of 500 Arrestees. Report prepared
    for U. S. Department of Labor, Manpower Administration, Re-
    search Contract No. 81-24-68-03. London, Ontario, Canada:
    Department of Sociology, University of Western Ontario, n.d.

_____. Television and the Riots. Mimeographed. London, Ontario,
    Canada: Department of Sociology, University of Western Ontario,
    June 7, 1968.

Swinehart, James W. "Socio-Economic Level, Status Aspiration, and
    Maternal Role." American Sociological Review XXVIII, 3 (June,
    1963), 391-398.

U. S. Government. Recent Trends in Social and Economic Conditions
    of Negroes in the United States. Current Population Reports,
    Series P-23, No. 26, BLS Report No. 347. Washington, D. C.:
    Government Printing Office, July, 1968.

Walters, James; Conner, Ruth; and Zunich, Michael. "Interaction of
    Mothers and Children in Lower Class Families." Child Develop-
    ment XXXV, 2 (June, 1964), 433-440.

Zunich, Michael. "Attitudes of Lower Class Families." Journal of
    Social Psychology LXIII, 2 (1964), 367-371.

SUBJECT INDEX TO THE
ANNOTATED BIBLIOGRAPHY*

---

* Page numbers refer to the opening pages of the bibliographic entries
    relating to the topics indicated.

ABOUT THE CONTRIBUTORS

BRADLEY S. GREENBERG is Associate Professor of
Communication at Michigan State University (MSU),
where he has been a faculty member for six years.
His M.S. degree in journalism and his Ph.D. in mass
communication are both from the University of Wisconsin, where he spent an additional year as a post-
doctoral research fellow in the Mass Communications
Research Center. From 1961-64, he was a research
associate at the Institute for Communication Research,
Stanford University. As a newspaper reporter and in
public information work Professor Greenberg has published more than 50 articles, chapters, and monographs in the area of mass communication plus one
book, The Kennedy Assassination and the American Public: Social Communication in Crisis. Most recently,
he served as a consultant to the President's Commission on the Causes and Prevention of Violence.

BRENDA DERVIN is currently Lecturer, School of
Library Science, Syracuse University, New York. Previously, she was Senior Research Assistant in the
Department of Communication at Michigan State University and Resident Lecturer-Coordinator for the MSU
communication seminars for foreign students studying
in the U.S. under Agency for International Development
auspices. Miss Dervin received her B.A. in journalism and home economics from Cornell University,
Ithaca, New York, her M.A. in communication from
Michigan State and is completing her doctorate in
communication at MSU. She has also worked as a public relations-program development specialist for the
University of Wisconsin Center for Consumer Affairs,
the American Home Economics Association, and other
non-profit organizations concerned with poverty and
development.

JOSEPH R. DOMINICK is Assistant Professor of
Communication Arts and Sciences at Queens College
of the City University of New York. He is a graduate of the University of Illinois, and holds M.A. and

Ph.D. degrees from the Department of Communication,
Michigan State University, where he was a senior research assistant during 1969-70. Professor Dominick
has published several articles in the area of broadcasting and mass communication and is the recipient
of a 1970 research award from the National Association
of Broadcasters.

JOHN BOWES is Assistant Professor of Journalism
at the University of North Dakota. He is a graduate
of Hamilton College, Clinton, New York, has an M.S.
degree from the Newhouse School of Communication,
Syracuse University, and is completing his Ph.D. in
Communication at Michigan State University. He was
assistant to the director of information services for
the National Assessment of Educational Progress Project in Ann Arbor, Michigan, during 1969-70. He
also served as a senior research assistant at MSU and
as a Research Associate at Science Research Associates,
Chicago.

56